Praise for Elizabeth Bard's

Picnic in Provence

"I love Elizabeth Bard's brave, funny forays into French life."
—Diane Johnson, author of *Le Divorce* and *L'Affaire*

"This charming follow-up to the author's bestselling *Lunch in Paris*... brings the tastes of Provence off the page and onto your table."
—*Woman's Day*

"Dotted with tasty recipes, this memoir about a young couple's adventures opening an ice cream shop in Provence is a treat." —*People*

"I was entranced by *Picnic in Provence* from Elizabeth Bard's very first encounter with spring asparagus in the French countryside. Her tale of delicious adventure left me drooling—and her sensitive thoughts on marriage and motherhood were like a heartfelt conversation with a true friend. A delightful book, filled with humor, heart, and the heady scent of lavender." —Ann Mah, author of *Mastering the Art of French Eating*

"Like the Provençal food and lifestyle it celebrates, Bard's book is one to be savored slowly and with care. Delectable reading."
—*Kirkus Reviews*

"A delicious journey through La Belle France....Funny, insightful, wicked, and wise, and the cherry on top is the delicious recipes."
—Jamie Cat Callan, author of *French Women Don't Sleep Alone*

"With funny, sharp, and insightful writing, not to mention a collection of delectable recipes, Bard reminds us what is important and that nothing's perfect." —Michelle Gable, author of *A Paris Apartment*

"A journey to the true heart and soul of living *la vie française*. Warm, thoughtful, and beautiful—a memoir to be savored one delicious chapter (and recipe) at a time. From truffle hunting to harvesting saffron, readers will discover that there is way more to France than just Paris. The simple things in life—love and cooking with love—make every struggle and adjustment worth it. *Bon app!*"

—Samantha Vérant, author of *Seven Letters from Paris*

"Talk about the sweet life: Elizabeth Bard's new chapter is filled with love, parenthood, and her very own ice cream shop, and she graciously shares the journey with a salty swirl of intelligence and humor." —Amy Thomas, author of *Paris, My Sweet*

"Once again, Elizabeth Bard welcomes us into a fantasy—this time, family life in a charming old house in the South of France. With its sharing of stories and recipes, *Picnic in Provence* is a friendship that deepens with every page." —Suzan Colón, author of *Cherries in Winter*

"This book takes delightful twists and turns. Not unlike the winding roads of Provence. *Magnifique!*"

—Janice MacLeod, author of *Paris Letters*

"Funny, sassy, and bittersweet: a heartwarming story with a delightful foodie twist. After all, who wouldn't want to run away, marry a Frenchman, and open an 'adventurous ice cream' store in a medieval Provençal village?"

—Karen Le Billon, author of *French Kids Eat Everything*

"The kind of adventure that makes you long for a fantasy of your own." —Maggie Harding, Bookreporter.com

Picnic
in Provence

ALSO BY ELIZABETH BARD

Lunch in Paris

Picnic in Provence

A Memoir with Recipes

Elizabeth Bard

BACK BAY BOOKS
Little, Brown and Company
New York • Boston • London

Back Bay Books / Little, Brown and Company
Hachette Book Group
1290 Avenue of the Americas, New York, NY 10104
littlebrown.com

Originally published in hardcover by Little, Brown and Company, April 2015
First Back Bay paperback edition, June 2016

Back Bay Books is an imprint of Little, Brown and Company, a division of Hachette Book Group, Inc. The Back Bay Books name and logo are trademarks of Hachette Book Group, Inc.

The publisher is not responsible for websites (or their content) that are not owned by the publisher.

The Hachette Speakers Bureau provides a wide range of authors for speaking events. To find out more, go to hachettespeakersbureau.com or call (866) 376-6591.

ISBN 978-0-316-24616-3 (hc) / 978-0-316-24617-0 (pb)
LCCN 2015930158

10 9 8 7 6 5 4 3 2 1

RRD-C

Printed in the United States of America

For my mother. *Now I get it.*

Contents

CONTENTS

CONTENTS

Author's Note

Some names and identifying details have been changed to protect people's privacy. Once again, poor Gwendal didn't get that lucky.

Picnic
in Provence

CHAPTER 1

Picnic in Provence

I don't, as a rule, introduce myself to cows. But these were important cows, essential ones. If for some reason they weren't available, our dream of locally made Provençal ice cream would be dead before it began.

"Hello, ladies," I said gamely, noting the bones jutting out from their hindquarters. To an American, they seemed a bit svelte for good lavender ice cream. But this is France, so it shouldn't surprise me that even the livestock look like they're on a diet. The cows observed me with perfect detachment as my heels sank into the early-spring mud. One finally looked up and gave me her full attention. She chewed thoughtfully on a mouthful of hay, her large liquid eyes perfectly ringed with black, like Elizabeth Taylor in *Cleopatra*. Suddenly her head bobbed down toward my boots and immediately back up again, as if to say, *Excusez-moi, madame, but it's clear from the cleanliness of your shoes that you're new around here. Very, very new. And, as a rule, we don't produce milk for anyone born in Manhattan.*

If you had told me on my wedding day that ten years later I'd be standing in a field in Provence making small talk with skinny cows, I would have nodded politely and with a twist of my graduated pearls, said that you must have mistaken me for someone else.

I would have been wrong.

༄

WE DIDN'T COME to stay. We had no intentions beyond a few days of sun and a busty bottle of Côtes du Rhône.

Céreste, an hour east of Avignon, is not what you'd call the chic part of Provence. It's a village of thirteen hundred tucked into a valley along the old Roman road; the locals are accustomed to tourists passing through on their way to more scenic hilltop towns—Saignon, Lourmarin—nearby. There is a single main street with a butcher, two *boulangeries*, and a café with plastic chairs and a thatched awning. From the moment you drive into town at the roundabout near the blinking neon cross of the pharmacy to the moment you drive out under a canopy of towering plane trees is about twenty-five seconds. If you duck to rummage in the glove compartment for an extra pair of sunglasses, you might miss it. But here we were, one exhausted French executive and his pregnant American wife, staying for ten days over the Easter holidays.

Gwendal and I rolled our bags, wheels noisy as a stagecoach, through the stone-paved courtyard of the B&B. La Belle Cour is a gracious house, full of books, sofas with deeply dented cushions, and the grave ticktocking of grandfather clocks. As we climbed the spiral stairs to our room (no one offered me a piggyback, though I might have accepted it), I ran my hand along the white plaster walls, chill to the touch. The plumped-up pillows on the bed were welcoming. I sat down, eased down, really, with my belly in the lead, on the quilted chenille spread.

I thought of another set of spiral stairs, three flights up to a cramped love nest in the heart of Paris. Ten years ago, I had lunch with a handsome Frenchman—and never quite went home. My French lover is now my French husband, and I'm an adopted *Parisienne*. I know which local bakery makes the best croissants, I can speak fluently to the man at the phone company (a bigger accomplishment than it sounds), and I can order a neatly flayed rabbit from the butcher without the slightest hesitation.

We had spent the past five years in nearly constant motion. Gwendal founded a successful consulting company and realized his dream of working in the cinema industry. I had made the precarious transition from part-time journalist to full-time author. My first book, as well as our first child, was on the way. We had a flat with a working fireplace and some semblance of a bathtub. In our mid-thirties, deeply in love (if completely exhausted), it was all coming together. When I was a child, I had projected myself ahead to this place; I'd waited my whole life to sit atop a well-tended mountain of accomplishments, admiring the view. But lately, there was another feeling creeping in. Call it lack of oxygen. Battle fatigue. Maybe it was just the baby pressing firmly against my bladder, but it felt more and more like the mountain was sitting on top of us.

When we came down dressed for dinner, there were already four glasses and a bottle of rosé on the wrought-iron table outside. Our English hostess, Angela, appeared with a plate of *gressins,* bread sticks long and thin as a flapper's cigarette holder, and a small bowl of candied ginger. She was tall and elegant with finishing-school posture, her shoulders draped in layers of cotton and cashmere with a dangle of silver earrings. Something in the way she kept her quick smile in reserve told me that she was the funny one. Her husband, Rod, wore pastel stripes that matched his pink cheeks. He had the bright eyes of someone who enjoyed crying at weddings, and movies. We liked them instantly. "So what brings you to Céreste?" asked Rod, pouring a blush of wine into Gwendal's glass. Though no one ever got arrested for having a glass of wine while pregnant—particularly in France—I contented myself, begrudgingly, with sparkling water.

Gwendal paused, trying to come up with an answer that wouldn't sound too much like we were on a pilgrimage. My husband is a great admirer of the French poet and World War II Résistance leader René Char. We knew Char had lived in Céreste during the war. Because I was entering my third trimester and wary of flying, we'd decided to explore the Luberon, the landscapes and events described in Char's most famous poems. If that sounds like an odd premise for a holiday, well, I suppose it is. Then again, some people bird-watch.

As soon as we mentioned Char, Angela put down her glass, disappeared inside the house, and returned with a small white paperback. "Have you read the latest book?"

As it turns out, history was living just up the road. During the war, Char had a passionate affair with Marcelle Pons Sidoine, a young woman from the village. They lived together and ran the local Résistance network from her family's home. Marcelle had a daughter, Mireille, who was eight years old in 1940. "She just published a book about her childhood with René Char," said Angela. "They're only a few houses up. On the left. Would you care to meet her?"

Gwendal's eyes got excited, then bashful. I could see his French brain ticking away: *But what will I say to a perfect stranger?* It takes more than ten years in bed with an American to cure a European of his natural reserve. In the end, curiosity trumped culture—there was no question of refusing.

A phone call was made, polite greetings exchanged. Mireille would be happy to see us in a few days' time.

⁊

OUR APPOINTMENT FIXED, we settled in to explore the region. The next morning, while I read my book in the flower-filled courtyard,

Gwendal went hiking. He needed to walk off the last few months at work. Two years earlier, he had merged his little company with a larger entity and worked his ass off (he belongs to the rare genus of French workaholics). Now he found himself at the point where he no longer had strategic control. He was like one of those mimes pushing at the ceiling of an invisible box; he had a great salary, a fancy title, but was trapped nonetheless. Angela and Rod sent him up the trail behind the local cemetery to the neighboring village of Montjustin. On a clear day you can see the snow-white summits of the Alps. Gwendal returned at noon, his dark hair slick with sweat, his boots muddy. As much as I like him in a suit and tie, I had to admit he looked five years younger in his shorts.

Even if I hadn't been six months pregnant, it's debatable how much hiking I might have done. Gwendal, raised on the wild Brittany coast, has always had a closer relationship to nature than I have. He likes panoramic views, the breeze coming up off the cliffs ruffling his hair and filling his lungs like white spirit. Me, I'm an asphalt princess, born and raised. I like the breeze coming up off the subway grates, ruffling my skirt and tickling my thighs, like Marilyn Monroe. The view I like best is of a well-laid dinner table.

To that end, we had some shopping to do. The B&B didn't serve meals, and since most afternoons were already a balmy seventy-five degrees, Gwendal and I decided to picnic. Ten miles to the west, down a road that hugs the curves of the Luberon hills, the market in Apt is an institution in this part of Provence. Every Saturday from eight in the morning to twelve thirty in the afternoon, it takes over the entire town, from the parking lot on the outskirts of the old city, through the narrow arches with their pointed clock towers, down the cobblestoned streets, into each alley, onto every *placette*—a jumble of cheese, vegetables, sausage, and local lavender honey.

Over the years, French markets have become my natural habitat. It's fair to say that almost everything I've learned about my adopted country I've learned *autour de la table*—around the table. The rituals of shopping for, preparing, and sharing meals have become such an integral part of my life in France, it's difficult to remember those days in New York when lunch was the fifteen minutes it took me to walk to the Chinese salad bar and back to my desk.

We had made our way no farther than the first archway when I was stopped in my tracks by the scent of strawberries. Not the sight; simply the smell. Over the heads of several passersby, I spotted a folding table and a dark-haired mother-daughter team arranging rows of small wooden baskets. The berries were heart-shaped with neat crowns of green leaves. They were smaller and lighter in color than the bloodred monsters that normally came our way from Spain.

We had been warned that Easter was the beginning of the tourist season, and sure enough, the prices were strangely Parisian, higher even. But a girl's got to eat. More specifically, she's got to eat the season's first strawberries from Carpentras, a purely local privilege. I bought one basket for us and one for Angela, and I asked the dark-haired woman to put them aside for later. I had a feeling we were going to end up with a lot to carry.

We passed a man selling quail's eggs, tiny and spotted, the real ones barely distinguishable from their Easter candy equivalents in the window of the *chocolatier*. Neat bundles of the first asparagus were laid gently on pallets of straw. Resistance was futile. I felt certain that if I asked nicely, Angela would lend me a pot and a spot at her stove to blanch them.

Our steps slowed behind the growing morning crowd. There was a bottleneck up ahead at the *boulangerie*. A wrought-iron cart, a more elegant version of the pretzel vendors' on the streets of New York, was posted outside. In addition to croissants and *pains au chocolat,* it was loaded with flattish ovals of yeasted bread. Some were covered with grated Gruyère cheese and bacon, some with a tangle of caramelized onions and anchovies. The script on the chalkboard sign said *Fougasse,* which I took to be a type of local focaccia. I leaned toward one topped with toasted walnuts, pungent with the smell of recently melted Roquefort cheese. This would be the perfect bread for our picnic, easy to tear and just greasy enough to give me an excuse to lick my fingers.

The crowd on the main pedestrian street was beginning to resemble Times Square's on New Year's Eve, all shuffling steps and jutting elbows. The weight of numerous plastic bags cut into my wrist, and I began to see the virtue in the brightly colored straw baskets on sale next to the Swiss chard. We ducked into a side street, passed stalls heaped with bolts of brightly colored cloth and bowls of glistening green olives, and entered a small square. I surveyed the morning's haul. All we were missing was that essential French food group: *charcuterie.* I approached an unmarked white van, the kind your mother warned you never to get into. The side of the van opened to reveal a pristine stainless-steel counter and a display case. It was packed with thick-cut pork chops, fresh sausages flecked with herbs, even *boudin noir maison,* homemade blood sausage (not very practical for a picnic, but I couldn't help plotting how I might get several lengths back to Paris in my suitcase). I settled on a *saucisse sèche au thym*—a horseshoe of dried sausage flavored with fresh thyme and black peppercorns. I was pretty sure Gwendal had remembered his father's pocketknife.

Shopping for food in France never fails to make me hungry. Armed with a few days' worth of supplies, we were more than ready for lunch.

༄

THE FOLLOWING TUESDAY, we arrived promptly at three for coffee with Mireille, the daughter of Char's wartime love. She greeted us at the door, a dark-haired woman in her seventies wearing a wool skirt, sensible shoes, and a pink cotton blouse with a matching scarf. We walked under the stone vaults of the meticulously renovated seventeenth-century coaching inn she shared with her husband and her mother, Marcelle, now ninety-four. We were on the ground floor, the former kitchen of the inn. The stone hearth of the fireplace was almost large enough for me to step into. It was easy to imagine a hulking great cauldron of daube or *soupe d'épeautre* hung low over the embers, ready to greet the travelers who stopped to water their horses and left at first light.

A table was set by the only window. On the starched white cloth were a wooden pencil case and a pair of leather-covered headphones attached to a tangle of aging wire. They looked like props for an old-fashioned magic show. I wasn't sure what to expect. Up until that moment, René Char was little more to me than a name on our bookshelf.

When you marry a foreigner—when you *are* the foreigner— cultural references are one of the widest gaps to leap. Gwendal and I worshipped at different altars. When we met, he had never seen *The Breakfast Club;* I'd never seen *Les 400 Coups.* My first slow dance was to Wham!; his was to some Italian pop star I'd never heard of. My adolescent angst (such as it was) was fueled by John Donne; Gwendal preferred Rimbaud. I won't bother to tell you what happened the first time I tried to get him to eat a Twinkie. I consider myself a reasonably well-read English major, but except for the snippets Gwendal read aloud when he was particularly impressed, René Char's poetry and history were new to me.

I knew Char had been a friend to Braque, Picasso, André Breton, at the crossroads of the intellectual life of Paris between the wars. During the Second World War, he was a leader in the French Résistance, receiving weapons drops from London and hiding arms, refugees, and young Frenchmen who refused the *service du travail obligatoire*, mandatory work service in Germany. In 1944, he went to Alger to help de Gaulle prepare for the liberation of the South of France. But as we sat down at the table, I quickly sensed that the public man was not the one Mireille wanted to share with us. "Char was like a father to me," she said, showing us a letter written in his hand. His writing was even, slanted, with a slight flourish—an uptick at the bottom of each capital L. She opened his cracked wooden pencil box and touched the darkened metal nib of a quill. Although the events we were speaking of were only seventy years in the past, she handled these possessions like ancient relics.

In true Provençal style, we lingered through the afternoon: one coffee, then a second, one cognac, then another. Mireille told us stories of false papers, village collaborators, and Char helping her with her homework by the wood-burning stove. Her expression wandered between the softness of nostalgia and the grim pragmatism of the local *paysans*. "He made me memorize 'Maréchal, Nous Voilà,' the Vichy anthem, and told me to sing extra-loud in school so no one would suspect what we were doing," she said.

"Do you have any other questions?" asked Mireille as we stretched over our empty espresso cups. Gwendal cleared his throat. "I read that even though Char refused to publish under the German occupation, he wrote all through the war. It is said that he buried his manuscripts in the cellar of the house where he lived and came back for them when the war was over." In fact, after the liberation, Char dug up the notebooks and sent them to Gallimard, the famous Paris publisher, where they were noticed by the future Nobel laureate Albert Camus. Published in 1946 as *Feuillets d'Hypnos*, these poems remain Char's masterpiece. "We've looked all over the village," said Gwendal. "Where," he asked, taking his roundabout French path to the point, "is this famous hole in the floor?"

"That's easy to show you," said Mireille. "We still own the house."

The next morning, we found ourselves walking past the remains of the medieval château and into the heart of the *vieux village*. The houses in this part of the village were huddled close together, stacked one on top of another like building blocks; it was hard to know where one residence ended and another began. We took a sharp left at the place des Marronniers, with its fountain and giant chestnut trees, and walked a narrow flagstone street to La Maison Pons.

Mireille unlocked a wrought-iron gate and took us under a porch into an interior courtyard. There was a wooden carriage wheel the height of my shoulder balanced against the stone wall: *"Mon grand-père."* Her paternal grandfather, she explained, had been a *carrossier*. We ducked through another doorway. Gwendal and I had to practically fold ourselves in half to avoid hitting our heads on the rough-hewn stones as we followed her down the steps into the wine cellar. Mireille cleared away some empty bottles and pointed to a low wooden shelf, about a foot from the earthen floor. *"Le voilà.* That's where Char buried his manuscript," she said. "Wrapped in an old parachute."

Gwendal looked down. *This is the man I love,* I thought. *A man who can be so visibly moved by a dent in the dirt.*

"We used to store pigs down here," continued Mireille, returning suddenly to more practical details. "In those days we ate everything. We sealed the cutlets in a layer of fat, and when you wanted one, you would dig it out." As we turned to leave, she stamped her foot on the packed-earth floor. "My uncle—he was Char's driver during the war—before he died, he said there might still be guns buried under here. We never looked."

Inside, the house was a maze, a series of small whitewashed rooms. Nothing was on the same level; to get from one room to another you had to take two steps up or two steps down. There were dark wooden beams and an open fireplace in the dining room that still smelled faintly of smoke. Up half a flight of stairs was the room where Char had slept. I looked out the window where he had had his writing table. I could see only a sliver of the street; just enough of it, I imagined, for the poet to distinguish the calves of a pretty girl from the jackboots of a German soldier. There were three more bedrooms and two bathrooms upstairs. The master bedroom, a former attic with a sloping roof, was flooded with morning light. "This is where we used to hang the hams," said Mireille. It was clear that everywhere she looked, she saw two worlds, past and present. She was born in this house; so was her mother. I ran my hand across a beam. There was a date carved into the wood: 1753.

Before we left, we went out to the garden, a large two-level stone terrace overlooking the surrounding fields. Shoots of new mint congregated at the foot of an heirloom rosebush. It was almost May Day, and the lilies of the valley were in bloom. Mireille picked one and pressed it into my hand. The tiny individual flowers shook like bells in the morning breeze. "C'est un porte bonheur; it's a good-luck charm," she said, "for the baby."

I didn't know what to say. Though it was only about four months away, motherhood remained abstract for me. Most women carry babies in their wombs, but for now this pregnancy was mostly in my head. Gwendal already felt like a father. I certainly didn't feel like anyone's mom. Not yet. I pressed the flower to my belly, wondering if the baby could smell the springtime through my skin.

Up the steps, I looked into the mouth of the outdoor brick oven, the opening covered with ash and cobwebs. I squinted into the morning sun; I could just make out two horses, heads nodding in the grass of a nearby ridge.

I'm not someone who knows a whole lot about contentment; my default settings tend more toward striving and mild panic. But the warmth of this place was intoxicating: the high walls of the garden cocooned between the neighboring houses, the small spirals of fern growing undisturbed between the stones. "I know it was a dangerous, terrible time," I said to Mireille, "but you can feel that your family was happy here."

"We were." Mireille smiled, briefly. "But I am sad now. I gave this house to my daughter, thinking she would come back to the village with her family. Instead, she wants to sell it."

"Ah."

People who know me will tell you: I almost never let reality get in the way of a good story. For most of my life, that's made me a dreamer, a dilettante, even—in my own head—a failure. But every once in a while, we catch up to our dreams and make them real. The best decisions of my life have been made this way—a feeling, followed by a giant leap into the unknown. I never regret these choices, though I often make myself crazy with worry along the way. I think most of us wish we had more appetite for risk, not less.

Gwendal and I didn't even exchange a glance. I know my husband. We were both thinking exactly the same thing.

We walked back along the gravel-strewn path that hugged the outskirts of Céreste. The houses were nestled on one side, the river and the open fields on the other. Mireille huffed slightly as she mounted the small hill toward home. Suddenly she stopped as if she had forgotten something very important. "The bed-and-breakfast doesn't serve meals," she said, crumpling her eyebrows together with concern. "Where have you been eating?"

"We bought some things at the market in Apt on Saturday," I said. "We've been making picnics."

"*C'est bien,*" she said with a nod of approval. "Picnicking is good. That's what we used to do."

⁂

It's impossible to say exactly what it was that moved us. Some heady combination of the history, the baby—not to mention those first strawberries. It took only a moment for the absurd to become the obvious. This is where we would live the next chapter of our lives. This is where we would become a family. Gwendal and I spent a sleepless night in front of an Excel spreadsheet and the next morning went back to ask if we could buy the house.

Recipes for a Picnic in Provence

FIRST ASPARAGUS WITH TAHINI YOGURT DRESSING

Asperges, Sauce Yaourt au Tahini

Angela did indeed lend me a saucepan to blanch my asparagus, and this was the result. The sauce, much lighter than a traditional hollandaise, has become my go-to dressing for steamed vegetables, poached salmon, even impromptu chicken salad.

1 pound thin asparagus
2 tablespoons dark (unhulled) tahini
3 tablespoons plus 2 teaspoons fresh lemon juice
1¼ cups plain Greek yogurt (whole-milk is best)
Small pinch of fine sea salt
Grinding of fresh black pepper

Wash your asparagus and cut off the tough ends of the stalk, then steam them over a large pot of boiling water for 3 to 5 minutes, depending on thickness. It is a sin to overcook asparagus (they get limp and smelly), so watch them carefully and take them out when they are still bright green and firm.

To make the dressing: In a medium glass bowl (or other nonreactive container) combine tahini and lemon juice until smooth. Add yogurt and a pinch of salt; stir to combine. Grind in pepper.

Serve the asparagus warm or at room temperature; pass the sauce on the side.

Serves 4 as an appetizer or side dish

CHICKPEA SALAD WITH SWEET PEPPERS AND HERBS

Salade de Pois Chiche aux Herbes Fraîches

Chickpeas grow abundantly in Provence, and they're used in everything from *poischichade*, the local hummus, to *socca*, traditional chickpea flour crepes made in Aix. Warm and colorful, this salad travels well. It's a wonderful accompaniment to grilled chicken or lamb chops.

1 red pepper, thinly sliced
1 yellow pepper, thinly sliced
1 yellow onion, thinly sliced
1 red onion, thinly sliced
Pinch of cinnamon
1 teaspoon ground Spanish ñora peppers or good-quality smoked paprika
½ teaspoon cumin seeds
½ teaspoon harissa (North African hot pepper paste) or a pinch or two of hot pepper flakes, to taste
½ cup olive oil
3 cups chickpeas (2 14-ounce cans), drained
Black pepper
A good pinch of coarse sea salt
1 cup (packed) flat-leaf parsley, with stems, finely chopped
1 tablespoon (packed) fresh mint, finely chopped
Lemon slices, to garnish

Preheat the oven to 350°F.

In a large casserole dish, combine peppers, onions, and spices (not the parsley and mint—you'll add those at the end). If you want the salad to be a little spicy, you can double the harissa or hot pepper flakes—the amount I've suggested adds flavor, not heat. Pour in the olive oil, toss to combine. Roast in the oven for 1 hour, stirring twice along the way.

Meanwhile, rinse your chickpeas in hot water. Take a bit of extra time to rub off and discard the waxy skins.

Remove peppers and onions from the oven—there will be a slick of lovely spiced olive oil at the bottom of the dish—and stir in the chickpeas. Add a good grinding of black pepper and a pinch of salt to taste. Let sit 5 or 10 minutes, then stir in the parsley and mint. Serve warm or at room temperature, with a slice of lemon to squeeze on top. This can easily be made a day ahead—it gives the flavors time to mingle.

Serves 6

CARAMELIZED ONION AND ANCHOVY FLATBREAD
Pissaladière

This is a classic at Provençal buffets and *apéritifs*. It may be the perfect food: sweet, salty, doughy, and portable—who could ask for anything more?

The French use fresh yeast sold in cubes at the *boulangerie* to make the crust. For a simple dough using active dry yeast, I turned to *Artisan Bread in Five Minutes a Day* by Jeff Hertzberg and Zoë François (Thomas Dunne Books, 2007). This is a supereasy no-knead olive-oil dough—and though you do have to let it rise for two hours, your active cooking time is almost nonexistent.

For the dough

6½ cups unbleached all-purpose flour
1½ tablespoons granulated yeast (I use Red Star)
1½ tablespoons kosher salt or coarse sea salt
1 tablespoon sugar
¼ cup extra-virgin olive oil
2¾ cups lukewarm water

For the topping

¼ *cup olive oil, plus one tablespoon for the cookie sheet*
2¾ *pounds sweet yellow onions, halved and sliced*
1 *teaspoon herbes de Provence*
1½ *teaspoons sugar*
1 *clove garlic, minced*
Pinch of coarse sea salt
20–30 *anchovies*
20–25 *cured black olives*

To make the dough: In a medium mixing bowl, measure out the flour. In your largest mixing bowl (5 quarts), whisk together the yeast, salt, sugar, oil, and water, then dump in the flour all at once and combine with a wooden spoon. You might want to finish with your hands; if so, coat your hands liberally with olive oil so the dough doesn't stick. There's no kneading in this recipe; just make sure flour is thoroughly combined. Cover the bowl lightly with a clean cloth and let rise for 2 hours. You can use the dough immediately after that, but it is easier to handle if you leave it in the fridge for a while (it keeps, covered, for several days).

Meanwhile, prepare the onions: Preheat the oven to 350°F. In a medium Dutch oven or stockpot with an ovenproof cover, heat ¼ cup olive oil until it sizzles, then stir in the onions, herbes de Provence, sugar, garlic, and a pinch of sea salt. Sauté over medium heat for 10 minutes on the stovetop, stirring occasionally, until the onions begin to become translucent. Place the onions in the oven, covered, for 1 hour. The goal is to evaporate the water without browning the onions—that will happen when you put them on the pizza. Both the dough and the onion mixture can be made a day or two in advance.

Preheat the oven to 500°F (bake, not broil). You need only half your dough to make the *pissaladière*, so tear off half the dough, form a ball, and store in the fridge for a weekday pizza. (Not to get off the subject, but my family likes cured ham, fig, and Gorgonzola...)

Line your largest cookie sheet with parchment paper (I use my oven tray, which is 14 by 18 inches). Spread 1 tablespoon olive oil over the entire parchment paper, including up the sides. Remember, this is no-knead dough, so all you have to do is shape the remaining dough into a ball by stretching the surface of the dough around to the bottom on all sides. On the oiled cookie sheet, stretch the dough into a large round (about the size of a Frisbee) and then flip it over to make sure both sides are coated with oil. Using your fingers, press the dough into a rectangle the full size of the cookie sheet. Using the back of a fork (or your fingertips), make lots of deep indentations (not quite holes) in the dough.

Using a slotted spoon to minimize the liquid, scatter the onion mixture evenly over the dough, right up to the edges (you should be able to see a bit of naked dough peeking out from underneath the onions). Make a diamond pattern on top with the anchovies, then place an olive at the corner of each diamond. Cover with plastic wrap and let sit for 20 minutes. Remove the plastic wrap and bake for 12 to 15 minutes, until the crust is golden brown along the edges; take a peek underneath as well. The exact timing will depend on the size of your cookie sheet and the thickness of the dough.

Cut into small squares; serve warm or at room temperature.

Serves 8 as an hors d'oeuvre

Tip: If you are not inclined to make your own dough (I used to be scared of yeast myself), you can substitute a high-quality premade pizza crust or focaccia dough and bake according to the manufacturer's directions.

CHAPTER 2

Last First Date

Paris in August is like the set of a science fiction movie—a planet devoid of life except for very pregnant women and stray cats. The civilized world is on holiday, walking in rolled-up jeans and summer cashmere on a beach in Brittany or donning white linen trousers and expensive sunglasses in, well, Provence. We'd been back to Céreste only once since our leap of faith in April, just long enough to sign the initial paperwork and taste the first white peaches of the season—reason enough to pack up our boxes and go. Our annual week in Greece had been canceled as soon as I learned my due date: August 21. Note to self: Next time, get pregnant *on* the vacation, not *instead* of the vacation.

Over the past three months we'd slowly introduced the idea of the move to our friends and family. It's helpful to explain your plans to other people. It makes them real. By *other people,* of course, I mean my mother.

We tackled my mom in the rush of breathless excitement just after our first visit to the house. I approached her via the avenue that seemed most promising: home decorating. "So," I said, taking a deep breath into the phone, "how would you like to come to

Provence and shop for a hundred and seventy square meters of new tiles?" Silence. I've been away from home since I was fifteen, and this was hardly the first crazy idea she'd heard from the other end of a long-distance call. She let me get through the whole story. More silence. "A *vill-age*," she said, giving the word a nice slow exoticism, like *Brigadoon* or *devil worship*. "What are you going to do in a *vill-age?*"

That's a fair question. What is a sushi-loving, window-shopping, museum-wandering city girl who can't drive a car or ride a bike going to do in the middle of all those trees? Most people don't up-root their whole lives for a crazy story about a poet and a good-luck garden. But I believe in stories, the way other people believe in religion, or free-market capitalism. I did my best to express what was essentially a hunch: We felt something of our future in those walls. Céreste was the answer to a question we didn't even know we'd been asking.

As word got around, reactions seemed to be evenly divided along cultural lines: Our French friends nodded with bewilderment: How could we possibly leave our jobs? We were so *settled*. Others nodded admiringly. They too thought about moving to the country-side—when they retired.

My American friends were more blunt: They give it six months.

⤫

WITH ONLY A month till my due date, this time feels precious, re-moved from the everyday rush. Without thinking, Gwendal and I are retracing our steps—visiting old haunts, craving familiar tastes. We have Paris all to ourselves again, like the bubble we lived in those first months together, before I could speak French, when we couldn't get ourselves out of bed before noon, and every *tarte au cit-*

ron and sprinkle of *fleur de sel* felt like a revelation. Tonight, we are in search of ice cream.

Gwendal and I were both students when we bumped into each other (okay, I bumped into him, a little bit on purpose) on the stairs at an academic conference in London. I'd noticed him sitting in the middle row of the lecture hall, the kind of earnest young man who would never hide all the way in the back. He was tall, handsome in a serious, scholarly way. He might have been German given his height and the hideous light blue windbreaker he was wearing. But the square jaw, dark hair, and tiny glasses were pure *café crème*.

A few months and one blissfully rare steak later, Gwendal lured me back to his tiny apartment in Paris with the promise of a steaming pot of mint tea. In those days the path to his place along the Canal Saint-Martin was full of soot and graffiti, a lone *papy* walking his dog down the cobblestoned quays. Ten years later, the retirees have given way to hipsters with strollers, screenwriters on the verge of a breakthrough, and, on summer nights like this one, hordes of students picnicking with bottles of wine, baguettes, and slices of pale pink ham from the Franprix. There's still graffiti, but it tends to be done by aspiring artists or as guerrilla marketing for chic new galleries and boutiques.

I remember everything about that first weekend in Paris. It was early December, freezing and damp, the flip side of tonight's soft August haze. The dirty little secret of Paris is that the weather is exactly the same as it is in London. But the places to hide, oh, the places to hide. We sat in cafés with fogged-up windows and tables so small you couldn't help but hold hands. We made out in secluded corners of the Louvre. Gwendal also took me to a special exhibition about death, complete with shrunken heads. I thought it took a certain confidence to suggest it, and a certain prescience on the part of a new lover to suspect how much I would enjoy it.

But mostly, we ate. He slipped out in the morning and came

back with crinkled waxed-paper bags of *chouquettes*—puffs of choux pastry studded with sugar. We went to hole-in-the-wall restaurants and lingered over *maffé,* a West African stew thickened with peanut butter, the white butcher-paper tablecloth wrinkling under our elbows.

When I met Gwendal, I had a very clear idea of what I wanted my life to look like: I was starting a master's degree in art history, on my way to a PhD and some version of my dream job as the chief curator of the Pierpont Morgan Library. There wasn't a lot of room for interruptions. Gwendal was a mass of contradictions to a type-A striver like me. He was finishing up a PhD in computer science while working full-time for the national TV and radio archives, but he slept on a mattress on the floor and didn't own a tie. He was smart and well read, but I sensed an inner goofiness (when I met him, he had just started tap-dancing lessons). He seemed to be willing to wait out some of my more quaint American neuroses: an obsession with financial security, status, and unending upward mobility. Some of my finer American qualities he licked like sugar from my lips—my confidence, my optimism, my sense of endless possibility. He knew that if I stayed in France long enough, *be happy* might well appear at the top of that endless to-do list I kept in my purse. Paris, and Gwendal, had that effect on me.

If I sound soppy about him, it's because I am. It's also because I know how close I came to pitching the whole thing into the Seine. It took me two years to agree to live with him, six months to accept his marriage proposal. Paris was enchanting, but I had no family there, no friends, almost no French-language skills, and definitely no job. It was hard to imagine this croissant-fueled fantasy as my real life. In the end, I sat on my doubts the way you sit on an overstuffed suitcase, just so you can close the lock. It was the right decision. Every day I feel like I'm living a life I almost missed, and it makes me grateful.

The high-summer light is fading and the clouds are lined with dusty rose as Gwendal and I make our way past the giant statue of Marianne in the place de la République and down into the narrow streets of the Marais. I never walk very fast in Paris; I still peek in doorways, admiring inner courtyards and secret gardens. The extravagant squiggles of the wrought-iron balconies and the groaning weight of the wooden doors are the very opposite of the utilitarian symmetry of my native New York.

We walk across the Pont Marie onto the Île Saint-Louis, the tiny island of aristocratic mansions with beamed ceilings in the middle of the Seine. Our destination is our favorite outpost of La Maison Berthillon, Paris's most famous ice cream maker. This family-owned institution has been open since the fifties, and in the true measure of French success (particularly in the ice cream business), they sell to other cafés and restaurants and take the whole summer off.

Choosing your Berthillon stand is of utmost importance. There are several on the island, each with a different assortment of flavors and all with a large number of tourists and regulars lined up in front. We always go to one on the eastern edge of the island, as far as you can get from Notre-Dame without falling into the river. This evening there are only four or five people ahead of us. Just enough time to consider my choices.

Berthillon's ice cream is dense and creamy—served, in keeping with French rules of moderation, in golf-ball-size scoops. You have to be a real purist to order a *simple* (pronounced "*samp*-le"). I usually order a *double* ("*doob*-le"). *Menthe* (fresh mint), *Créole* (rum raisin), and *nougat-miel* (honey-nougat) are at the top of my list. But as good as the ice cream is, it's the sorbets that are Berthillon's real standouts. I almost always order *cacao amer*, a bitter chocolate sorbet so dark it's closing in on black. My second scoop depends on the season: pear, melon, rhubarb, or *framboise à la rose* (raspberry with a hint of rose). But habit often sets in and I go back to my old favorite:

fraise des bois (wild strawberry). These tiny gem-like fruits are the equivalent of strawberry grenades, releasing a tart, concentrated flavor that downgrades every other strawberry I've tasted to the level of Bubblicious.

We take our cones, wrapped in single paper napkins, and walk along the river. It is just dark enough for my favorite Parisian pastime, staring into the fifteen-foot-high windows of the grand *hôtels particuliers*. I like to imagine myself inside the wood-paneled libraries or speculate which Saudi prince installed that gaudy chandelier. We pass a long-haired teenager in sweats and a silk bathrobe—I guess you'd have to call it a smoking jacket—walking a bichon frisé. The shaggy wave of the boy's hair, his aquiline nose and easy but slouched posture (not to mention the smoking jacket), clearly mark him as a member of the aristocratic class. "White Russian," says Gwendal emphatically. This is one of our favorite games. When I first arrived in Paris we would walk the streets for hours inventing identities for people we saw along the way. "Sacha-Eugène," Gwendal purrs now, imitating the high-pitched voice of the boy's mother. "It's the butler's night off. Be a dear and walk the dog, *chéri*."

Still nibbling the tips of our cones, we walk hand in hand down the stone steps to the quay, a steep descent, considering I am nine months pregnant and can barely see my toes. Just a few feet above the Seine, we hear the lapping of the water. We step over boys with bongos, wave at the passing Bateaux Mouches. We make our way down to the tip of the island, dangle our feet over the edge. From here we can see the conical fairy-tale towers of La Conciergerie and, as the clock strikes ten, the sweep of the giant spotlight on top of the Eiffel Tower. We've been here dozens of times since we met, but this precious month before the baby is born feels like a last first date. There's a different kind of romance beginning. We will never again be entirely alone in the world. I've been younger, God knows I've been lighter, but I've never been happier.

∽

TWO WEEKS TILL my due date, and I suddenly feel like I'm developing a split personality: Dr. Jekyll and Mrs. I Wouldn't Leave This Bed If There Was an Atomic Blast in My Kitchen.

Yesterday I was so exhausted I couldn't even muster the will to hit the supermarket. I'd been told I needed more iron in my diet. So I found myself staring into the open refrigerator, surveying this week's odds and ends.

When I first moved to Paris, Gwendal would often come upon me meditating in front of the open fridge, contemplating world peace or choosing middle names for our unborn children. This studying of the culinary stockpile seems to be a uniquely American habit. The French never open the fridge in passing just to check if everything's still there. Personally, I draw comfort from it—like a king surveying his realm.

To be fair, I had quite a bit to contemplate. Growing a person is a heady business.

Gwendal had been patient with me. The French tend to start their families early. He'd been ready to have kids since the day we met, maybe the day before. I kept waiting for that feeling to arrive, the one where you see a baby on the street, your eyes well up, and your ovaries do a little dance. But it never happened. I'm extremely close to my own mother, and I knew I wanted to be one, but the timing never seemed right. Moving to another country set back the clock on my independence. It took me years to get my sea legs in Paris; when I woke up I was suddenly thirty-five. The expression is exactly the same in French: *Tic toc.*

The discussion began in earnest two years ago. It had been a busy time. I had just put every ounce of my (somewhat lost) soul into helping Gwendal start his consulting business in the field of digital cinema. He was successful and contented—even a little bit arrogant. Exactly, I suppose, what I hoped he would be. On New Year's Day, over espresso at our local café, he blithely announced: "It's a new year; I'm ready to move on to the next stage of my life—let's have a baby." I burst into tears. I didn't know what else to do. "How can I be someone's mother," I said, gulping between sobs, "when sometimes I feel like I don't even *exist* here."

Gwendal is not an insensitive man. But he walks through life's doors of decision easily, while I often have to be pushed through, white-knuckled, clinging to the moldings for support. From that moment, I knew that if I wanted my life in France (not to mention my marriage) to move forward, I had no choice but to build something for myself, and in a hurry. I'd cobbled together some work in Paris—writing articles for art magazines and newspapers, giving museum tours—but nothing that met my definition of a career. I am a master procrastinator; I knew if I had a baby before I got my professional life up and running, I might never have a career at all. I could see myself using a child as an excellent excuse to never get anything done—ever again. A few months after that New Year's conversation, I started work on my first book—and threw away my birth control pills. I had to create something for myself before I could create someone else.

When I finally did get pregnant, my first decision was not to read any books about pregnancy. I know myself, and my natural paranoia doesn't need any encouragement. I don't want to know what to expect when I'm expecting. I want to sleep at night.

At first, I thought I would do it the American way. I wanted a doctor, preferably one with a fancy degree and a cell phone I could call in the middle of the night. Someone who would accompany me to the delivery room and whose office would send a card on the kid's birthday. I gave it my best shot: On the first of every month, I dutifully called the hospital, and every time I was told that my doctor was skiing, or at a conference, or just fully booked. Why didn't I see a *sage-femme,* a midwife, instead? Doctors in France are technicians. They don't talk a lot. They look at test results and nod. Like car mechanics, they go in only when something needs to be fixed. The few times I did manage to see MDs, they would squint and stare, no doubt searching for the reason I was there. In France, doctors are people you see when there's a problem. I didn't have a problem. I was just pregnant.

It's not that I didn't have fair warning. As soon as I peed on the stick, I called a family friend, an older man who was a family practitioner on the Breton island of Belle-Île. "I'm being really careful," I said. "Not standing on any chairs."

"Attention," he scolded playfully, *"tu es pas malade."* You're not sick.

After five months of silent nodding from taciturn doctors, I decided that if I wanted some advice about hemorrhoids or someone to actually ask me how I was feeling, I would have to approach pregnancy *à la française.* To this end, I decided to put myself in the hands of the System. The French are excellent at systems. The trains run on time. You just put yourself on a track and wait to be swept along like a letter in one of those pneumatic tubes. I made an appointment with one of the rotating cast of *sages-femmes* at the hospital where I was planning to give birth. *Sage-femme* translates literally to "wise woman," and now I understand why. All of a sudden, the process seemed more human. The *sages-femmes* asked me how I was sleeping and what I was eating and scolded me gently when I gained more than the allotted amount of weight. I didn't know which one would be with me in the delivery room; they all blended into one reassuring pink uniform with a manila folder.

Now, two weeks before my due date, I shut the fridge with a thud. There was officially nothing in there. So I went hunting for a bag of orange lentils I was sure I had stashed at the back of a cabinet some months ago. For iron and pep, I wanted to make a cold lentil salad with a zingy orange-ginger vinaigrette, handfuls of chopped herbs, and slices of white peach. (The purple-green Puy lentils, more common than the orange ones in France, just seemed too dark for a summer salad.) After unpacking half the kitchen while standing, against my better judgment, on a kitchen chair, I ended up not with orange lentils, but with a bag of yellow split peas. That would have to do.

The split peas had been hiding up there for a while—I'm pretty sure I bought them after a trip to Puglia, where we were served warm split-pea puree drizzled with wonderful glass-green olive oil and a grind of fresh pepper. Still hankering after a cold salad, I tried cooking the dried peas al dente, as I would the lentils, but a half hour later, when the lentils would have been perfect, the split peas were a chalky, starchy mess. I decided to boil on past defeat and transform my salad into the silky puree I'd eaten with such gusto in Italy.

When the peas were sweet and tender and the liquid almost absorbed, I got out the power tools. I'm deeply attached to my hand blender—the dainty equivalent of a serial killer's obsession with chain saws. The orange-ginger vinaigrette was already made, so I dumped it in. The recipe's necessary dose of olive oil would have some lively company.

The result was a warm, golden puree with just enough citrus to deviate from the classic. I toasted some *pain Poilâne,* slathered the bread with the puree, and chopped some dill. My *tartines* were still lacking a bit of sunshine, so I placed a slice of white peach on top.

Lunch was delicious, but more effort than I'd anticipated. Time for a nap.

⁂

I'M TRYING TO multitask, cooking rabbit with pastis while packing for the hospital. Pastis is the universal aperitif of Provence, the anise-flavored symbol of the south, a subtle reminder of our life to come. Frankly, I think the pregnancy hormones are blocking full consciousness of our decision. That and the sheer number of things left to do before the baby arrives.

I know the very idea of eating rabbit makes most Americans want to run home and hug the Easter Bunny. When I first arrived in France, the small flayed heads in the window of the butcher took some getting used to, but over the years it's become a one-pot staple—more interesting than chicken, fancy enough for a dinner party but easy enough for a weeknight dinner with leftovers for lunch.

While the rabbit was browning, I cut the tags off some baby clothes. I was beginning to notice a disturbing trend. When I laid the French baby items on top of the American ones my mother sent, I found that the American clothes were about two inches wider—not longer, but *wider*—than their French counterparts. There's a book in here somewhere: *French Babies Don't Get Fat.* The baby-clothes discrepancy was one of many I'd noticed during my pregnancy, particularly with regard to weight. The doctors and midwives, as well as the official government handbook (of course there's an official government handbook), recommend a weight gain of one kilo (just over two pounds) per month—that's a total of twenty to twenty-two pounds. When I first read it, I thought it was a typo. *Twenty-two pounds—that's a pimple, not a pregnancy.*

It's true that French women have babies the way they tie scarves: with an ease that belies effort and years of cultural conditioning. In fact, unless you saw the basketball belly peeking out from under a French woman's shirt, you wouldn't know she was pregnant at all. You can't tell anything from the back; they continue to wear high-heeled sandals and tight little sweaters, or ironed white blouses with low-rise jeans and polished ballerina flats below their decidedly unswollen ankles.

Now, I'm hardly a French pixie to begin with. I come from

hardy Russian-peasant stock; I have what my grandma would politely call "buzooms" and hips designed to give birth in a field, digging potatoes. I'm an American size 10, which, to put it kindly, puts me at the top end of the sizes sold in French boutiques. Yet so far (fingers crossed, ankles crossed, everything crossed), I seem to be pregnant the French way. Frankly, I can't imagine gaining any more. As it is, I'm running my hands over my stomach every day, looking for the eject button. I'm carrying around the equivalent of a Butterball turkey in here.

I shook the rabbit, added a big splash of pastis. To finish it off, I added a cupful of fresh peas, but also a quarter-cup of crème fraîche. There is certainly nothing inherently virtuous about French cuisine. And while I'm sure there's no ideal weight for a pregnant lady, I'm more and more convinced that my Parisian eating habits help keep things calmly and, I must say, rather deliciously in line. I know I can't take any credit. If I were home in the States right now, I'm pretty sure I'd be eating Pillsbury vanilla frosting out of the can with a plastic spoon. This is nurture, not nature, at work. The reason that French women are back in their jeans a few weeks after giving birth is the same reason they can slip into their bikinis every summer with a minimum of fuss—they make sure they never have more than a few pounds to lose.

I think there's another reason why I'm clinging so tightly to the French prescription for weight gain: I don't want there to be a before and after. It's taken me such a long time to carve out a life for myself in France. I've just started spreading my personal and professional wings in Paris, and I can't help wondering how motherhood will change my identity. I don't want to belong to the "woman" tribe one day and the "mommy" tribe the next.

There's something else: I'm an only child, and to ask if I'm close to my mother is like asking, as Angela would say, "Does the pope have a balcony?" My mother and I have one of those relationships a French psychoanalyst would call *fusionnelle*—as in nuclear fusion. Nothing less than perfect synergy or catastrophic meltdown.

When my mother wants to tell me she's proud of me (and, I'm lucky to say, this happens quite often), she says: "You're the best thing I've ever done." Since I got pregnant, this phrase has started to irkle me, by which I mean it wakes me up in the middle of the night so I can stare at the ceiling.

To be fair, I don't know any daughter who isn't living at least a little of her mother's stolen life. I went to Cornell because it was a good school and a good deal for in-state students, but also because my mother once had a chance to go and didn't. She's supported all my crazy (and minimally remunerated) professional choices partly because her own parents refused to pay for full-time law school for a girl. My mother had a safe career at the New York City Board of Education, which at times she loved. She had health insurance for her type 1 diabetes and an excellent pension plan to balance out an ex-husband who wasn't always capable of holding down a job or paying child support. I'm not sure how much of her life turned out exactly the way she'd imagined, except for me. And this scares the bejesus out of me. It sounds so final, as if all my future dreams are about to be transferred onto this tiny person. I want my life to be full to overflowing with stuff I haven't even thought of yet. I have an inkling that someday I might feel differently. But right this second, I'm not sure I want my kid to be the best thing I've ever done.

IT'S BEEN A heavy week. Literally. Here I was, so pleased with myself for being pregnant like a French woman, only to discover at yesterday's appointment with the *sage-femme* that I'd gained eleven pounds in the past ten days—most of it, it seems, in my toes. With ten days to go, I am filling up with water like a fish tank.

I used to have very long skinny toes, but now they look like little sausages. Pigs without their blankets. It's depressing and uncomfortable. I shudder to think of the opinion of a certain foot fetishist I dated after college. He would flee in horror.

It's also been quite a French week—by which I mean a week in which I find out something stupid and ridiculous about this country that I must learn to accept. It's about my family name. Or, more specifically, my child's family name.

As an only child, I'm the last to carry the Bard name, and I feel strongly that I want to pass it on. But in France, it seems to be illegal to use the mother's maiden name as a middle name. Okay, not exactly illegal, but problematic. The French state has a judge who is responsible for approving the name of every child born in France, to keep parents from burdening their children with stupid (*Caca Rhubarbe*) or offensive (*Hitler*) names. In the States, of course, the First Amendment guarantees our right to be as stupid or offensive as we like.

Apparently, this judge sometimes rejects the use of the mother's maiden name as a middle name, thinking it should be part of the last name instead. Even more bizarre, there is a new law that if you want to hyphenate your last name and your husband's last name for your child's surname, you have to use a *double hyphen* (- -). I think it's to distinguish plebs like my husband and me from people who are born with proper double-barreled aristocratic names. This absurdity can only lead to spelling mistakes and administrative woe for the rest of the child's life. I imagine my sixteen-year-old son stuck in the purgatory of secondary passport control at JFK trying to explain to a pasty-faced security officer that no, it's not a typo, no, he's not a terrorist, he's just...French.

I try to be philosophical. Some days I succeed, some days I don't. Who knew when I moved here that I'd willingly trade my civil liberties for a decent slice of pâté.

Despite the heat, I had some dry-cleaning to fetch, so I hunted around for a pair of flip-flops that wouldn't bother my swollen toes. Just as I opened the door, I heard the jangle of keys on the other side of the hall, and I immediately shut it again. *Non, merci.* I simply couldn't face her. Just across the landing was my nemesis or, rather, my platonic ideal of womanhood, my neighbor Juliette.

Let's be honest, every woman has someone like this in her life. Maybe it's the Pilates-toned high-school friend you run into at the supermarket *only* when you haven't washed your hair. Perhaps it's the red-soled powerhouse that stands in front of you every day at Starbucks. The one woman who makes you feel like you should retreat back into the cave and seriously reevaluate your eye shadow. These women have two distinct qualities: They always look their best, and they always show up when you look your worst. Mine has an additional, home-court advantage: she's French.

Juliette is a thoroughbred—a pure *Parisienne,* raised in the sixteenth arrondissement. She's an editor at a popular magazine, married to the equally gorgeous and scruffy Luca, who, after business school, went to work for UNICEF. She wears fashionably louche sweaters with suede elbow patches in touch-me-soft fabrics that *do not* allow for a ring of fat bulging out of the bottom of one's bra. What's more, she's unbearably, unfailingly nice. On a good day, I admire her. On a bad day, I pray for an open manhole cover.

Juliette and Luca have two children: Horace, five, and Zoé, two. Naturally, Juliette came home from the maternity ward in her skinny jeans. She always has on eyeliner, mascara, and chunky high-heeled boots when she takes the kids to school.

She seems genuinely excited that I'm pregnant. At thirty-eight and thirty-five, Gwendal and I are on the old side for French parents; many of Gwendal's childhood friends have near-teenagers by now. It's always difficult to get together—Parisian couples are so busy—but one afternoon, the four of us paired off over beers at the local café.

French women can be notoriously hard to get to know, but childbearing seems to bring you into a sorority where otherwise off-limits personal topics are discussed with abandon. Juliette tucked her dark hair behind her ear and took a sip of her *blanche*. "No," she said, "I didn't breast-feed. *J'avais pas envie*. It just wasn't for me," she said casually. No guilt, no judgment.

"*Tu fais la rééducation?*" she inquired earnestly, referring to the ten sessions of state-subsidized Kegels that are supposed to keep me from peeing on myself for the rest of my life and, more important, get me back to having sex with my husband in short order.

I'd heard about this from other Americans who'd had babies in France. How shall I put it? *La rééducation périnéale* is basically physical therapy for your vagina. You pick up an electric wand (not unlike a vibrator) at the pharmacy, find a way to discreetly slip it into your purse, then head to the *kiné*'s office—mine works in a nice converted apartment complete with fancy moldings and fireplace. Then, with a mix of electrical stimulation and exercises, the therapist shows you how to tighten all your interior muscles again. The sessions are completely free, and absolutely everyone does it.

Juliette checked a message on her phone. "Don't wait too long to *faire l'amour*," she whispered. "Six weeks is ideal."

I must have looked stricken, or at least not appropriately ecstatic. "*Tu vas voir.* You'll see," she said, lightly squeezing my arm. "The day my children were born was the most beautiful day of my life." She made it sound so simple: she was beautiful, it was beautiful. And that's when it hit me. For the French, there is clearly no before and after. I was meant to be exactly the same woman, but with a reeducated vagina—and a kid.

Recipes to Substitute for a Summer Vacation

YELLOW SPLIT-PEA PUREE WITH ORANGE-GINGER VINAIGRETTE
Purée de Pois Cassée Jaune aux Agrumes

I first tasted this in Puglia. It's a great alternative to traditional hummus at a party. Try serving with prosecco, just to keep the Italian vacation fantasy alive.

2 cups yellow split peas
6 cups cold water
3 tablespoons best extra-virgin olive oil
3 tablespoons freshly squeezed orange juice
3 teaspoons sherry vinegar
1½ teaspoons freshly grated ginger
Generous ¼ teaspoon coarse sea salt
Thinly sliced sourdough bread, toasted
Fresh chopped dill, to taste
½ white peach, thinly sliced

In a medium saucepan, combine peas and water. Bring to boil, lower the heat, and simmer for 50 minutes to 1 hour, until most of the water is absorbed.

In a glass jar or airtight container, add the oil, orange juice, vinegar, ginger, and salt. Give it a good shake to combine.

Stir the vinaigrette into the peas; puree with your hand blender (or in a food processor).

Serve warm on toasted sourdough bread with an extra drizzle of olive oil. Top with the chopped dill and a slice of white peach.

Serves 4 as a light lunch (add a mixed green salad) or 8–10 as an hors d'oeuvre

Tip: This dish will thicken as it cools. To reheat, add a dribble of white wine.

RABBIT WITH PASTIS, FENNEL, AND FRESH PEAS
Lapin aux Pastis

I was only a week from my due date when Gwendal went to sign the deed for the house in Céreste. We were so nervous that I might have the baby on the train that I stayed behind in Paris. In this recipe, I've re-created Provence from afar. It's such a pretty summer dish, and the pastis gives it a unique licorice kick. If even after my elegies, you're still feeling squeamish about rabbit, try making this with a good-quality chicken.

2 tablespoons butter
2 tablespoons olive oil
1 rabbit, with liver, cut into 8 pieces
Coarse sea salt
2 carrots, coarsely chopped
1 half bulb fennel, coarsely chopped
4–6 small shallots, left whole
2 tablespoons pastis or anisette
1 cup dry white wine
4 small carrots, halved or quartered lengthwise
1 additional bulb fennel, cut into large chunks
¼ cup crème fraîche or heavy cream
1 cup fresh peas
1 handful of chervil, chopped

In your largest frying pan or Dutch oven, heat 1 tablespoon butter and 1 tablespoon olive oil. Brown the rabbit well, along with the liver, on all sides; sprinkle generously with coarse sea salt. Remove the rabbit to a plate. Add the additional tablespoon of butter and oil and sauté the chopped carrots, fennel, and shallots until softened and slightly golden, 5 to 6 minutes.

Add the rabbit back to the pan, add the pastis, let sizzle for a minute. Add white wine. Tuck the large chunks of carrots and fennel in between the rabbit pieces. Bring to a boil, then lower the heat, cover, and cook for 40 to 45 minutes, turning the meat once at the 20-minute mark.

Remove the rabbit to a plate; cover with aluminum foil. Bring the sauce to a boil and reduce for 5 minutes. Add cream and stir to combine. Add the rabbit, peas, and chervil to the pan; heat through.

Serve with wild rice.

Serves 4

Tip: If you make this with a whole chicken, you might not need to add the second tablespoon of olive oil and butter to the pan when you sauté the veggies, as the chicken skin will probably render some fat of its own.

CHAPTER 3

The Sushi at the End of the Tunnel

"No," I grunted, my white-knuckled fingers gripping the footboard of the hospital bed. "I will. Not. Go. Downstairs. The nurse *promised* us a single room. I don't care if I have this baby right here on the linoleum floor, I'm not going till it's done." Even in my slightly altered state, I'd been in France long enough to know that if we went down to the delivery room before this was taken care of, someone would forget, or make a mistake, or give the room away. Giving birth seemed to me a rather private process, and I didn't relish the idea of spending the first week of motherhood in the same room with another hormonal human and her howling newborn.

Right up till the moment the first contractions hit, I had not made a decision about the epidural. I thought about toughing it out, not because I'm so attached to the cosmic authenticity of natural childbirth but because I was afraid the doctor might paralyze me. It was Friday the fourteenth of August, the eve of the biggest holiday weekend of the year. Surely all the truly competent doctors were on the beach in Saint-Tropez, not stuck here on call with me.

Also, I was in no rush to get downstairs because I knew it wasn't going to be any cooler down there. The French air-condition their operating theaters, but that's to keep the machines from overheating, not the people. Ask your average *homme* on the street, and he will tell you that air-conditioning is bad for your health—that it gives you colds, gout, acne, what have you. This idea seems to have its origin in a 1990s outbreak of Legionnaires' disease spread through the ventilation system at the Hôpital Pompidou in Paris. Cooling systems never got over the bad press, and we pregnant women have been suffering the consequences ever since.

Because it was August, and all normal people were away, the hospital had taken the opportunity to rip up half a wing. A small window in the delivery room was missing its glass; the space was covered with a plastic sheet and sealed with duct tape. I could hear the jackhammers going on the other side. If air-conditioning wasn't sterile, how about this?

I would tell you what happened next, but I dozed through almost the whole thing. In theory, there are lots of reasons I'd rather have been born in another century: I like chamber music, and I think I would have looked good in a bustle. But here we are in the twenty-first—so give me the drugs. French women seem to be casually pragmatic about this as well as other childbearing rituals. I think this is part of what they mean in France by women's liberation. To most, natural childbirth is a bit like nineteenth-century dentistry; we've moved on.

In between naps, I appeared to be meeting with everyone's approval. A doctor came in, took a look below the sheet, said, in classic French fashion, "Everything looks great, you don't need me," and promptly walked right out again.

The presence of the sheet brings us to the small but not inconsequential question of who looks where. (Add this to the list of things, like nipple cream and the dangers of kitty litter, that I never thought about before getting pregnant.) My gynecologist, who, like me, was a relative newcomer to France, said that when she had her first baby in Paris, her French obstetrician counseled that if—*if*—her husband was present for the birth, she should make sure he didn't see exactly what was going on down below or he would never want to have sex with her again.

In the States, people put their birthing videos on YouTube, and a friend at a big law firm once got a sonogram picture from a colleague over the office intranet. I'm pretty sure that in the U.S., the privacy ship has sailed. The French take a more discreet tack.

Unsure how to proceed, in the weeks before the delivery I decided to take an informal survey. I began with my friend Keria, a platinum-blond American also married to a Frenchman. Keria is a teacher by day, a jazz singer by night—and the mother of five-month-old Theo. She has the kind of split personality I love: consummately intelligent, cool under fire, but with a gift for high drama and the potty mouth to go with it. We sat down over cocktails one afternoon at a busy intersection near Jaurès, the alcohol carefully timed to fit between her breast-feedings. "Oh, yeah," said Keria when I asked her where her husband was positioned during the birth. "That's a big ten-four. I told Marco, 'Eyes forward, mister.' Nobody needs to see that shit."

Frankly, I'm with her.

It may sound old-fashioned, but I like the idea of maintaining an aura of mystery, not to mention dignity, during childbirth. I think of it like this: When my parents were first married, my father made the mistake of offering my mother an automatic garage-door opener for Valentine's Day. Forever after, practical gifts were outlawed in our house. No one wants to have sex with a garage-door opener.

❧

AFTER THE STRONG epidural, the next few hours were mostly hurry-up-and-wait. I felt like I was meeting a train, the kind of big steam locomotive that makes a satisfying hiss when it pulls into the station and cuts the engine. I imagined myself in a long dress, a hat with a veil, a big bunch of roses in the crook of my arm. I was waiting for an honored guest—who just happened to be staying eighteen years. To make matters more interesting, we didn't know exactly who would be stepping off onto the platform.

Since we'd decided we didn't want to know the sex of the baby in advance, speculation these last few weeks had been intense. *"Alors, comment va le fiston?"* said the Tunisian man who sells me my melons at the Saturday market as he handed me a sweet juicy slice. He is sure that it is a boy. I agree. As the only daughter of a mother who is one of a pair of daughters, I always imagined myself as the mother of a tiara-obsessed little girl. But my life is already so different from what I imagined it would be—different country, different man, different vegetables—that I've learned to enjoy (okay, *tolerate*) the off-piste-ness of it all. If I can stand the suspense, life never gives me exactly what I want—it gives me something better.

After a mere six hours in the delivery room, the *sage-femme* laid the baby on my chest, curled up like a cat, warm and sleepy. I brushed my lips to a tuft of hair. "Is it a boy or a girl?"

"Oh," said Gwendal, slightly dazed. "I forgot to look."

Gwendal picked up the baby, long skinny legs dangling in the air. The melon man was right: it was our son.

⌒

AFTER A PERFECTLY normal birth, Alexandre and I spent six days in the hospital, for free. I repeat: for free. I don't know what that sounds like to the rest of the civilized world, but for an American, that's like a week in Aruba. The single room I had huffed and puffed my way into was a whopping 367 euros extra on our private insurance. I doubt that amount would cover the cost of the rubbery chocolate pudding on my lunch tray in the States. Yes, you have to bring your own diapers. It seems a small price to pay for universal health care.

I like to think of that precious week as what the French call a *palier de décompression*—the time you take to decompress when you come up from scuba diving; if you go too fast, your head is going to explode. The nurses teach you how to bathe the baby, how to breast-feed. If you need extra help after you leave the hospital, you can arrange for home visits from a *sage-femme*. For a few days they let you float in a liminal space—senses are heightened. Somewhere between the girl you once were and the mother you are in the process of becoming.

I WANTED TO get to the market early so I wouldn't roll over too many toes with the stroller. Gwendal had gone back to work after his eleven-day paternity leave (another federally mandated Gallic perk) and Alexandre and I had some time to get to know each other one on one. I tend to do the bulk of my worrying in advance, so as soon as he arrived, most of my existential angst about motherhood evaporated, replaced with a sleepy routine of feeding and changing and napping and bathing.

I showed Alexandre Paris the way I would a tourist friend, albeit one who comes with a lot of excess baggage. Bouncing the stroller down two flights of spiral stairs was a challenge. Whether to leave the baby at the top of the stairs or the bottom while I performed this operation felt like a life-or-death decision. (I opted to leave Alexandre in his seat just outside our front door; at least anyone trying to snatch him would have to get through me first.)

After ten months of pasteurized cheese and a week of hospital food, one not inconsiderable pleasure of coming home was access to my own refrigerator, and the right to fill it with all the forbidden favorites I hadn't tasted in almost a year. Friends rushed over to meet the baby bearing seasonally inappropriate treats: squat glass jars of foie gras and sweet golden Sauternes wine, *saucisson* marbled with fat. Watching the butcher weigh my half pound of chicken livers felt like catching Santa in the act. The good sushi place, the subject of so many midnight reveries these past few months, wouldn't open for another ten days.

My first stop at the market was the fishmonger. The team greeted Alexandre like he was a long-lost nephew; one of the men dangled a sardine over the carriage in welcome. I chose two whole sea bass, slick and glistening in the early September light, and some dark meaty tuna steaks—I would make tartare to tide us over until the chirashi got back from vacation.

Personally, I love dinner that stares back. Gutting my first fish in Paris was an initiation on par with losing my virginity—who knew there was such a dangerous, bloodthirsty individual hiding behind this neo-Victorian facade?

I've also been practicing my fifteen-minute meals, because as much as I love to putter around the kitchen, my time there is likely to be reduced in the coming months (and I would hate to fall asleep standing at the stove). Whole fish doesn't sound like fast food, but it is. You put in the time later, boning it at the table (which is better for digestion and conversation). I know most Americans don't like to work for their food, but deconstructing a whole fish is one of my favorite culinary activities. It looks so decadent on the plate—you feel you are playing a game (Operation comes to mind). The protective skin makes quick methods like broiling a real option; there's no risk of dry, charred flesh. The eyeball is basically like one of those Purdue self-timers—when it pops, chances are it's done.

My Tunisian friend gave me an extra melon for the baby, gratified to know his prediction was correct. I weaved between the morning shoppers, past the roasting chickens and sizzling potatoes, past the last blackberries and the ripening figs, to my cheese monger, Madame Richard.

Madame Richard must be nearing seventy; she wears her hair in a bleached-blond pixie cut and has an affection for hot-pink parkas. She took a motherly interest in my pregnancy. In fact, I've found the relationship between a woman and her cheese monger to be one of the more intimate in French life. They know if you buy quite a lot that you are having important guests or your in-laws are in town. They know if you buy just a little that you are on a diet or your husband has a problem with his cholesterol. They know your moods, your desires. They know if you're feeling brave enough for a sharp blue or need to hibernate with the rich drippy comfort of a Mont d'Or so ripe you could serve it with a spoon.

Madame Richard was among the first people in Paris to find out I was pregnant. Sometime in February, I rolled up with my red polka-dot granny cart and said I had a friend coming for dinner who was expecting and couldn't eat raw-milk cheese. The next Saturday, my poise and creativity somehow deserting me, I tried the same lame excuse. No doubt she had seen this look on the faces of a thousand women, cheeks flushed with excitement, nerves, and the genuine regret of knowing they will spend the next nine months without a single mouthful of pungent Camembert. Madame Richard smiled knowingly and gently ushered me toward all things pasteurized.

When she spotted me with the stroller, Madame Richard quickly handed the change to her previous client and bounced out from behind the counter. *"Félicitations,"* she said, kissing me on both cheeks. *"Coucou, toi,"* she said, leaning to get a good look.

While she was staring adoringly at Alexandre, I was staring adoringly at the cheese. I chose the drippiest, moldiest, smelliest one I could find—an Époisses soaked in marc (a kind of grappa made from the leftovers of Bordeaux grapes). I tucked the round of red-and-white-checkered waxed paper into the basket of the stroller and rolled down the hill toward home.

SO THIS IS the supermom challenge: Two of the most important events of my life—the birth of my son and the publication of my first book—are happening right around the same time. My editor in New York called only once, just as I was going into labor. When I arrived home, I reviewed the galleys of *Lunch in Paris* with two-week-old Alexandre asleep in my lap.

I was sitting at my desk wearing a hands-free breast pump: a 1980s-Madonna-esque contraption engineered, at the suggestion of a very organized American friend, by cutting two holes in an old sports bra to hold the suction cups in place. Three weeks in, I was getting antsy, bored, nutty. There seems to be a dearth of vocabulary for describing these feelings. The modern cult of motherhood has left women with very few options; the only acceptable emotions are pure joy and/or jocular exhaustion. I was turning in circles—dying to get out of the house, but loath to leave the cocoon, the safe little triangle between the café, the market, and the corner *boulangerie*.

As my first real outing, I'd decided to accept an invitation to the new-members cocktail party of the Association of American Wives of Europeans. Putting myself into smiley networking mode was a bigger production than it used to be. I stared into my closet, eventually choosing a black Donna Karan dress with an Empire waist that I thought was fairly flattering. But even as I took it off the hanger, I wavered. In the English tradition, Empire waists are associated with ballroom scenes in Jane Austen novels, but in France, there's something about a seam underneath your bust that just screams *Lactating over here!*

But I was already late. The dress would have to do. I found some red lipstick and a pair of flats that didn't pinch, kissed my boys, and ran out the door. What I didn't have time to do before I left was eat. It was six o'clock, and somehow lunch had escaped me. In the middle of my power walk to the Métro at République, I stopped at our local *boulangerie* for a *pain au chocolat*. I knew I was breaking ranks, flouting etiquette. The French simply do not stuff their faces on the run. They do not eat on the street, on the Métro, at their desks, or anywhere, in fact, but in a restaurant or at the family table. Adults do not eat between meals; that is a privilege reserved for schoolchildren—the 4:00 *goûter*. Books in the stores, trailers at the movies, and philosophers on the national radio will tell you: Anything else leads to chaos, anarchy, the decline of French culture, and the rise of obesity. Scarfing my pre-dinner pastry on the sidewalk was the culinary equivalent of waxing my legs on the downtown A train or answering my cell phone at the opera—simply not done. But the New Yorker in me had kicked in—and I couldn't stop her. She had places to go, people to see. She was late, and she was going to multitask.

I was chomping away on my pastry, waiting impatiently to cross the avenue Parmentier, when I heard a comment aimed in my general direction. *"Attention aux kilos."* Watch your pounds. I turned around; maybe the voice was in my head? But then I heard it again. *"Attention aux kilos."* I looked down. There was a homeless man on the sidewalk, sitting cross-legged, like a prophet, among the empty bottles overflowing from the recycling bin. *"Attention aux kilos, madame,"* he said, wagging a finger unsteadily at my knees.

I had sinned, and now I'd been punished. The light changed, and I ran.

I had just enough pregnancy hormones left in my system that I wanted to cry. Thankfully, I had the Métro ride across Paris to collect myself. The event was in the chic eighth arrondissement, land of embassies, gleaming Haussmann apartment buildings, and boutiques selling cashmere cardigans. There were no homeless men to comment on my figure, or on anything else.

I felt relaxed as I mounted the sweeping marble staircase of the *hôtel particulier*—one of hundreds of grand private residences now transformed into mundane offices. Alexandre was snug at home with his dad drinking a bottle of breast milk. Thanks to the Star Trek–like miracle of breast pumps, it really *is* possible to be in two places at once. I found my name tag and followed the crowd into a high-ceilinged reception room with ornate plaster moldings and polished wood floors. I love meeting new people. I let myself enjoy the frisson of anticipation that accompanies a roomful of strangers.

An older woman in a trim wool jacket and a gold brooch—the welcoming committee—spotted a newcomer and came right over. She glanced at my name tag and immediately launched into small talk. "When's the baby due?" She smiled, tilting her head to indicate what a good listener she was.

"I gave birth three weeks ago," I croaked, doing my level best to smile in return. I took a sip of my wine and vowed to throw all Empire waists in the trash as soon as I got home.

༄

THOUGH HE IS not quite ready for a fork, Alexandre did start smiling this past week. Why didn't I know that humans have to learn how to smile? The effect was electric, like watching the lights go on on top of the Empire State Building. It changes everything. He doesn't just need me; I think he likes me. Of course, he also smiles at Mimi the musical chicken, who has orange polka-dot legs and a rattle inside her left foot. I think I could take Mimi in a fight, but for now I'm hanging back. In the immortal words of John Wayne: Never come between a man and his musical chicken.

It has been a good day—an ordinary one that somehow feels special. Gwendal is away on business, and Alexandre and I spent the afternoon browsing my favorite spice shop in the Marais and sitting under a tree in the courtyard of the Hôpital Saint-Louis, a seventeenth-century building that once housed Paris's first wards for patients with infectious diseases. At that time, the neighborhood was still open pasture—safely outside the city walls.

I plucked the falling leaves off Alexandre's blanket; they were already brown and crinkly, despite this past week of Indian summer warmth. On days like this, I wonder why I sometimes feel so insecure in my new role. It's not the practical bits that worry me; I just can't seem to figure out the proper distance to maintain. Some days Alexandre makes me feel crowded, claustrophobic; some days he makes me feel lonely in advance. Maybe it's because he's a boy, but I have this feeling that even though he just got here, he's already got one foot out the door. *A son is a son till he takes a wife; a daughter's a daughter the rest of her life.* Look who's talking—I live three thousand miles away from my mother. But no matter how far away, I'm still hers. I'm brave in the ways she's made me brave and scared in the ways she's made me scared. I'll never belong to anyone the way I belong to her. Maybe it's a self-fulfilling prophecy, but Alexandre already feels so independent of me.

That night, I laid him down, as gently as possible, in his bed. This doesn't always work. As often as not, he stretches and coos, then jolts himself suddenly awake, arms spread, eyes wide, as if he's been struck by lightning.

But not tonight—tonight, when I laid him down, one arm fell instantly behind his head; the fingers flexed and released. The other arm fell more slowly, across his chest, then he gave a graceful outward wave, as if he were conducting a symphony.

I realized that, right up until the moment of his birth, all my thoughts about motherhood had been about myself: my fears, my work, my time, my body, my marriage. It was mysterious, fascinating, to discover the range of *his* feelings. That he could smile, scream, laugh, and conduct a symphony in his sleep.

Recipes for Forbidden Favorites and Fifteen-Minute Meals

BROILED WHOLE SEA BASS WITH LEMON AND HERBS
Loup de Mer au Citron et aux Herbes

I know making a whole fish doesn't sound like an easy weeknight dinner, but if I were writing one of those dinner-in-fifteen-minutes cookbooks, this is the first recipe I'd include.

4 sea bass, 9–11 ounces each, gutted and scales rubbed off
1 tablespoon olive oil
Sea salt
2 slices of lemon, cut in half
Fresh flat-leaf parsley, thyme, dill, or other herbs

Preheat your oven to broil. Put a double layer of foil on a cookie sheet.

Lay out your fish; drizzle with oil. Rub the oil all over the fish, including tails and heads; this will keep them from sticking to the foil when you need to turn them. Sprinkle the cavities with a pinch of sea salt and stuff each with a lemon slice and herbs.

Position your cookie sheet on the highest rack, about 2 inches down from the heat. Broil fish for 5 or 6 minutes (you can start checking at 4), or until the skin bubbles and chars in a few spots (sometimes the skin splits instead of bubbling). Don't worry if the fins stick straight up and burn a bit. Turn carefully; you'll need a spatula and a fork for this operation. Cook for 2 to 3 minutes more. You can tell if the fish is done by inserting the tip of a small knife next to the bone; if the fillet is opaque and pulls away easily, it's ready. Always err on the side of caution—it's better to undercook slightly and put it back than to turn a perfect piece of fish into mush with overcooking.

Serves 4

Tip: Of course, individual fish can vary in weight; a slightly larger fish (11 or 12 ounces) might need 7 minutes on one side and 4 to 5 minutes on the other. You'll soon get the hang of it in your oven.

CHEF SALAD WITH CHICKEN LIVERS
Salade Composée au Foie de Volaille

The French long ago mastered the art of serving salad so it doesn't feel like punishment for something. This one is in the tradition of a *salade composée*—a favorite bistro lunch. In Paris you might find one with duck gizzards, cured ham, even a poached egg—all things I missed desperately during my pregnancy—but my favorite is the velvety texture of warm chicken livers. You can mix and match ingredients, throw in some leftover roast potatoes to sizzle with the bacon, or top with nice-size chunks of Comté cheese. The final impression should be one of abundance, not restriction.

1 small head red leaf or butter lettuce
1 large handful green beans
1 large tomato
3½ ounces lardons (slab bacon or pork belly), cut into ½-inch cubes
8 chicken livers
Black pepper

For the dressing

½ cup olive oil
1 tablespoon plus 2 teaspoons red wine or sherry vinegar

1 scant teaspoon Dijon mustard
1 good pinch of coarse sea salt

Wash and dry the lettuce; set aside. Boil the green beans until dark green and tender, about 8 minutes.

Meanwhile, in a glass jar or other airtight container (I use an old jam jar), add all the ingredients for the dressing and shake vigorously to combine. This is my favorite kind of classic French vinaigrette, cloudy with mustard and grounded with good olive oil. This recipe makes enough dressing for several salads—it keeps in the fridge for weeks.

When the beans are done, rinse them under cold water to stop the cooking process and pat dry, then cut into 1½-inch pieces. Cut the tomato in half, discard the seeds, and chop into 1-inch cubes. Put the tomato and green beans in the bottom of a large salad bowl.

In a medium frying pan, cook the lardons, then remove with a slotted spoon—don't discard the fat, you'll need it to sauté the chicken livers. Add the bacon to the tomatoes and green beans. Toss to combine.

When you are almost ready to serve, sauté the chicken livers in the bacon fat, with a grind of black pepper, 2 to 3 minutes on each side. They should stay pink in the middle—overcooked chicken livers get kind of rubbery.

Add the lettuce to the salad bowl. Give the dressing a good shake, then add 2 to 3 tablespoons to the salad. Toss the whole lot. (If there's nobody watching, I tend to do this with my hands.)

Divide the salad between two plates, making sure to scatter an even serving of green beans, tomatoes, and bacon on each. Top each salad with 3 or 4 chicken livers. Serve immediately. A glass of light red would be nice.

Serves 2

TUNA TARTARE
Tartare de Thon

I had dreams about sushi all through my pregnancy. This is the postpartum recipe that tided me over until the owners of the good sushi place got back from vacation.

2 teaspoons olive oil

1 teaspoon sesame oil

2 teaspoons rice vinegar

½ teaspoon fresh ginger, finely grated

Good pinch coarse sea salt

10½ ounces sushi-grade tuna steak

¼ cup cucumber, seeded and diced

1 teaspoon pickled ginger, diced (optional, but very nice)

1½ teaspoons chives, minced

1 small avocado, halved

In a glass jar or other nonreactive container, combine oils, vinegar, fresh ginger, and salt, then whisk or shake to combine. Cut the tuna into ¼-inch pieces; store in the fridge until ready to use. Five minutes before serving, combine fish, cucumber, pickled ginger, if using, chives, and dressing. Let rest for 5 minutes (if you leave it any longer, the vinegar starts to cook the fish and you have ceviche, not tartare). Divide into two portions and press each portion into a bowl or a biscuit cutter to mold it. Unmold each onto a plate. Serve with half an avocado and mixed green salad on the side.

Serves 2 as a main course, 4 as a light appetizer

Tip: If you want to serve this as an hors d'oeuvre, you can make it portable: put a spoonful on top of an endive leaf.

CHAPTER 4

Sacrificial Lamb

Today we sacrificed a lamb in honor of my firstborn son. I always hoped I would have a reason to write a sentence so thoroughly biblical.

Le méchoui, a North African lamb roast, is a long-standing tradition in my husband's family. There was one when Gwendal was born, and one for the birth of each child since. Somewhere in the archives, there is a photo from the 1970s of my father-in-law with a waist-length beard munching—Neanderthal-style—on a leftover leg of lamb. This meal is a rite of passage, both hello and good-bye. It's a celebration of the transition to our new life as parents, from city dwellers to *villageois.*

The past year had seen as many changes as one person has a right to live through in 365 days. Alexandre was five months old when we took our first trip to New York for the book launch; I had to hold him up for his passport photo. When the book hit the stores, just before Valentine's Day, I waited for some current of electricity that would send me a jolt whenever someone read the first line. I wasn't sure what this day would feel like. Would I wake up in a fairy-tale ball gown—or turn into a pumpkin?

I was fortunate to get some advice on this very topic from Diane Johnson, author of *Le Divorce* and other tales of expat adventure. (I suspect she has a dark side. She is also the coauthor of the screenplay for *The Shining*.) She agreed to meet me one afternoon for macaroons at Ladurée in Saint-Germain. The interior of the tearoom resembles the drawing room of an eccentric English aristocrat—one who never quite returned from colonial service in Shanghai. The walls are painted with exotic palm fronds, and red lacquer screens cover the sign to the bathrooms. After we both poured our tea, I looked up from my Darjeeling and lemon macaroons. "So," I began, trying not to sound too much like an eager beaver, "what did it feel like when you published your first book?" Diane leaned over the small table—her chin was not much higher than its rim—and looked me in the eye: "Don't expect your life to change," she said. "Not one bit. When my first book came out, I was so disappointed, I went straight to the hairdresser and said, 'Make me a blonde!'"

I suspect my mouth was hanging open. My first thought was *My God, am I that transparent?* My second thought was *My God, what if she's right? The next time she sees me, I might be a flaming redhead.*

The fact is, I did expect this book to change my life. It was my way of staking out a little place in the world, independent of my husband, my child, my parents. Planting a flag: me, here. Even if I didn't sell a single copy, just getting it out there made me more relaxed in my own skin. My great expectations and my real life inching toward each other—page by page.

♋

WE ARRIVED AT Gwendal's godparents' house at dusk. The fields were recently shorn of summer wheat; the hay rolled and tied in bundles neat as giant spools of thread. The *apéritif*—wherever my mother-in-law goes, champagne will follow—was served on a cracked wooden wheelbarrow in a shady corner of the garden.

Affif and Annick have been my in-laws' best friends for forty years, back to their 1968 student days. Even now, it's easy to imagine them at a café, hand-rolled cigarettes and beer in hand, arguing the merits of the Beatles versus Brassens.

Affif and Annick live in a stone farmhouse that has been in her family for several generations. They've turned the old barns into a gallery and the hayloft into a sprawling bedroom for their two daughters and pack of grandsons. They keep chickens out back. There are two tortoises, the color of fallen leaves, who roam the grounds, looking for table scraps. They eat very well. There is a kitten with one blue eye, one brown, who rubs herself up against the glass of the kitchen window each morning. Affif keeps a pair of binoculars handy, to show his grandchildren the foxes that sometimes sprint across the neighboring fields.

The next morning I rose early—but, as usual, not quite early enough. Affif had been in the kitchen since dawn, roasting peppers, peeling onions, and plunging tomatoes into boiling water to remove their fragile skins. Affif was born and raised in Algeria, and though he has been in France for thirty years, his meals are often a marriage of two cultures—a lamb tagine cooked with white wine instead of water; stuffed cabbage laced with cumin but topped with a handful of grated Gruyère. When he heard the creak of my footsteps on the wooden staircase, he looked up from his knife. His curly hair was gray and cut short now, but it must have made for quite the afro back in the day.

"Bonjour, ma belle. S'il te plait, will you fetch me some thyme from the garden and some bay leaves from the tree in the corner of the yard?" I saw him watch me from the window as I ran to the far end of the lawn. Even after all this time, he's never sure his favorite city girl will come back with the right thing.

Over the past decade Affif has become a cooking mentor to me.

He is an artist, and he cooks the way he paints, with the confidence of long-practiced technique and a flourish of inspiration. His "recipes," such as they are, are not much more than a list of ingredients. I stick close to him in the kitchen as he beheads a handful of parsley, mixes olive oil with a thick dab of spicy harissa. It's the only way. Precious bits of advice drop like pebbles that I sort and collect over time.

The side dish to the roast lamb would be a traditional stew of white beans with tomatoes and herbs. The beans had been soaking overnight in a cool corner of the kitchen. In a bowl on the counter were bunches of fresh coriander and onions stuck with cloves.

After breakfast, my mother-in-law sat down to peel a pile of carrots. Alexandre sat beside her in the highchair, trying out his new teeth by gnawing on the skinny end of a carrot. With her dancer's posture and her gray-blond hair cascading halfway down her back, Nicole remains my paragon of French womanhood. She adjusted the sleeve of her simple black top as it slipped off her shoulder. I thought to myself, and not for the first time, that she was far too glamorous to be anybody's grandmother. She, like most French women *d'un certain âge,* would not see the contradiction in terms.

I sat down beside her and picked up a knife. I was still doing a bit of tiptoeing around my mother-in-law. My book had had some unintended but nonetheless serious consequences.

It had begun a few months before at the dining-room table of our apartment in Paris. I had given Nicole the galleys of the book, and I was looking forward to hearing her opinion.

She began softly. Nicole is a psychoanalyst; she speaks in a calm, even tone that I imagine is very soothing to her patients. *"J'ai été choquée.* I was shocked that you used our real names." I put down my fork, leaving a large leaf of lettuce half pinned to the plate. The French don't cut their salad, they fold it, and this intricate origami still required some concentration on my part.

The scope of my error rose like a lump in my throat. I had read every chapter aloud to Gwendal. I showed each of my friends the passages that concerned them and asked if they would like their names changed. My own parents were so excited for me that it simply never occurred to me to ask them. Why hadn't I asked Nicole? I suddenly felt like one of those clueless tourists who take a picture of a remote African tribesman and steal his soul. It was the faux pas of the century—a white elephant so enormous, I didn't notice it until it sat on me. Though her English was good enough for her to read for content, I was pretty sure she hadn't caught the tone, which was warm and affectionate. I simply never considered that she might view the book as an invasion of her privacy, a deeply wounding form of voyeurism. I just assumed that, like my own parents, she would be proud of me. My dad had a saying: *Assume* makes an *a-s-s* out of *u* and *m-e.*

My mistake was cultural as well as personal. The division between public and private life in France is strict and nonnegotiable. There are laws against the paparazzi taking pictures of famous people's children, and you won't catch a Parisian telling his life story to a stranger on an airplane. Although French politicians now Tweet and the First Lady is an ex–model/pop star, the culture doesn't reward the kind of confessional, Oprahesque catharsis we Americans are used to. Nicolas Sarkozy's minister of justice had a baby out of wedlock, and no one knew (or, rather, no one was allowed to say) who the father was. Imagine Hillary Clinton or Nancy Pelosi trying to pull off something similar.

"*Et la maladie de…*"

Nicole didn't even have to finish her sentence. It had been four years since my father-in-law passed away, at the age of fifty-eight, of colon cancer. I welled up with shame and self-recrimination. I should have known better. *She's still struggling to put her life back together, and here you are describing his funeral to a bunch of strangers as part of an airy-fairy piece of entertainment. You deserve to be put in the stocks and shit on by pigeons for the rest of your life.*

"Je suis désolée"...I didn't mean...

I started twenty phrases, each more inadequate than the last. My French vocabulary deserted me, as it often does in times of stress. There was something else I wanted to say, but couldn't: *I lived through it too.* The book was not a senseless act of voyeurism. I didn't lose a husband or a father, but I did lose someone I had come to love, an integral part of my new family. I also lost a profound sense of cultural innocence. Gwendal and I had been married for only six months when my father-in-law was diagnosed. I was just dipping my little toe into French life. Standing in hospital corridors, furious with doctors who spoke from on high or refused to answer our questions, *that* was the moment France became real for me, became more than a collection of cream-filled pastries and cobblestoned alleys. It was then I realized that I had given myself over to a country, a language, a professional ethos, even a health-care system that I didn't completely understand. I was powerless, and terrified.

"Je ne comprends pas," Nicole continued. *"Ce n'est qu'une description de notre vie."* It's just a description of our life.

There's a quote by Victor Hugo that French students learn early: *"Chateaubriand ou rien."* Hugo decided when he was very young that he would be a famous canon-worthy author like Chateaubriand—or nothing. In other words, if you're not going to write a masterpiece, don't write at all. In the mythic realms of French literature, there is little acknowledgment of writing as craft—something you can practice and get better at. There is a high premium on genius, provocation, and inspiration.

To be fair, my mother-in-law wasn't the only one who was confused. As much as I tried to explain to our French friends what I was doing, they couldn't quite wrap their heads around the fact that I was telling a true story about something as itty-bitty as my own life.

The memoir genre simply doesn't exist in the same way in France as it does in the States. *Mémoires* in the French sense are written by former prime ministers, scientists who cure polio, and explorers who climb Everest without oxygen, not twenty-something Americans in Paris learning to whip up mayonnaise or gut their first fish. The book was hardly Tolstoy, but I hoped it had something real to say about what it meant to build a life in another culture.

I'd spent the rest of the evening stammering through an apology; there is no direct translation for *inconsiderate*. By ten o'clock I felt like a wet rag wrung out from one end to the other.

"What just happened?" I said to Gwendal after I finally closed the door behind Nicole with a thud. I felt like someone had punched me in the stomach. I was so busy apologizing for my own insensitivity that I barely had time to process her dismissal. It was the *n'est qu'une* that killed me. But it's *just* a description of our life. With a few words, she had reduced the sum of my experiences in France (not to mention two years' worth of meticulous writing and editing) to the level of mere secretarial work, requiring no more talent or effort from me than if I'd transcribed the conversations from a tape recorder. The evening was a slap in the face for both of us, and it left a red welt that would take some time to fade.

⌘

For my first *méchoui*, several years back, Affif bought the lamb from a local producer, slaughtered it, and prepared it himself. But restrictions were getting tighter on this sort of thing. So this year, he decided to order. At a quarter past nine that morning, Gwendal hurried out of the supermarket carrying something the size of a small child. (What would happen, I wonder, if one tried to order a whole lamb from my mom's local ShopRite in Hackensack?) If we had any hope of eating before nightfall, it had to be over the fire by 10:00 a.m.

I'd never seen a whole carcass up close; I must have slept through this part last time. The dining-room table had been laid out with a pristine white cloth, an enormous sewing needle, two pairs of pliers, and a roll of wire. It looked like the equipment of a Wild West surgeon, the kind who operated with impunity on both horses and people.

Affif stuffed the stomach cavity with a mix of quartered onions, tomatoes, peppers, and whole handfuls of herbs. As the spit went in one end of the lamb and out the other, I took a deep breath (on the lamb's behalf). The lamb's feet were secured on either end.

"*Désolée, mon petit,*" Annick apologized (to the lamb) as she approached with the needle and the wire to sew up his tummy. The final image was strangely dignified: the animal resting on a white cloth, surrounded by colorful ceramic bowls full of carrots, tomatoes, and branches of fresh bay leaves, as well as several wooden cutting boards with half-finished tasks. It looked like a Dutch still life—or a Martha Stewart snuff film. I shredded the edges of a clean rag and used a bit of wire to attach it to a long stick—a homemade basting brush. A pot with wine, butter, olive oil, salt, and a bunch of thyme followed the lamb to the fire. Affif's rotisserie is a homemade affair, rigged with rusting bicycle gears. But hey, it turns just fine.

Friends trickled in throughout the morning and were immediately put to work. There were more carrots to be grated for salad; tables and chairs to set up on the patch of grass between the house and the barns. I was in the kitchen chopping liver. To keep everyone going until the main event, the *méchoui* always begins with brochettes of grilled lamb's liver, marinated briefly with a slick of olive oil, spicy red harissa pepper, salt, and a good earthy dose of cumin. When Affif butchered the lamb himself, he would save *la voilette*, the delicate, lace-like membrane of fat that surrounds the internal organs, to wrap the hunks of liver and give it a bit of sizzle on the grill. Unfortunately, the supermarket butcher had chosen to throw this part away.

Gwendal's colleagues arrived from Paris. After five years of working on the bleeding edge of the digital-cinema industry, they were like an army unit, full of banter and private jokes. Alex brought reinforcements: two cases of Bordeaux. My eleven-month-old son *loved* the liver, proving, more than any passport, the French blood coursing through his veins.

During those lazy hours when the lamb browned slowly and it was too hot to sit outside, I found myself perched on some fading couch cushions in the barn with our friend Marie. She's a teacher in a small town in the Pyrenees. She speaks classical Greek, and she'd refused to fill out administrative forms asking for the professions of her students' parents: "What difference should that make!" she said indignantly. She's the kind of warm, intelligent, thoughtful person who makes a new friend feel like an old friend in a hurry. She also speaks fluent English.

"I read your book," she said. I braced myself, waiting for another literary sledgehammer. "I really enjoyed it. It was very thoughtful and well written."

I was sure I didn't know her well enough to throw my arms around her neck and sob with gratitude. Because the book was not published in French, and because talking about work in France is bad form in general, aside from the family drama, there had been little reaction on this side of the Atlantic. I was living parallel lives, one in which the book was an event to be celebrated, one in which it was barely acknowledged. I managed to clamp down my reaction to an acceptable European level. "*Merci*, Marie. *Ça me touche beaucoup.* That really means a lot to me."

THERE IS NOTHING fundamentally graceful about a woman with a greasy oven mitt lugging forty pounds of lamb across a field. It's more about tradition, tribal ritual. I was honored with the first piece of lamb crackling, burning-hot, slick and shiny like the leather on a fine first edition. I had to resist the urge to pick my entire meal off the spit with my bare hands. I sunk my teeth into the crispy fat. *Take your diamonds, boys, just give me the skin.*

As the afternoon heat gave way to an early-evening breeze, Gwendal and I took Alexandre to the yellow cherry tree in the garden. I'm sure my father-in-law once ate cherries off this tree; he was tall enough to reach deep into the branches without a ladder. (We keep the photo we took that day on the mantel: Alexandre raised above Gwendal's head, his chubby fingers grabbing at the leaves.)

After the day's feast, it seemed impossible that anyone would want dinner, yet somehow the spicy *merguez* on the grill lured everyone back to the tables. Marie had brought a case of melons with her across the Pyrenees. Alexandre didn't seem to mind when the juice dripped past his elbows.

I can't say this *méchoui* went as late as the one I remembered, with wine and the lilting melodies of *chansons réalistes* stretching late into the night. The kids, the rare Brittany heat wave, and the good Bordeaux wore us out. We were moving in a few days. I went to bed thinking about the people and places we would miss, all the boxes left to pack. We slept like little lambs, and woke up—if you can believe it—hungry.

A Recipe to Mark an Occasion

SEVEN-HOUR LAMB WITH NORTH AFRICAN SPICES

Gigot de Sept Heures aux Épices Orientales

I admit it, it's not every day that one roasts a whole lamb on a spit in the backyard. This recipe is a take on the slow-cooked *gigot de sept heures*, using the scents and spices—the inspiration—of Affif's kitchen. Get out your grandest serving platter and make this with couscous for a big family dinner—or any occasion that requires a warm welcome and a flourish of presentation.

3 tablespoons olive oil

5-pound bone-in leg of lamb, shank bone trimmed (to fit your pot), meat tied with kitchen string

Freshly ground black pepper

1½ pounds onions, halved and sliced

2 teaspoons whole cumin seeds, crushed

1 tablespoon turmeric

1 cinnamon stick

2 large pinches of saffron threads or ¼ teaspoon ground saffron

2½ cups white or rosé wine

1½ cups water

2 branches of celery with leaves

1 14-ounce can of chickpeas, drained

5 small carrots, scrubbed and halved

2 zucchini, cut into 2-inch chunks

½ cup green olives with pits (about 12), rinsed

12 strips of preserved lemon rind, about ¼ inch wide and 1 inch long

Fresh coriander for garnish

Preheat the oven to 300°F. Make sure your butcher has tied the meat with kitchen string, otherwise it will fall apart during the slow cooking.

In your largest Dutch oven (I treated myself to a huge Le Creuset for this recipe), heat 1 tablespoon of olive oil. Brown the leg of lamb on all sides as best you can. If you are restrained by the size of your pot, ask your butcher for a deboned leg of lamb with the bones on the side, brown the bones with the meat, and add to the pot for flavor. (Deboned lamb will cook more quickly.)

Remove the meat from the pot, season with black pepper, and set aside. Add the remaining 2 tablespoons of olive oil to the pot. Add the onions and spices and sauté until softened, about 10 minutes. Add ¼ cup wine, scrape the bottom of the pot, let sizzle a minute. Add another ¼ cup wine, let sizzle a minute as well. Add remaining 2 cups wine and the water and tuck in the celery branches. Bring to a boil.

Cover and put in the oven for 2 hours. Flip the meat, add chickpeas and carrots, bring back to a boil. Cover and bake for another 2 hours. Carefully flip the meat again. Add zucchini, cover and bake 1 hour more. Remove from oven and let rest. Twenty minutes before serving, add olives and preserved lemon and reheat. Carefully remove the meat to a large shallow serving dish (you'll need two large spatulas or slotted spoons to keep it intact as you lift it). Surround the meat with the vegetables, pour over the sauce, and garnish with coriander. Serve with couscous that has been tossed with a pat of butter, a handful of golden raisins, and a pinch of cinnamon.

Serves 6

Tip: Preserved lemons can be found at Middle Eastern groceries and specialty stores. I use only the outer rind (usually about ¼ inch thick) and discard the inner pulp. I don't add any salt to this recipe because the pre-

served lemons will take care of that at the end. If you can't find preserved lemons, sprinkle some coarse sea salt on the leg of lamb as you brown it and garnish the roast with a bit of lemon zest along with the coriander.

WHITE BEANS WITH TOMATOES AND HERBS
Haricots Blancs aux Herbes

Fresh beans are a summer treat—I like to make a simple warm salad with herbs, olive oil, and the sweetest tomatoes I can lay my hands on. Excellent with grilled lamb chops.

For the beans

4½ pounds fresh white beans, unshelled (2 pounds shelled)
Handful of flat-leaf parsley with stems
6 or 7 sprigs of fresh thyme
1 bay leaf
Pinch of cinnamon
A good grinding of black pepper
1 onion stuck with 5 cloves
9 cups cold water
2 medium tomatoes
2 teaspoons coarse sea salt

For the dressing

2 tablespoons olive oil
2 tomatoes, seeded and coarsely chopped
¼ cup cilantro, chopped
Coarse sea salt and black pepper to taste
Lemon wedges, to garnish

Place the beans, herbs, cinnamon, black pepper, and onion in a medium Dutch oven. Cover with 9 cups of cold water. Bring to a boil, add the whole tomatoes, and blanch for 3 minutes. Remove the tomatoes and rinse under cold water until cool enough to handle; peel, seed, and chop them, then add them to the pot.

Simmer with the cover ajar for 30 minutes. Add the salt and continue to simmer until the beans are tender, about 30 to 45 minutes more. Using a slotted spoon, remove the beans to a serving dish.

While still warm, toss with olive oil and chopped tomatoes. Just before serving, add the cilantro and black pepper. Pass with lemon wedges. Serve warm or at room temperature.

Serves 6

CHAPTER 5

Pas Mal

The French have a habit of polite understatement. Something good gets a slight nod of the head. Something marvelous might elicit a firm *bien*. But anything truly spectacular, knock-it-out-of-the-park nirvanaesque gets a resounding *pas mal*—not bad. We've been here only a few weeks, but already I can tell you: summer in Provence is *pas mal*. The heat is positively shimmering. It makes everything undulate, like the landscape in a fever dream. If you can bear to roll down the windows in the car (I could write a sonnet titled "Ode to Air-Conditioning"), the perfume of the fresh-cut lavender fields rushes in, making everything else you've ever inhaled a distant memory.

The drive from Paris took just over twelve hours. Since we left at rush hour, it took us nearly three hours just to clear *le périphérique*—the giant ring road that encircles the city like a manacle. The movers had forgotten to pack the contents of the coat closet, so in addition to my jewelry and the family silver, the backseat was stuffed to the gills with every scarf, hat, mitten, umbrella, spare button, and bottle of shoe polish we'd accumulated over the past ten years. To the passing cars, we must have looked like a band of gypsies off to join the circus. We pulled into Céreste, wheels crunching through the heavy silence, at four in the morning. We laid Alexandre in his crib and fell asleep on a bare mattress.

The first sign of our neighbors was a small wicker basket on the kitchen stoop. I disappeared upstairs with a carton of books and when I came down there it was, like a valentine from a secret admirer. The basket was carefully arranged, overflowing with small batons of zucchini, their delicate yellow flowers still attached. There were also green peppers, longer and slimmer than the ones I knew. Balanced on top were two squat, roly-poly eggplants and *le pièce de résistance,* a bright yellow heirloom tomato so large it barely fit in my hand.

It didn't take long for Jean, our next-door neighbor and vegetable benefactor, to appear. When he heard a string of French curses (Gwendal almost lost control of a box of dishes), he sauntered out; the metal gate at the entrance to his house shut with a clank behind him. Like a cow's bell or a teenager's ringtone, the sound was something we would learn to associate with his comings and goings.

Seventy-eight years old, Jean has close-cropped white hair, round glasses, and a belly that precedes him. *"Alors, les jeunes."* He was still dressed in his gardening clothes, a white undershirt and loose gray sweatpants. Come to think of it, those may have been the only pair of sweatpants I'd seen since I arrived in France.

He leaned against the stone wall of the courtyard and wiped his forehead with a handkerchief. At 9:00 a.m., he'd already done a full day's work, leaving the house at six, back before the late-morning heat set in.

I kissed him on both cheeks. *"Merci beaucoup,"* I said, turning the basket to admire the vegetables from all angles.

He pointed to the zucchini. "You will make soup for the baby." Over the past few months, I'd noticed that the French, particularly those of a certain generation, are positively dictatorial about babies and green vegetables. This has less to do with torture or nutrition than with introducing kids to the diverse flavors of the French table as early as possible. Almost as soon as they start on solid food, French children are expected to eat a miniature version of their parents' meals. Zucchini and leeks are favorite places to start.

"You add a bit of olive oil, a bit of cream." He looked over at Alexandre, still working on his morning bottle. *"Miam, miam,"* he said, patting his stomach. (That's French for "yum, yum.")

"Regarde ça," he said, picking up the yellow tomato and bouncing it a bit in his hand to emphasize its heft. "From my garden."

"J'adore cuisiner." I love to cook.

"Ah" he said. "You will come any time you like."

"You are American?" he said, narrowing his eyes. Though he'd met me several times and no doubt had had this piece of information since we'd bought the house the year before, the tone was suspicious, a vague rumor that required confirmation or denial. Could a woman born in the land of McDonald's really have a proper appreciation for French cuisine?

"Oui," I said, smiling hopefully.

"Before the war, my grandmother was the *chef de cuisine* at the American consulate in Nice."

"Ah, *oui?*" I said, nodding and blinking rapidly. I hope I sounded suitably impressed. Sometimes the most tenuous connection is all it takes. Between Grandma and the tomato the size of a small pineapple, perhaps I had found my first culinary mentor.

The clang of Jean's gate had brought Denis and Marguerite out onto their front steps. We heard the rattle of the heavy beaded curtain covering the front door. The subtle movement of the beads is meant to keep the flies out. We had our own hideous, if necessary, example over the kitchen door.

"Ho, Playboy." Denis calls our eleven-month-old son Playboy, pronounced with a broad Marseille accent: "Play-bo-yah." He's a big man: big voice, big belly, big heart. He identifies himself as

"L'Arménien," though his family came over from Armenia more than a century ago. It's very possible that if my great-grandchildren were to live in the village, they'd still be known as "Les New Yorkais."

Though I had been speaking French every day for the better part of ten years, I strained to understand the speed, lilt, and expressions of France's deep south. The Provençal accent has an extra *g* at the ends of words: *vin* becomes *ving*, *pain* becomes *paing*. But Marseille natives, with their love of one-upmanship, add a whole extra syllable, an *eh*, *oh*, or *ah* that sounds like the one-two jab of an amateur boxer. As Denis bent forward to kiss my cheek, his large cross and nazar, a glass amulet in the shape of an eye, dangled on a gold chain into space. Marguerite appeared on the stoop with a watering can, her red hair cut Anna Wintour–style over her full cheeks. Although they are a generation older than us, they are newlyweds, recently married at the village town hall, complete with white dress and pink Cadillac.

I heard the creak of a heavy wooden door as Claire and Arnaud joined us in the middle of the narrow street. Their house was literally stuck to ours; their daughter's room was once a part of our house, and we passed under her window to enter our small inner courtyard. Their little girl, Clémentine, scampered out from behind Claire's knees. Two and a half years old and intensely verbal, she showed me a pigeon feather she had found, carefully smoothing its edges between her small fingers. I felt the fuzzy spring of Arnaud's beard as we exchanged three rapid kisses. Depending on the region, one can spend quite a bit of time on perfunctory morning kisses in France. Two in Paris, and it seems to be the same here in Céreste, but just over the river in Apt it's three, and if you happen to meet someone from northwestern France, it could be four. Plus, I've never found a consistent answer to the question of which cheek to offer first. I just close my eyes, lean forward, and hope for the best. If you get it right, it feels like a dance; if you get it wrong, you can end up in a head butt like a pair of contentious goats. I'm sure there are times when kissing people you barely know has a lot of advantages, especially for teenagers. Imagine—you're seven-eighths of the way into someone's personal space from birth.

I haven't worked in a proper office in a while, but I imagine this is what it's like, the proverbial gathering around the water cooler. But instead of discussing reality television or basketball, the men were talking about firewood. Arnaud chops his own. With his beard, plaid shirt, short ponytail and calm, steady gaze, it is easy to imagine him taking a meditative pleasure in wielding an ax at dawn on some misty spring morning. I looked up, squinting to protect my eyes from the searing light coming through the branches of the apricot tree. *Firewood?* How can anyone talk about firewood when it's ninety degrees in the shade? I felt the moving boxes lurking behind me, waiting to be unpacked. It was unclear when or how we could excuse ourselves. It was Tuesday, and only two of our group were retired, yet no one seemed to have anywhere urgent to be.

Paris seemed impossibly far away—too far for a comparison. Still, I guess we won't be lonely here. It was ten in the morning, I'd barely left my doorstep, and I'd already kissed eight—no, actually, nine—people.

⟋⟍

TURNED OUT OUR neighbors weren't our only neighbors.

I was on my way to the cellar for a broom and heard a rustle. I opened the door a smidgen, heard distinct flapping, and immediately shut it again. "Gwendal, I think there's a bird stuck in there."

"It's not a bird," said Gwendal, stamping on the last of the cardboard boxes, "it's a bat."

"A what?"

"A bat. It probably moved in because there was no one living in the house."

"Well, can you tell him to move *out*," I said, backing away from the door. *There's a new sheriff in town, and she doesn't like vampire movies.*

"Don't worry," he said. "They eat the mosquitoes."

Buying an apartment in Paris had taught us all about squatters, and the bat wasn't our only encounter with the local wildlife. There were also scorpions—probably not the kind that could kill you, but even so. They hide in damp corners and behind laundry hampers, lounge in shower drains. No bigger than a matchbook, they seem completely unaware of their own puniness. When confronted with a shoe, they raise their pincers and flail around like Godzilla. You have to admire their pluck. Spiders are considered positively friendly. When the carpenter came by to measure the bookshelves, he patted the plaster walls and nodded up to a spiderweb across the kitchen ceiling. *"Ça veux dire que la maison est saine."* It means the house is healthy. Flies are considered an acceptable nuisance; instead of screen doors, most homes sport beaded fly curtains. When we bought the house, I wondered about this decorative touch. The last time I'd seen one of those was in the ladies' room of our local Chinese restaurant. In 1978.

At least I recognized the pigeons. I used to count the ones lined up on the roof of the A&P on the corner of Eighth Avenue, just around the corner from my dad's apartment. These pigeons had decided, like the bats, that a house that hadn't been lived in for twelve years was more theirs than ours.

The locals told us to buy an anti-pigeon sonar—which accomplished nothing at all. Then one day on my way to the café I saw a guy walking around the place des Marronniers with a long leather glove and a sleek, glassy-eyed falcon perched near his elbow. At first I thought the bird might be stuffed, which was weird enough, but then I saw its eyes dart back and forth, its feathers ruffle with impatience. I looked around for the cameras, sure they were filming a costume drama of some kind—Robin Hood was about to prance out from behind the iron gate of the château in tights. Not wanting to miss a village movie-star sighting, I asked the man what was going on.

"*Ça fait peur aux pigeons,*" he said. The falcon is supposed to scare the pigeons.

Scare them? Pigeons, if I remember correctly, have very small brains. This brings up existential questions: Do pigeons experience trauma? Can they even remember being scared, from one day to the next?

Sometimes translating from one language to another leaves a mental lag that allows concrete consequences to fall through the cracks. Just after our arrival, I started finding enormous wasplike creatures in the dining room, two or three each evening. They were yellow and black and made a sound like a remote-control helicopter. I brought a dead one in a plastic bag over to Arnaud. *Frelon,* I was told, very dangerous; a few stings can kill a small child. But somehow the word *frelon* just didn't sound that serious. If I'd known then what I know now, that there was a hornets' nest at the base of my chimney, I would have gone after them with something sturdier than a paperback copy of *Me Talk Pretty One Day*.

And then there's the scratching. It's no wonder people used to think their houses were haunted. It began during one of Gwendal's trips back to Paris for work. Thinking maybe the bat had migrated from the cellar to the upstairs hall, I gathered my courage, rolled last week's *New Yorker* into a makeshift baton, and went to face the enemy. There was no one there. At least, no one I could see. I sat up most of the night listening to the claws of the invisible intruder racing to and fro above my head.

"It's probably a *loir,*" said Angela. Over the year we were preparing the move to Céreste, Rod and Angela, our English B&B hosts, had become dear friends, not to mention a valuable source of local information. My hands were still shaky from a sleepless night when she gave me a much-needed espresso the next morning.

"What's a *loir?*" I said, imagining a huge slinky rodent with eight feet and four eyes.

"I think it's a dormouse."

"It didn't sound like a dormouse. It sounded like a yeti."

And then there's Guy. Stealthy as a fox, silent as a dead mosquito, and hunted by his clients with the zeal of the wild boar. Guy is our plumber. He walks around town in a royal-blue jumpsuit, which should make him easier to spot than a general in the Napoleonic wars, but just when you see him and think you can catch him without breaking into an undignified run, he manages to dip around a corner, or through a gate, and disappear. The extraordinary calcium levels in the local water require the timely replacement of our hot-water heater. It has been a few weeks now, *timely* being a relative term here in Provence. Guy has an excellent reputation, but like the hares that scamper across the roads at night, you can never tell when there's going to be a sighting. I don't run around the house naked anymore because one day, on a non-aforementioned date—weeks, perhaps months, after my urgent call—I'll find him staring, patiently, through the window of the kitchen door at eight a.m., waiting for the key to the cellar.

I SET OUT to follow Jean's soup instructions. The first thing I noticed when I walked into the minimart on the main street was that the olive oil was almost the same price as the bottled water. There were supermarket varieties and local ones, glass-green or clear and golden, like honey. I'd been cooking almost exclusively with olive oil since I moved to France—mostly because I can't stand the smell of melting butter (forgive me, Julia Child). There was even a three-liter *bidon* with a plastic screw cap, like a jerrican of gasoline.

Angela had warned me to leave some extra time for the butcher.

When we first signed for the house, she wrote us a letter.

I met Mireille at the butcher's this morning and she said again how happy she was that you were buying the house because it was the home of René Char. There were several people in the shop, so no doubt the whole village will soon be au courant *with the news.*

Apparently, if you had a rumor to spread, gossip to chew over, or simply needed to hear the hum of other human beings, the butcher shop was the place to be. I walked in the door to the murmur of a Greek chorus. As each customer joined the line, he or she was required to greet and be greeted by the entire cast. Following the example of the man in front of me, I sang out, *"Bonjour, messieurs, dames,"* to nobody in particular.

My butcher shop in Paris was a razor-sharp affair, gleaming white, clinically efficient—this was more laissez-faire. Women chatted with neighbors; two kids pressed their noses against the glass display, and when they looked up, they were each given a mini-*saucisson,* the size of a Tootsie Roll, cut from strings hanging like party streamers from the ceiling. A long wooden bench had been installed against one wall for older customers who preferred to sit while they waited. No one sat at the butcher in Paris.

After my general greeting, I went mostly unnoticed. Seeing my straw hat (I had a fantasy that living in Provence, coupled with my sensitive skin, would give me license to wear such things) and hearing my slight accent, they must have taken me for a tourist, just another of the many English, Dutch, and Germans who had summer homes in the area.

I began to consider my purchases. On one side were cuts of meat and neat little *caille*—tiny quails with their legs tucked primly underneath them. The summer selection was clearly skewed toward the BBQ: thin sausages spiced red with smoky *piment d'espelette* and something called *rouleau de Céreste* that looked like rolled pork belly with paprika and *persillade*. Without giving the impression of cutting in line, which would surely cause a diplomatic incident, if not an arrest by the local gendarmes, I pressed myself closer to the corner of the glass case. Unlike my butcher in Paris, who sold only meat, in Céreste, the butcher is also a *traiteur,* which means he sells a number of prepared foods—homemade pâtés, goat cheese wrapped in paper-thin slices of *jambon cru* soaking in olive oil and herbs, a classic salad of grated carrots in vinaigrette.

I felt an odd sensation—not exactly déjà vu, but *déjà vécu,* already lived. Suddenly, I was eight or nine, staring at the long glass case at Zabar's.

My parents divorced when I was seven, and my father moved from our house in northern New Jersey back to New York City. Sometimes, on a summer day like this one, there would be an open-air opera in Central Park, or we would wait in line for tickets to Shakespeare in the Park. A picnic from Zabar's, the famous grocer on the Upper West Side, was a special treat. A quarter-pound container of orzo salad with roasted red peppers and shrimp cost twice the weekly allowance my grandparents sent me from Florida.

Even as a small child, I understood it was better not to ask my father for things. No one had explained his diagnosis to me—in 1982, bipolar disorder was still called manic depression; it was mysterious and not discussed at the dinner table. If I didn't quite understand his illness, I absorbed its central theme, its underlying current of unpredictability. There were years he was so depressed he hardly spoke, others when he was so full of grandiose schemes that there was a new woman and a new business every month. Zabar's meant things were on the upswing. I remember so clearly the queenly thrill of choosing my calamari with cold sesame noodles, the feeling that, at least this week, things were going well. My father has been dead for almost fifteen years, but as I get older, as I move from city to city, country to country, I sometimes find myself back at that counter, an odd sensation of being in two places at once. Time collapses, a new experience layered with memories of other homes, meals, conversations.

I was so busy daydreaming about Zabar's and broccoli knishes that I didn't notice when the man in the apron was finally standing in front of me. *"Alors, madame."* He put his hands together like a pastor and gazed expectantly at me over the rim of his glasses. His voice was soft, hesitant to disturb my thoughts. I looked up, slightly startled. After twenty minutes surrounded by the hum of morning chatter and cuts of lamb, I'd almost forgotten I'd come to place an order.

⁂

BY DINNERTIME, my arms ached—my twin passions of heavy books and international travel were finally catching up with me. We decided to go for a walk; the days were long, twilight stretching almost till bedtime.

We stopped to sit at the edge of the fountain in the place de Verdun. The locals call it the place des Marronniers, after the four towering chestnut trees that grow in the center. A year ago, when we crossed this way for the first time, Mireille told us a story.

"This square used to be named after René Char," she'd said. "After the war—the first mayor of Céreste was a fellow Résistant—he named this place Capitaine Alexandre." Capitaine Alexandre was Char's nom de guerre.

Why isn't it called that anymore? I asked.

"Ah, c'est compliqué..." Which translates to "If you have a half hour to spare—it's a really good story."

During the war, she told me, Char had to feed his men, so from time to time he would go to the local farmers. He went to see one of the prominent landowners, a man who raised sheep. "Would you mind if occasionally one of your *bêtes* went missing…eaten by a wolf?" He let the question hang in the air.

The farmer refused. *"Je fais pas de politique."* I don't involve myself in politics, he said.

After the liberation, this same man came to Char and asked for an official *attestation* certifying that he had been part of the Résistance during the war.

Char looked up from his desk: "My guys eat fine now, thanks," he said and sent him on his way.

During the 1960s, this same farmer became the mayor of Céreste. *"Et voilà,"* Mireille told us, "the first thing the new mayor did was strip away any trace of Char and rename this square the place de Verdun. It was only recently that the village finally got a rue René Char, just below your street, where you'll find La Maison Taupin, the house that Char rented with his wife when he first came to Céreste."

People, and places, have long memories.

We walked down the main street, the facades of the buildings painted yellow, peach, and a fiery red—pigments reminiscent of the local ocher. We passed the town hall, a tall narrow edifice, its steps neatly swept of leaves, its balcony festooned with flags and flower boxes. We turned back into the old village; the warren of narrow lanes was already deep in shadow. The stroller jumped and rattled along the uneven pavement. There was light from a small window, the muffled sound of a television, the clinking of silverware and glasses. The rue de la Liberté was so narrow I could almost touch the walls with my outstretched arms. There were shutters of light blue and dark green, some freshly painted, others that needed a touch-up. I had walked down streets like this as a tourist, out at the wrong time of day, as tourists often are. It had never occurred to me that I would live here.

Two boys threw a ball back and forth in the small *placette*. We walked under a low stone arch. In the walls around me I saw echoes of other arches, a filled-in window, a going-nowhere door. These houses had been transformed so many times over the centuries that their entrances and exits, never mind their owners, were constantly subject to revision. Instead of making a jumble, these corrections gave an air of permanence, of survival. One more pair of new arrivals wasn't going to change a thing.

We took a sharp left and found ourselves in the open air. The oblong tower of the church, with its wrought-iron steeple, caught the last reflections of the sun against the hills. This is what a cinematographer would call the golden hour, the glowing time just after the sun sinks below the horizon and before the dark sets in. It's the hour of watercolor skies—discreet layers of cotton-candy pink, dusky rose, and periwinkle, when the fields are their deepest green, and the wheat has a halo that rises from the surface. We were standing on the medieval ramparts, the walls that once protected this small community from the hostilities of the outside world. Just below us was a field of lavender, the rows tidy and symmetrical. Just behind, a hedge of rosemary bushes. In the distance I could make out the summit of Reillanne, golden city on a hill. We enjoyed the view in the company of a set of flowered sheets, some undershirts, and two graying, pendulous brassieres. This part of the ramparts, due south, is now the site of the communal laundry line.

✢

FIVE GENERATIONS OF my Russian peasant ancestors are rolling over in their graves. Long did they toil, sweat, struggle, to escape the shtetl. Hopeful, they passed through Ellis Island to live the American dream of a chicken in every pot and a dryer in every mudroom. And now one of their progeny is reduced (*voluntarily*, no less) to hanging her washing on the line in the garden. Oy.

Gwendal, of course, thinks it's perfectly normal to hang our undies out under the stars. It smells good. It saves electricity. It's 110 degrees in the shade.

Yes. But.

I'm an American. And God help me, I love a good tumble dryer.

Not only does the sun not fluff your towels, it comes with folklore as well. One night, Gwendal hesitated on his way out with an armful of sheets and pillowcases. "I feel like there's something about not hanging your white sheets out in the full moon," he said.

Huh?

This was how I felt the first time I burned my finger in our apartment in Paris. Gwendal sliced open a raw potato and put it on my hand. The starch, he said, would soothe the skin. Where do they learn this stuff? Where's the Bacitracin? Sometimes it's like being married to a Trappist monk.

That said, the potato thing actually works. As for the sheets in the moonlight, I've since heard various theories, all having to do with the combination of UV rays and bleach. Anyone? Anyone?

That night, I looked at my brightly colored silk underwear, swaying in the breeze like the pennants at a jousting tournament. My once plush sage-green wedding towels were hopelessly matted and rough. Then again, I mused, thinking back to the brassieres-at-large over the lavender field, at least I got to hang my underwear in private.

The T-shirts were warm—I stuck my nose into one, looking for that special smell. It must be an acquired thing. Alexandre's socks hung in tiny pairs, each clipped with a single plastic clothespin. They were more than dry. But my mother was arriving from JFK in the morning.

I decided, with a pinch of irony, to leave everything exactly where it was.

Recipes from Our First Summer in Provence

CREAMY ZUCCHINI SOUP
Velouté de Courgettes

Jean was right, and zucchini is still among my son's favorite foods. *Creamy* here refers to texture, rather than ingredients, since there's not a drop of dairy. Good olive oil gives the soup a rich quality without diluting the bright flavor of the vegetables. As with all recipes that count on one ingredient, buy the best zucchini you can find.

⅓ cup fruity olive oil
1 large onion, coarsely chopped
2½ pounds zucchini, preferably organic, unpeeled
1 chicken or vegetable bouillon cube
3 cups water
¾ cup dry white wine

In a stockpot, heat the olive oil, add the onion, and sauté over medium-low heat for 10 minutes, until translucent and just beginning to color.

Meanwhile, wash the zucchini (leave the skin on) and cut in half lengthwise. Cut the halves into ¼-inch slices. Add the zucchini to the onions. Stir to coat. Cover the pot, but leave the lid slightly ajar—about an inch or so. Reduce the heat a bit and sauté for 20 minutes, stirring occasionally.

Dissolve the bouillon cube in ½ cup boiling water. When the zucchini is tender, add wine, stir, then add the ½ cup of bouillon and the remaining 2½ cups water to the pot. Let simmer for 2 to 3 minutes.

Using a hand blender, puree the soup. Leave the flavors to blend for a few minutes before serving.

Serves 4

Tip: Every once in a while I get a batch of very bitter zucchini and end up having to throw my whole pot of soup away—very disappointing indeed. It's rare in commercially produced vegetables, but if you are using zucchini from the garden or the farm stand, always taste an unpeeled slice before you start. If the skin tastes unusually bitter, peel all your zucchini before you proceed with the recipe.

ZUCCHINI GRATIN
Gratin de Courgettes

All through that first summer, the zucchini never stopped coming. Often, the vegetables were so abundant we made a full meal of them.

3 pounds of zucchini, cut into ⅛-inch slices
1 red onion, diced
¼ cup olive oil
¼ teaspoon coarse sea salt
1 good pinch cinnamon
¼ cup (packed) dill, chopped, with some stems
1 cup aged sheep's milk cheese or Parmesan, freshly grated

Preheat the oven to 350°F.

In a large mixing bowl, toss all the ingredients, except the cheese, together. Transfer to a 9-by-13-inch casserole dish. Bake for 1 hour. The key is to not move the zucchini around, so it takes on the nice layered look of lasagna. Remove from the oven. Let it rest for 10 to 15 minutes.

Turn on the broiler. Top the zucchini with the grated cheese—I use an aged sheep's milk cheese with a texture close to Parmesan. Put the oven rack a bit higher and cook until cheese is melted and beginning to brown, 3 to 4 minutes. You can serve this alongside meat or fish, but we usually eat it as a vegetarian dinner with wild rice.

Serves 4 as a side dish, 2 to 3 as a light main course

WHITE PEACH AND BLUEBERRY SALAD WITH ROSE SYRUP
Salade de Pêches Blanches à la Rose

It's nearly impossible to improve on the white peaches in Provence, but I did find a bottle of locally made rose syrup in the *boulangerie* that piqued my interest. This makes a quick but surprisingly elegant dessert for guests.

4 perfectly ripe white peaches, cut into ½-inch slices
1 cup blueberries
1–2 teaspoons rose syrup

Combine all the ingredients.

Serves 4

Tip: Rose syrup is available online and from some specialty supermarkets. A small bottle will keep forever in the fridge. You can use it to make champagne cocktails or raspberry smoothies, or to flavor a yogurt cake. You may find rosewater, *which is unsweetened (and very concentrated), at a Middle Eastern grocery. Use it sparingly (a few drops plus 1 or 2 teaspoons of sugar for this recipe), otherwise your fruit salad will taste like soap.*

CHAPTER 6

Leftovers

I'm reconquering my kitchen. Clearing the counters and throwing out the rice cakes. Pitching the leftovers and Wildberry fruit roll-ups. After my mother's five-week visit to our new home, I'm in need of a scorched-earth campaign: leave nothing behind that the enemy can use. Not her instant Vietnamese noodle soup, not her Skippy chunky peanut butter. Following in her Napoleonic wake, I had no choice but to dump it all, exorcise it with the ritualistic pleasure that some girls get from burning pictures of old boyfriends.

Let me be clear. I love my mother and I *hate, hate, hate* throwing away food. Yet every time my mom leaves France, I'm saddled with a huge bag of leftover, canned, partially hydrogenated horrors that neither I nor my family want to eat. Food is one of the central pleasures of my life here, and particularly at a time when I am doing my best to lose the last of the baby weight, I simply cannot tolerate putting (excuse my French) shit in my mouth.

When we lived in Paris, the evening she left I would discreetly deposit the bag outside our building, where it would be recycled by the local population in less than fifteen minutes. Here in the village, there is no spot to discreetly do anything. I can't imagine what my neighbors would say if they saw me throwing away a shopping bag full of instant Raspberry Cool iced tea and processed chorizo pizza. Would anyone here even know what to do with Raspberry Cool iced tea? For now, the bag is sitting in the vaulted stone cellar, awaiting further study.

✍

I THOUGHT THE August heat and the extra leg to Céreste would force my mom to pack light, but no. As we hauled the five suitcases, the four carry-ons, and the computer bag down the hill, my mother looked exhausted. "We're never doing this again." She sighed. Which is exactly what she said the last time.

"What the hell is in here?"

"Paul has to bring his mask." Paul is my stepfather, a title that doesn't describe at all how I feel about him. Since he came into our lives, the year I turned twenty-one, he's been my third parent. Introduced by a mutual friend, Mom and Paul had their first date on a Friday night. My mother called me in my dorm room on Saturday morning—way too early—and announced: "If this man is still around on Monday, I'm going to marry him." He moved in on Wednesday and has been with us ever since. I sometimes call him my fairy godfather, because he appeared out of nowhere and made so many things better. Paul loves his gadgets: computers, adapters, telephones—you name it. He also has a super-cool Darth Vader–like mask he wears for his sleep apnea. As if this contraption the size of a dust buster could account for the camel caravan that just arrived in my courtyard.

After clomping the suitcases up the stairs, my mother began the ritual unpacking. Along with a pair of silver grape shears, out came a package of marshmallow Peeps (I do love a good marshmallow Peep) and the apricot Jell-O.

"Look," she said, as if pulling a rabbit out of a hat. "Instant pistachio pudding!" I knew that this display of powdered American ingenuity was partly for me and, now, partly for Alexandre.

The parade of American objects began almost as soon as I moved to France. At first it was nice; my mom brought over the serrated bread knife with the wooden handle that we used when I was a kid. She brought over the chipped flowerpot in the shape of a Tudor house that resembled our own; it once held an ivy plant in our den. Some of it was practical: she brought over sheets and towels (they were so much cheaper at Marshalls) and clothes for the baby (you could buy a whole toddler wardrobe at OshKosh for the price of one impossibly cute French-made Catimini sweater). She brought over the silver asparagus tongs, a treasured family heirloom. I think it comforted her to see familiar objects take their place in my new, and often perplexing, foreign life. I call it the "stuff is love" theory: If you transfer enough objects from your old home to your new home, you never left.

Overpacking aside, my mother has always been supportive of my living abroad. Once, when I was giving tours at the Louvre, I took around an American couple whose daughter had done her junior year abroad in France and was now applying for a job in Paris. "I can't help it," said the woman, reaching into her handbag for a mint, "I really hope she doesn't get it." My mom was never that person. She supported each and every one of my far-flung decisions—boarding school in Massachusetts, junior year abroad in Scotland, grad school in London, new life in Paris—even as they took me farther and farther away from the world she knew.

But now it wasn't just me living thousands of miles away; I had kidnapped her grandson as well. And if he didn't grow up with a taste for meat loaf made with Lipton's onion-soup mix, some part of him would remain distant, unknowable. "What if he doesn't speak English?" she said to me, staring down into Alexandre's crib. "What if I can't talk to him?" As if stuffing his face with instant pistachio pudding would somehow make him bilingual.

I always try to keep mom and Paul awake for as long as possible on that first day, to help them get over the jet lag. "So," said my mom, readying herself for the highlights tour, "where to?" This is the part of village life that might take some explaining. There is not, strictly speaking, anywhere to go.

We tried taking them for a walk around the village. Between the time change and my parents' retiree lifestyle, this required more organization than you might imagine. I tried to explain that with the summer heat (and Paul's history of skin cancer), it was best to run errands before 11:00 a.m. But somehow they never got out of bed before 10:30, and they were still sitting at the table drinking their morning coffee when I started preparing lunch. Early afternoon was nap time all around, and in any case, the shops were closed between 12:30 and 4:00. It was 5:00 before we managed to get everyone out the door.

Before our move to Céreste, my mother and I shared a rather Gertrude Stein attitude toward nature: a tree is a tree is a tree. It helps to understand that she was born in Brooklyn and has spent her entire life within a twenty-mile radius of the Empire State Building. (Paul, as Mom never tires of reminding him, was born in the Bronx.) Her family made a brief foray into Connecticut when my mother was in her teens, but after my grandmother discovered a cow blocking the entrance to the kitchen door, they gave up and moved to Levittown. Wide-open spaces didn't play a big part in my childhood. After my parents' divorce, my mother and I went on a "girl-bonding" trip, canoeing down the Delaware River. The six other people on the trip turned out to be a group of psychologists on a professional retreat. All I remember is the skinny-dipping.

We followed the curve of the village downhill (downhill was better; no one in my family could be described as athletic) to the parking lot past the small stone chapel. I'm not sure it's been open since Char and his band hid guns in the rafters. The sun was still high. The lavender field had been shorn down to gray-green stumps, and thousands of white snails, no bigger than my thumbnail, clung to the tall grass at the edge of the road. Alexandre sat on Gwendal's shoulders, his chubby hands holding clumps of his father's hair. He seemed perfectly at home in his new surroundings.

On the Pont Roman, Paul stopped to study the text of the plexi-glass explanation panel. "It's not actually a Roman bridge, or even Romanesque," I said, feeling that even our historical monuments were slightly inadequate. "It's a nineteenth-century copy. There was a real Roman bridge, with two arches, a bit further down near the edge of town; they uncovered the foundations a few years back."

The stream that ran under the bridge was almost dry; small pools of water fluttered with insects. This was the quietest part of the day, after the bees have turned in for the night. We passed dense hedges of quince trees, hard green knobs of fruit just beginning to form among the leaves. I wondered what my parents were think-ing, if they saw what we saw. If they thought it was beautiful or just...empty.

⁘

"Why not?" asked my mother.

"We just don't need it," I said, trying to keep the irritation out of my voice.

"There's not even a park."

"Mom, we live in the *middle* of a national park." We do—you can't put up so much as a cable antenna without asking how it's go-ing to affect the local flora and fauna.

The subject at hand was a green plastic slide in the shape of a di-nosaur that my mom wanted to buy for Alexandre. A few days into their visit, my parents found a familiar landmark, the local *hyper-marché*—a reassuringly vast supermarket in the industrial outskirts of Apt. It doesn't close for lunch. On the last run there, my mom spotted the slide, and she's been nudging me about it ever since. I imagined a six-foot monstrosity that would block the view and take Gwendal the better part of a month to put together. Instead of just giving in and then throwing it off a cliff when she left, I decided to dig my heels in.

"Fine," said my mother brightly, meaning *This discussion is not over.*

It's not that I don't understand the appeal of a good supermarket. When I go to a foreign country, I love to browse the aisles, check out the tins of preserved octopus and sweet sesame paste, look at the different girls on the shampoo bottles. What my parents can't fathom is the limited—very limited—role the supermarket plays in my life in France. For most Americans, the supermarket remains weekly one-stop shopping. Here, I go to the supermarket once every three or four *months;* we buy pasta, baking chocolate, toilet paper, cleaning supplies, and a brand of Indian-style lime pickle imported specially for the Brits. When my mom goes to the supermarket in France, she buys flabby Danish salami (I get fresh sliced ham at the local butcher) and rubbery processed Babybel cheese (I prefer the oozy Gorgonzola at my Sunday cheese monger).

And then there's the salmon roll. It's a con. Each and every time my mother comes to France, she falls for this attractive Yule log wrapped in appealingly pink smoked salmon. But—aye, there's the rub—lurking underneath is a dense grayish cylinder of fish paste. *The horror, the horror.* I eat blood sausage, *fromage de tête, andouillette,* but I've simply never been able to get near this thing. It's become a running gag, like the uncle on a sitcom who's always farting. She often buys it when it's marked down on *offre spéciale*—which translates roughly as "two days away from giving you food poisoning."

If seeing the salmon roll once is bad, seeing it twice is a violation of the Geneva Conventions. My mom has an affection for leftovers and a long-standing love affair with plastic containers. From thirty paces, she can judge exactly what size Chinese soup container will hold the chili you need to put in the freezer.

"Mom, the cheese is *alive*. It needs to breathe. Or else it gets damp and moldy. Bad moldy." In France it's important to distinguish between good mold and bad mold. Good mold makes Roquefort; bad mold is what is growing on our bedroom ceiling. Despite my warnings, all sorts of things get hermetically sealed and shoved to the back of the fridge—wilting salad, slices of red onion, half a piece of quiche. I could be excavating for weeks.

The fridge stuffing made me feel squashed; violated even. Since I've come to France, cooking has become an essential everyday pleasure. The kitchen is my territory, and by filling it with things my family would never eat, she was ignoring my wishes, my independence—simply turning my house into a version of hers. Ease up, you say, she's just trying to be helpful. I know, I *know*. She can see I'm a little underwater with the move, the baby, trying to get back to my writing. And yet, this kind of help makes me want to curl up in a ball in a dark corner of the coat closet and suck my thumb.

One morning, Gwendal slunk off, bewildered, to Angela and Rod's bed-and-breakfast for an espresso and a croissant. I think he might have been tempted to check in for the week. "Sorry I snuck out," he said when I handed him a tray of tomatoes and fresh mozzarella to take out to the garden for lunch. "I opened the refrigerator," he said, "it was completely full, and there wasn't a single thing in there that I wanted to eat."

WE FOUND A great babysitter for Alexandre. Amandine is a few years younger than me, but she had her first child right around the time I was sitting for my AP European History exam, so she's fifteen years and three kids ahead of me in experience. Her daughter Rose is four months older than Alexandre. They look like twins, two blond heads bent over a set of blocks.

As the weather cools and the tourists and summer-home owners head back to London and Brussels, the locals have begun to notice our presence. Older women with their woven straw shopping baskets now stop me in the street with the stroller. "You are staying the winter?" they ask. *"Si c'est pas indiscret."*

I've noticed that whenever people ask me a question that doesn't involve the time or the weather, they first ask if they are being indiscreet. I find this charming, but it also makes me giggle to myself. It makes me think of a friend of mine in New York. He introduced himself to me for the first time *after* he'd walked up behind me at a table in Starbucks, put his hands on my shoulders, stared at the grad-school application on my computer screen, and then said in an incredibly snide tone: "Why would anyone want to go to Yale?" He, of course, went to Harvard. Sometimes, a little discretion wouldn't kill anyone.

One afternoon, when I came to get Alexandre, Amandine was outside with a broom. Like us, she is in a constant battle with a flock of pigeons roosting over her door. *"Tu veux un café?"* She has tan shoulders and a trim, girlish figure that belies her three pregnancies. She had been sorting a wooden crate of tomatoes. "Would you like some?" she said, already filling up a plastic bag. "They are from my friend's garden." I watched Alexandre and Rose crawl up and down the two steps between the kitchen and the dining area. There were no baby gates, no plastic covers for the sockets. I've never seen a French home that meets the American definition of *baby-proof.*

Sitting at her kitchen table, I asked questions gingerly, not wanting to violate the code of discretion that has so kindly been extended to me. *"Non, non. Je suis pas d'ici, moi."* No, no, I'm not from here, she said, laughing at my surprise. Her local accent was thick enough to cut with a scythe. *"Je suis Parisienne, moi.* We left Paris and came here when I was nine." Nine? Twenty-five years, a local husband, and three kids later, and she's still not *d'ici*, from here. The French take the idea of *terroir* very seriously. Just like the wine and strawberries are proudly, irrevocably *from* somewhere, people are too.

❧

"I DO LOVE to watch you squeeze the fruit," said my mom, peeking over my shoulder at the Sunday market in Reillanne. "You used to do this with the Rembrandts." Not squeeze them, exactly, but it's true that I now study figs with as much attention and enthusiasm as I once studied Old Master paintings.

Like the magnificent wrinkles in a Rembrandt self-portrait, figs are something my mother and I can agree on. Every September, I throw myself a little fig festival. A fig par-*tay*. Figapalooza, if you will. One of the many pleasures of living in Provence is that fig season seems to go on and on. I made my first fig tart over a month ago, and my favorite fruit is still very much at the market.

A fresh fig is a coy fruit. Fresh figs hide out a bit. Their exterior is sober, matte—a dignified, often dusky, royal purple. But crack one open, and you have a pulpy, fleshy kaleidoscope of seeds. A ripe fig, like the cheeks of a well-fed child, should give slightly when you squeeze.

Figs make an excellent transition from summer to autumn cuisine. This is particularly useful this time of year in Provence, when we are eating in the garden one day, turning on the heat the next.

Fresh figs are at home alfresco, in a rocket salad with Golden Delicious apples, pine nuts, and picnic cheeses or roasted with slices of Roquefort and a drizzle of honey to begin a fall fireside dinner.

The other day, Amandine let us in on a little secret: the village has a public fig tree. It's just behind the post office; I pass it every morning on the way back from the *boulangerie*. *See,* I wanted to say to my mom, *we may not have the Metropolitan Opera, but we have a communal fig tree.* Like paid maternity leave and Camembert for school lunches—that's my kind of public service.

That afternoon while Alexandre was asleep upstairs, my mom and I decided to make a fig tart. It was not just for us. We would be deepening our village social life that week—inviting the neighbors over for tea. Between you and me, I had an ulterior motive. I was trying to sweet-talk (or feed) Jean into taking me mushroom hunting with him when the rains came.

My mother and I talk best while doing things—cleaning out closets, shopping for clothes. She didn't necessarily get all the fun bits of my childhood. My father did the weekend things, museums, theater, Christmas windows at Bendel's. My mom handled the weekday necessities: homework, laundry, dirty ol' chicken on the barbecue grill. We've had some of our best conversations just sitting side by side in the car headed to the dry cleaner. We could talk about anything.

"I'm just nervous," I said, measuring out the sugar. "The book is out there, doing its thing, and I'm completely cut loose, without a concrete next project."

"I wish you could stop worrying and enjoy all this." My mom has been telling me to stop worrying since—I can't even remember when. Where, she says, did I inherit this lousy habit of accomplishing a goal and then ten minutes later pushing it aside in favor of something new to panic about?

"You just don't know how lucky you are," she said, putting the measuring cup in the sink. My mother and father had been through a miscarriage and a still birth and were on the verge of adoption when I came along. I too had been through a miscarriage before Alexandre was born; I was not oblivious to the gift of a healthy child.

My mother is a very clean cook, always washing and wiping as she goes. I'm a messy one—I use every pot, spoon, and spatula in the place, then leave most of it in a sticky jumble in the sink. She was rinsing the whisk when she said:

"You just don't seem invested enough in being Alexandre's mom."

"How dare you say that to me?" I said, tears suddenly streaming down my cheeks. "I'm his mother!" I was as close as I'd ever been to walking out of the room during an argument. "Take it back."

"What about the stroller?"

"*Oh!*" I said, raising my voice in a way I never did to my mother. "We're back to the stroller? I'm a bad mother because I wasn't excited to go shopping for *a stroller.*"

Apparently, I had failed my first test of motherhood before Alexandre was even born. I couldn't fathom it. Why would my mother think that her daughter, who loves vintage coats with fur collars and rare Victorian picture books, would be ass-over-teakettle excited to shop for a stroller? It's not a hot pair of stilettos or even a hand-embroidered bassinet cover. It's a stroller. As long as it rolls and turns and doesn't fold up like a Venus flytrap with the kid inside, what do I care? It needed to be light enough so I could drag it up three flights of spiral stairs in Paris, sturdy enough to handle the paving stones and potholes in Céreste. It didn't matter if it had a coffee-cup holder; there's no such thing as takeout coffee in France.

But my mother was right; this argument was part of a larger—and, as I was quickly learning, unacceptable—ambivalence. There's no other way to say it: Babies, and certainly all the trappings that accompany them, just don't interest me that much. There are people who are gaga for small children. My mother is one of them. I prefer kids a little later, in the Greek-myth and first-crush stage. My mom took five years off from work; it was never my intention to be a stay-at-home mom. The judgment was enormous, the guilt was even worse.

This was not the first time I'd been made to feel this way. Before Alexandre was born, my gynecologist recommended something called *haptonomie*—an affective technique invented in the 1950s by Dutchman Frans Veldman. If there is an American equivalent, I haven't heard of it. The goal is to bring the new family together. We did this cool exercise where Gwendal put his hand on the side of my stomach, and the baby actually moved over to nestle in his palm. I think *haptonomie* is useful for bringing fathers closer to their future children. But in our case, Gwendal wasn't the one who needed to be brought into the process—I was.

The sessions were at the hospital with a female pediatrician who was trained in this technique. Things immediately got off on the wrong foot. The first thing the doctor told me to do was stop my twice-weekly yoga lessons, which I loved. "If you are thinking about your own *respiration*—breathing—during the birth, then you will not be fully present with your child."

Then she asked me to lie down on the table and put my hands over my stomach. *Haptonomie* begins when you're about four months pregnant, right after the baby starts moving. "How do you *feel* about your child?" she said, staring down at me with a beatific smile.

I panicked. I'm a good student, and I don't like to give wrong answers. It was clear what was expected of me: *I feel joy. I feel wonder. I feel life.*

What I actually felt was…pregnant. Afraid. Worried about whether the child would be healthy. Unsure if I would enjoy the first years of motherhood. Gwendal and I had talked about this. One day, we were walking down the street, trying to imagine who this little person would be. "I love it already," Gwendal said with the calm yet elated tone he maintained throughout my pregnancy. I answered truthfully. "How can you love someone you've never met?" It seemed a wonderful, but illogical, leap of faith.

On the table in the doctor's office, I searched for an answer to her question. I paged through my mental dictionary, looking for an adjective that was true but inoffensive. The only thing I could come up with was *responsable*. "I feel responsible." I knew as soon as I said it that this was inadequate. Apparently, there was no window to settle into the idea of motherhood. As soon as the egg was fertilized, I was supposed to be *on*—like an actress who never suffers from stage fright. When Gwendal and I left the office, I was in tears. I felt completely alone, damaged. As if my feelings were somehow deformed.

Now here we were, a year later, a beautiful baby boy thriving, and I was getting the same treatment from my mother as I'd gotten from that doctor—a complete refusal of my doubts, a negation of my feelings. I consider myself a fairly confident person, but having a baby has made me as wobbly as the apricot Jell-O, hypersensitive to criticism yet doubting myself at every turn.

And yet, I knew in my heart that we were doing something right. Alexandre was born smiling, and he hasn't stopped since. He slept through the night at two and a half months. At one year old, he feeds himself with a spoon. He eats fish and broccoli—and liver. At least by French standards, we were right on target. *Just look at him*, I wanted to say, *he's happy all the time.*

A baby is a wishing well. We walk by every day and throw our pennies in. Most are bright and shiny, full of smiles and possibility. Some are tarnished with bad memories, unlucky genes. Others have been hiding under the couch cushions all these years, just waiting for someone to dig them out.

A baby is a wishing well. Everyone puts their hopes, their fears, their pasts, their two cents in.

ON THE WAY to Alexandre's new babysitter (Amandine, like the vast majority of French women, was going back to work), we passed by the *boulangerie* and picked up two baguettes for lunch. We rolled down the narrow asphalt path bordering the fields. I enjoyed these morning walks. I think my mom was pleased to be out and about, participating in my daily routine.

Valerie is a brisk grandmotherly type who has been watching village children in her home for fifteen years. Her house has a sunroom with lots of toys, a big garden with a birdbath, and a friendly, fluffy dog who ran to greet us at the gate. But what caught my mother's eye was the sandbox. It was made from an old wooden construction pallet, and the corners had four rounded metal prongs that stuck up about two inches over the edge. After my mother retired from the board of education she took a position as the executive director of a day-care center. So she knew all about the latest playground regulations—foam tiles, heights of swings, appropriate plastics. She stared at Alexandre, who was happily scooping sand into a purple bucket. Valerie was sitting just beside him, nodding in enthusiastic agreement every time he burbled with excitement and raised the shovel. My mother seemed oblivious to Valerie's supervision and Alexandre's pleasure. I could see the wheels turning in her head. Maybe it's the fact that one in three hundred U.S. citizens is a lawyer, but where the rest of the world sees fun, Americans see liability.

One problem with my mother and I being as close as we are: I can read her mind. Paris was far away from home, but it was logical, beautiful, sophisticated. Céreste, it seemed, was a bridge too far. A mysterious step sideways, if not downright backward. All parents want their kids to live better than they did, and my mother couldn't see the "better" in this. On the one hand: *Oh, those crazy kids, but*

never mind—you know Elizabeth, she steps in shit and it turns to gold.
On the other hand: *All those degrees. I paid for a field trip to* Venice, *for God's sake. All this so you can hang your laundry on the line like a peasant and bring up my grandson in some backwater where they don't have a decent Chinese restaurant or a natural history museum?* As if just by leading our lives in this different place, in a different way, Gwendal and I were somehow damaging our son.

Underneath the incomprehension was fear. *You are slipping away from me.* This is the ultimate paradox of good parenting. I'm certain that my mother raised me to live a life that is wider, grander, and more free than what she grew up with. But in giving me my liberty, she sent me running straight into the arms of a world she doesn't always understand. This makes her uncomfortable. I could hear her internal monologue. *What about the schools? Won't you be lonely here?* Barely having unpacked the moving boxes, I couldn't answer her questions. The truth of the matter was, I didn't know.

We walked back from Valerie's house in silence, wheeling the empty stroller in front of us. *"Bonjour, mesdames,"* said Mr. André as he overtook us on the path.

I meet old Mr. André every morning as he heads to the sunny stone bench in front of the *mairie.* There he sits, with two other men for company, until it is time to return home for lunch. He's always very friendly, though his two remaining front teeth and long tobacco-stained fingernails do suggest the character in a fairy tale who carries a sack of tasty little children over his shoulder. Even in the heat of summer, he wears so many layers it is difficult to know if that lump is the hunchback of my overactive imagination or just an arthritic stoop. He shook my hand, pointed at the baguettes in the empty stroller, said something, and laughed and laughed.

"What did he say?" asked my mom.

"He asked if I sold the baby for a loaf of bread."

"Is he kidding?"

"Maybe." I shrugged, in no mood to lessen her discomfort.

I can't say for sure if it was the sandbox, Mr. André's fingernails, or just an overdose of chlorophyll, but the very next day my mother came home from the supermarket with Paul lugging the green plastic dinosaur slide behind her. It was only three feet tall, but it was so wide it barely fit through the garden door. I was crisp with rage. Alexandre, of course, was delighted. "See," she said, bending to give him a kiss, "Grandma knows what you like."

❦

THE NIGHT BEFORE my mother left, I made lentils with sausage. It's normally a winter dish, warm, slow, and hearty, the big hug I often forgot to give my parents this month. By the time she began repacking the endless suitcases, we were both exhausted. I felt overwhelmed; she felt marginalized. I felt judged; she felt stupid. A baby was supposed to bring everyone together. This was as far from each other as we'd ever been.

The next morning, I sat with Alexandre on the edge of the fountain in the place des Marronniers. He waved as Gwendal inched the car down La Grand Rue, a radical misnomer for this narrow path to the main road. My eyes stung. I missed them before they were even gone. Having them here was torture; not having them here was worse.

I put Alexandre down for his morning nap and stripped the sheets off the bed in Char's room. I wandered around the house, fingering the ugly curtains left by the previous owners. *These have got to go.* This wasn't my house, it wasn't her house. For the moment, it didn't quite feel like anyone's house.

I knew she'd get home, unpack, and then we would talk about all this—make our way past it. Maybe I could make her more aware of how I was feeling—ask her to take care to treat me like an adult in my own home. I hoped it would make me a better guest when I went back to the States, rather than my classic reversion to a child who comes and goes as she pleases and leaves her underwear on the bedroom floor. That's the difference between my mother and Napoleon. Napoleon never made up with anyone.

I started clearing out the plastic containers in the back of the fridge. When Alexandre woke up for lunch, I reheated some lentils in the toy-size copper pot my mom had bought for me in Paris a few years before. He didn't seem to feel my mood. The spoon made a few detours between the bowl and his mouth. There was a brown paste of lentils and green flecks of parsley all over his face and down his bib. He smiled. So did I. Then I realized: he was eating leftovers. But they were *my* leftovers, and somehow that made all the difference in the world.

Figapalooza

ARUGULA SALAD WITH CHICKEN, FRESH FIGS, AND AVOCADO

Salade au Poulet, Figues Fraîches, et Avocat

This is an easy option for lunch with the girls; the fresh figs make it just that extra bit special. You could add some crumbled blue cheese or, if you want to make a vegetarian version, replace the chicken with warm goat-cheese toasts.

4 chicken breasts, or the meat from 1 small roast chicken, sliced
1 small peppery salad, or 1 bag arugula
1 tablespoon olive oil
½ teaspoon balsamic vinegar
1 good pinch coarse sea salt
8 fresh figs, cut into quarters
2 small avocados, cut into ½-inch slices
2 tablespoons raw pumpkin seeds

In a large frying pan, cook the chicken breasts in a bit of olive oil; season with salt and pepper. (I often use meat from a roasted chicken I buy at the Sunday market.)

Just before serving, toss the salad with the olive oil, vinegar, and salt. I like to go easy on the dressing; there's nothing worse than soggy salad. Divide the salad among 4 plates. Top with the chicken, figs, and avocados. Scatter the pumpkin seeds on top. Voilà!

Serves 4

ROASTED FIGS WITH ROQUEFORT AND HONEY
Figues Fraîches Rôties au Roquefort

These are a nice surprise with drinks. Or serve them after dinner with a green salad—a combo of cheese course and dessert.

8 perfectly ripe fresh figs, cut in half lengthwise
1 teaspoon olive oil
A drizzle of honey
A small wedge of blue cheese—Roquefort, Bleu d'Auvergne, Stilton, or
  Gorgonzola

Preheat the oven to 350°F.

Place the figs in a ceramic baking dish and drizzle with olive oil and honey. Bake for 15 minutes, until tender. Meanwhile, cut ¼-inch slices of blue cheese; make them slightly smaller than the figs. As soon as the figs come out of the oven, top with a slice of cheese. (Gwendal prefers the bite of Roquefort; I like the milder creaminess of Gorgonzola.) Let the cheese soften for a minute or two. Serve immediately.

Serves 4 as an appetizer or cheese course

FIG AND ALMOND TART
Tarte aux Figues

I've been in search of the perfect frangipane (almond cream) for most of the time that I've lived in France. The solution came from an old colleague of Gwendal's in Paris. This is the almond cream she uses to stuff her *galette des rois*. It's easy to make, sweet but not overwhelming, and the rum gives it the right to vote.

For the crust

This shockingly easy pastry recipe is from our dear friend Anne. It's essentially a stir-and-go choux pastry without the eggs.

9 tablespoons butter
¼ cup water
1 tablespoon sugar
1¾ cups flour

In a small saucepan, combine butter, water, and sugar. When the butter is melted, turn off the heat and add the flour all at once, stirring with a wooden spoon to combine. Roll out the crust with a rolling pin until it is about 13 inches in diameter.

For the filling

7 tablespoons salted butter; if you can find it with sea-salt crystals, so much the better
½ cup plus 2 tablespoons granulated sugar
3 eggs
1 tablespoon dark rum
½ teaspoon almond extract, or a few drops of real bitter almond essence
½ teaspoon vanilla extract
1½ cups almond meal (ground almonds)
6 or 7 ripe fresh figs sliced about ⅓ inch thick
Small handful of pine nuts
2 tablespoons powdered sugar

Heat the oven to 375°F.

Whip the butter until soft and airy. Add the sugar, and cream the two together until light and fluffy. Add two eggs, whisk to combine.

Break the third egg into a cup, stir lightly. Pour ½ of the third egg into the batter. Put the cup with the remaining ½ egg to one side. Add the rum and almond and vanilla extracts to the batter; whisk to combine. Add the ground almonds and stir to combine.

Place the crust in an 11-inch tart pan (preferably a metal tart pan with a removable bottom—metal helps the crust cook through). Let the extra crust hang over the edges. Prick the bottom of the crust with a fork. Top with the almond cream. Slice the figs on top. Scatter the pine nuts. Fold the extra crust over the top of the tart to form a little border. Mix the remaining ½ egg with the powdered sugar and brush the top of the folded-over crust with the egg wash.

Bake for 30 to 35 minutes, until golden and cooked through.

Serves 8

CHAPTER 7

The Big Chill

I've nicknamed our new wood-burning stove Bertha, and if I wouldn't burn myself in the process, I would hug her.

Summer fled suddenly. One day we were sitting in the garden watching the swifts circle low above our heads, drinking beer, and grilling sardines. Then it rained for two days straight. When the sun came out, the trees had lost half their leaves and the temperature had dropped thirty degrees. Every morning while I give Alexandre breakfast, I hear Jean shuffle out in his bathrobe and slippers to check the thermometer in his garden: *"Moins trois ce matin."* It gives him his topic of conversation for the day.

In our poetic assessment of the house, we had overlooked several things—not least among them, heat. There were only two outdated radiators in the whole house, nothing upstairs in the bedrooms or the bathrooms. At least there *were* bathrooms. The village didn't have running water until the mid-1950s, and Mireille told us stories from her childhood about the *pipi* freezing in the chamber pots at night. In July it seemed funny. In November, not so much.

The thick walls that provided a welcome retreat from the summer sun were now glacial. The charming nooks and crannies were just more corners to heat. Central heating was not an option; there was no central gas line in the village, and we couldn't install an oil burner because the truck to deliver the petrol couldn't make the turn onto our narrow street. We were left with the choice of either electric radiators (super-expensive to run) or wood. Upstairs, we settled on radiators (there's a limit to the number of chores I'm willing to do to warm up the toilet seat), but for the living room, we decided on Bertha, a squat cream-colored wood-burning stove with a glass window so we could watch the fire. The day she was installed I felt a little like Laura Ingalls Wilder.

Now I understand why everyone had been talking about firewood in the middle of July. When you order your firewood in July, the nice men from the company come and stack it neatly in the cellar. If you order your wood in November, they come with a pickup truck and dump the whole lot unceremoniously by the front door. Ten cubic meters of tree. The pile was as high as Gwendal's head and blocked the entire width of the street. Getting it into the cellar would take till sunset.

The neighbors must have heard the rumble, the rusty crank of the truck, and the thundering crash of the wood hitting the pavement, because no sooner had Gwendal picked up the first log then Denis appeared in the doorway, already wearing work gloves, a support belt for his back, and his old SERNAM vest, from when he used to move freight in Marseille.

"Where do you want it?" he asked as he chucked three thick logs under his arm.

Jean and his wife, Paulette, came out next, then Arnaud. Jean is a retired *contremaître*. He and his teams worked all over France, fitting airtight windows for nuclear submarines. He was particularly proud to have installed the shock-proof windows on the first TGV, France's famous high-speed train. Standing at the foot of our woodpile, he directed operations, instructing the men in the proper Lincoln Log technique to make a tight, stable stack. When it fell over, the uneven ground, *bien sûr,* and not the method was to blame. Alexandre was still a little unsteady on the steep incline of our street, so Paulette held his hand while I grabbed slender logs to stack outside the kitchen door for kindling.

People who grew up in small towns might be used to this kind of helping hand. When I was growing up in Teaneck, New Jersey, our neighbors the Maddens were an older couple, distant figures. The only significant interaction I can remember was the time my best friend Sarah and I decided to make purple scrambled eggs and leave them in the middle of the path to their garage. My mother forced me to apologize in person. Mrs. Madden may be the only person who ever looked at me and honestly thought to herself: *Bad seed.*

My last neighbor in New York, through no fault of his own, watched all my comings and goings through the keyhole. He was only a little older than I and, as far as I know, left the apartment only on Tuesdays, when his mother came and took him out for dinner. I think he may have had a hoarding disorder. The one time I got a glimpse of his place, I saw what looked like a ski slope of brightly colored rags piled all the way to the ceiling.

Our nearest and dearest neighbor in Paris was Marie-Claude, who used to bellow her hellos from the open window of the apartment building across the street. She was a huge woman. Each morning, she would heave first one breast, then the other, onto the windowsill and stay there all day long, watching the traffic back up behind the garbage trucks. We later found out she had an Egyptian husband, as reedy as she was rotund. A mental picture was unavoidable. She liked the fact that I was American. She must have heard me speaking English on the phone. One day she approached me while I was writing at a local café. "My mother," she bellowed—the fact that she was standing right in front of me and not across the street had no effect on her volume—"had American pots during the war."

Two hours later, the woodpile was done and the street swept clean. I made a mental note to triple the number of chocolate chip cookies I'd be making for Christmas.

Marguerite kept looking out the window. Apparently, Denis was supposed to have spent the morning fixing the dishwasher.

PS: There's another reason why locals order their firewood in July. Wood ordered in July has time to dry out. Wood ordered in November is wet and green and smokes like a lounge singer. It took us a half hour and an entire crumpled *Monde Diplomatique* to get our first real spark. It was the dumbest kind of newbie mistake. We deserved a wedgie.

⌀

THE OTHER SOLUTION to the heating problem was to work from the inside out.

There is something about the first frost that brings out the caveman—one might even say the vampire—in me. I want to wear fur and suck the meat off lamb bones, and on comes my annual craving for *boudin noir*, otherwise known as blood sausage. You know you've been in France for nearly a decade when the idea of eating congealed blood sounds not only normal, but positively delightful.

When I was pregnant, my body craved iron in silly amounts. I could have eaten a skyscraper. It's a shame that it's not on the French pregnancy diet—forbidden along with charcuterie, liver, and steak tartare.

It's true that *boudin noir* is not the sort of thing I'd buy at any old supermarket. Ideally, you want a butcher who prepares his own. I bought mine from the mustached man with the little truck in Apt market, the same one I'd spotted during our first picnic in Provence. Since our first visit, I'd returned many times to buy his delicious, very lean, *saucisses fraîches* and his handmade *andouillettes,* which I sauté with onions, Dijon mustard, and a bit of cream.

I serve my *boudin* with roasted apples—this time, some Golden Delicious we picked up from a farm stand by the side of the road. I tossed the apple slices with olive oil, sprinkled the whole lot with sea salt, and added a cinnamon stick and a star anise to ground the dish with cozy autumn spices. *Boudin* is already cooked through when you buy it, but twenty minutes or so in a hot oven gives it time to blister, even burst. I'm an adventurous eater, but the idea of boiled (or cold) *boudin* makes me think about moving back to New Jersey. No, not really.

I admit, when you first take it out of the oven, there are some visual hurdles. There's always a brief moment—particularly when I serve this dish to guests—that I think, *But that looks like large Labrador shit on a plate.* True enough. But once you get past the aesthetics, you have one of the richest savory tastes I can imagine. Good *boudin* has a velveteen consistency that marries perfectly with the slight tartness of the roasted apples. Add mashed potatoes (with skin and lumps), a bottle of Châteauneuf-du-Pape, and wake me in the spring.

❧

THIS WINTER HIBERNATION period also presented us with the decorative realities of the house.

When people think of a house in Provence, they think of a villa, a vineyard, a pool—and a couple of hundred thousand dollars in renovations done by a genial but not entirely reliable builder. We don't have a couple of hundred thousand dollars. As it is, we are up to our earlobes in mortgages. As for the not entirely reliable builders—you're looking at 'em.

When we first arrived in Céreste, I was asked to write an article for the Home section of an English newspaper. The editor loved the René Char connection, but the paper's readers were accustomed to multimillion-pound restorations of Jacobean manors and innovative storage solutions for Devon cottages. Our wagon-wheel chandeliers and two-tone orange tiles were clearly not what they had in mind. I sent pictures, shoving myself as far into the corner as I could to make the rooms look bigger, the ceilings higher.

A few weeks later, the piece appeared as a double-page spread. The top half was a picture of a vast stone farmhouse, maybe even an entire hamlet, perched on a low hill among the lavender fields. It was a magnificent photo—of someone else's house. It must have been one of the paper's stock images of Provence. When a colleague of Gwendal's at the head office in London saw the article, he fired off a short e-mail: Now we understand why you moved down there. It seemed pointless to disabuse him.

Our first priority were the tiles. It was simply impossible to decorate around them. Shiny, dark orange, and arranged in a zigzag pattern, they sucked the light out of a room like a black hole. The house was covered with them top to bottom, including the steps, halls, even the moldings. They made a particularly pleasing contrast to the green-flowered wall tiles and pink bidet in the upstairs bathroom.

Picking out new tiles (lovely light-colored stone with plenty of natural variation) was something I knew how to do. Laying tile was another slice of *saucisson* altogether. Angela and Rod suggested we talk to Alain and Evelyne, a Belgian couple who lived just up the street on the place des Marronniers. They were retired but sometimes did remodeling projects for fun. Just asking was humbling. We were quickly woken up to our urban uselessness, our flabby graduate-school muscles. This was something we would have to get used to in Provence—people twice our age easily doing physical tasks that six months ago would have sent us running for the chiropractor.

Alain and Evelyne were worn out from painting shutters on a villa up the hill toward Montjustin, but they agreed to lend Gwendal their tools and supervise him for a day, teaching him how to tile the floor himself. Gwendal started taking measurements and cutting tiles to size in the courtyard. With grouting on his fleece, dust in his hair, and glue on his knuckles, it was a whole new vision of my husband. Kind of a turn-on, actually.

Denis, Jean, and Alain stopped by at regular intervals to check his progress. "We all saw you," Denis said to Gwendal, "with your computer and your telephone. *Maintenant, c'est bon.* Now you do something really *créatif.* Creative. Something with your hands." Gwendal's masculinity quotient went through the roof that day, a rite of passage on par with nailing the Torah portion at your bar mitzvah. PhD, shmee-hD—this was more praise than I'd ever heard one French person bestow on another.

Alexandre and I went off on a trip to the States. When we returned, the whole first floor of the house was done. If Gwendal was the proud creator of this decorative marvel, I was the grateful recipient. For weeks after I got back, every time Denis saw us in the street, he clapped Gwendal on the back and winked in my direction.

"*T'as tiré le bon numéro, toi.*" You hit the jackpot.

⁂

MY NATURAL CURVES don't lend themselves to layers—more than one sweater, and I end up looking like a long-haired version of the Michelin Man. I haven't quite mastered the Provençal style of dressing—it's always several degrees below freezing in the morning; at noon, if you find yourself a spot in the sun, you can strip down to a T-shirt. Most mornings, I meet Jean's wife, Paulette, fetching wine or ham or firewood from their cellar. She keeps sticking her hand underneath my single sweater. "*Il faut te couvrir.*" You need to cover up.

These are the shortest days of the year and also the quietest. No stir of insects, only the occasional whistle of birds heading south. You can smell the wood smoke, see the flash of flames in the hills: farmers burning their piles of leaves.

We have not seen much of Mireille and Jacques since we arrived in Céreste. Her mother is not well. As the cold sets in, we see less and less of the village in general. With the time change, the light begins to fade at 3:00; by 4:00, everyone is inside, shutters closed tight for the night.

✐

IT'S THE THIRD Thursday in November. As I roll down to the babysitter with Alexandre, the morning frost on the fields looks like a dusting of powdered sugar. By the time I make my way back along the path to the *vieux village,* the sun has come out and you can see the black crows hopping from branch to branch among the naked plane trees.

Thanksgiving snuck up on me this year. I doubt anyone in our tiny Provençal village even knows it's a holiday; there might have been something on the news this morning about Obama pardoning a turkey—the French can't resist a joke about a nation that executes people but pardons turkeys. I will go on with business as usual: buy some salmon and *dorade* from the fishmonger at our Thursday market, work for a few hours in my local café. I'm organizing my winter pantry: cocoa powder and lots of whole-wheat pasta. They are predicting snow this weekend.

One thing that happens when no one around me is frantically cooking, polishing silver, or planning the 5:00 a.m. Black Friday shopping marathon is that—alone in my kitchen—I have a little time to think about what Thanksgiving really means. I'm a perfectionist, which means I am often ungrateful. I expect too much—of myself, and of everything and everyone around me. I often forget to give thanks for the many gifts life has given me: a son who smiles all the time, a man who can tile a floor *and* recite poetry, a family who love me even when I bite back, friends who can finish my sentences, neighbors who reach out with a helping hand, a job that engages my head and my heart, and a new, glorious landscape to explore.

So this year, I'm going to stage a private celebration. I've decided to take the day off. From myself. Today, I will not feel behind. I will not worry about being a better wife, mother, daughter, house-keeper, or writer. I'm not making a fancy dinner. I'll be having quite an ordinary day, but I'll be thinking and thanking—instead of fret-ting and fixing. We all need one day a year when we meet our own expectations and allow the world to be as it is instead of exactly how we would like it to be.

❧

You know it's Christmas in France when the refrigerator looks like this: the fruit drawer is full of cheese, the cheese drawer is full of foie gras, the four bottles of water on the door have been replaced with champagne, and the lettuce (wrapped loosely in a dish towel) is wedged in over two broad, beady-eyed live crabs (nicknamed Gérard and Gaston). Last year, Gwendal forgot the crabs were in there. When he opened the door, they started rustling. He thought it was a poltergeist.

I was happy for the distraction. It had been a busy, bumpy year, and our little family arrived at Christmas feeling slightly bruised, like an apple left too long in the bottom of someone's handbag. Thankfully, the preparations for a Provençal Christmas are so com-plex that every thought not directly related to mistletoe and candied orange peel is happily put aside until Lent.

The bus for Apt market leaves at 7:32. Without a French driver's license (it's on my to-do list), I'm stuck taking the bus, so I'm up at the hour of the stray cats and the dog-walkers. It's still dark, the midnight blue getting paler each minute I wait. The streetlights are hidden in a Dickensian veil of fog. Despite the cold, the butcher is sitting on the terrace of the café across the street in his paper hat and apron. One more espresso before he pulls up the front window shade and starts his day.

Like the buyers at Macy's, the citizens of Provence start planning Christmas in September. One day in the early autumn, I was on my way to the *boulangerie* when I noticed the open door to Jean's cellar. *"Bonjour, ma puce."* He had taken to calling me his little flea, which is a term of endearment, though it doesn't quite sound that way. Amid the carefully stacked firewood and five-liter jugs of *vin ordinaire,* Jean was hanging a bunch of just ripe muscat grapes from a hook on the ceiling. A few inches to the left, suspended in a mesh bag, was a last-of-the-season melon. Long and mottled green like a German torpedo, it was supposed to survive in this dangling position until Christmas Eve.

These fruits are part of the Provençal tradition of *les treize desserts,* the thirteen desserts served on Christmas Eve. Contemporary France is an overwhelmingly secular place, but the country's Catholic past is so enmeshed in local life that it is impossible to entirely separate the Apostles from the almond brittle. Everyone must taste a piece of each dessert (for luck), and, best of all, you *must* leave the dishes and food on the table all night, so hungry travelers can come and dine if they like. In my opinion, anything that gets me out of doing the dishes is a tradition worth adopting.

Gathering *les treize desserts* is a bit like a scavenger hunt designed by mischievous Keebler elves. When I arrived at the market, it was only ten after eight, so I had a coffee and watched the men set up their stands of tablecloths and soaps and stir the huge, flat cast-iron skillets of paella that would be ready for lunch. The sun was glinting off the clock towers by the time I took the side street up to the North African grocery. I picked out medjool dates and tender teardrop-shaped figs from Portugal. I would need fat muscat raisins and moist prunes. Jean had already given us a large plastic bag filled with walnuts from his tree. *Where, oh, where is my silver nutcracker? I need to call my mother.* I bought a package of pink marzipan so Nicole and I could make *fruits déguisés,* dates stuffed with marzipan, each topped with half a walnut and rolled in sugar.

There was a bustle of people in the street as I made my way to La Bonbonnière, which is, quite simply, the most beautiful candy store in the world.

The best thing about La Bonbonnière is that it's all windows. Before I even walk through the door I am greeted by a fuzzy three-foot-high statue of a polar bear trying to dip his paws into a copper cauldron filled with *marrons glacés*—whole candied chestnuts. Each one was meticulously wrapped in gold foil, a miniature gift in and of itself. If nothing else, Christmas in Provence reminds you of a time when sugar was a luxury as fine and rare as silk.

Back to my assignment: I needed two kinds of nougat: white soft nougat made with honey, almonds, and fluffy egg whites (the angel's part) and hard dark nougat—more like honey almond brittle—for the devil.

Where are the *calissons d'Aix?* There they are, hiding behind the cash register, small ovals of almond paste covered with fondant icing. Traditional *calissons* are flavored with essence of bitter almond, but I couldn't resist some of the more exotic variations: rose, lemon verbena, and *génépi,* an astringent mountain herb.

Though I love the tender chew of nougat and the pliant sweetness of marzipan, my favorite of the Provençal Christmas treats is the *mendiant*—a small disk of dark or milk chocolate topped with dried fruit and nuts representing four religious orders: raisins for the Dominicans, hazelnuts for the Augustinians, dried figs for the Franciscans, and almonds for the Carmelites. When Alexandre is a bit older, I think we'll make these together. They seem like an ideal family project—essentially puddles of melted chocolate with fruit and nut toppings. See, as soon as you say "puddles of melted chocolate," everyone's on board.

Though *fruits confits*—candied fruit—are not, strictly speaking, part of *les treize desserts*, I can't resist. I think of them as the crown jewels of French *confiserie*, and Apt is the world capital of production. Dipped in sugar syrup, the fruits become almost translucent; whole pears, apricots, and strawberries glow from within like the gems in a pirate's treasure chest. Slices of kiwi, melon, and angelica catch the light like the panes of a stained-glass window. All the dazzling tastes of a Provençal summer, frozen in time.

Knowing that I would have too many packages to carry, Gwendal took Alexandre and came to pick me up. I met them at the café on the main square. I kept dropping bags in Gwendal's lap and hurrying off to the next errand.

I went to the organic-produce man for fresh grapes (since there were none hanging in my cellar), apples, pears, almonds, and hazelnuts still in their shells. There wasn't a single fresh melon to be had, so I'd make due with a candied slice. The *pompe à l'huile,* an olive oil–based brioche flavored with anise or orange-flower water, I could order from the village *boulangerie.*

I couldn't leave La Bonbonnière without the tiny sugar Santa Claus driving a marzipan car for Alexandre. He just turned sixteen months, so he'll be a more active participant in Christmas this year. When I put the car down in front of him, he looked confused: Eat the toys? Don't eat the toys? Oh, well, I guess parental consistency can go out the window once a year.

I DON'T KNOW if it's the Christmas tree lights or running the oven and three stove burners at once, but the electricity keeps blowing. I'm doing my best to cook around it, but at this rate, we could be eating Christmas dinner for New Year's.

After the gas went out for the third time under my stuffed squid, I decided to concentrate on the main course. One of the things that happens when my mother-in-law comes to town is that I end up cooking with leftover champagne. I know "leftover champagne" sounds like the culinary equivalent of a unicorn, but it does exist. I wrapped a large sea bass in cured ham and scattered some green olives with herbes de Provence alongside. Then, instead of reaching for my usual bottle of white cooking wine, I poured in a flat glass of bubbly that I'd forgotten to empty the night before.

While the fish was in the oven, Nicole went into the dining room and lifted Alexandre so he could see the crèche on the mantelpiece; it was one of Nicole's gifts to us this year. The small painted figurines are still handmade in several towns in Provence. In addition to the three Wise Men, there was a recalcitrant donkey, a painter with his easel, and a row of lavender plants. We would be able to add to it year after year until we had a whole tiny village. A neighbor up the road told me I was supposed to go out into the forest before Christmas Eve and find a springy piece of moss for the whole thing to sit on. I didn't quite get around to it.

The fish was delicious, though I can't swear if it was the champagne or the idea of the champagne that made it taste so good. After dinner it was time for the recounting of the Myth of the Christmas Cheese, one of my favorite family stories. Every year, Gwendal's great-aunt Jeanne, who lives in Auvergne, sends an entire ashy discus of Saint-Nectaire and a wedge of Salers the size and weight of a family Bible. During the general strike in 1995, the cheese was held up at the postal depot. The postman arrived three weeks later, holding the odoriferous package at arm's length. *"Ça. C'est à vous."* This story has all the elements of a classic French tale: smelly cheese, a national strike, and a comically put-upon civil servant.

It was nearly midnight when we each put the thirteen symbolic desserts on our plates: figs, almonds, hazelnuts, raisins, prunes, white nougat, dark nougat, candied melon, grapes, pears, clementines, the anise-flavored *pompe à l'huile* brioche, and the sweet almond paste of the *calissons d'Aix*. True to tradition, we left the half-empty wineglasses right where they were, and the peels from the clementines went straight into the fire. They sent up a spark before they flamed out and disappeared.

Recipes for a Provençal Christmas

BLOOD SAUSAGE WITH APPLES AND AUTUMN SPICES
Boudin Noir et Pommes aux Épices

Don't knock it till you've tried it.

4 Golden Delicious apples
1½ tablespoons olive oil
1½ pounds best-quality boudin (blood sausage)
Sea salt
2 cinnamon sticks
1 star anise
A glass of sweet white wine, like muscat

Heat the oven to 400°F.

Core the apples and cut into ½-inch slices (I leave the skin on). Toss apples with the olive oil.

In a large ovenproof casserole dish, arrange the *boudin* (cut into individual portions) and the apples. Sprinkle with sea salt and nestle in the cinnamon sticks and star anise. Cook for 20 minutes or until the *boudin* starts to sizzle and the apples have begun to brown.

Add a glass of white wine to the bottom of the pan. Cook 5 to 10 minutes longer. Serve immediately. If you want to double the comfort-food factor, add some fluffy mashed potatoes. Although this dish is prepared with white wine, I serve it with a medium-bodied red.

Serves 4

Tip: If you'd like to make this an appetizer for 8: Line a baking sheet with aluminum foil and carefully slice the boudin into coins (1 inch thick). Sur-

round with the apples as above. I'd serve it with the muscat I use to cook it—ideally, in front of a roaring fire.

SEA BASS WITH PARMA HAM, GREEN OLIVES, AND CHAMPAGNE
Loup de Mer au Jambon Cru, Olives Vertes, et Champagne

This is a spectacular holiday dish—the fish look so grand when you bring them to the table. It is important that you ask your fishmonger to scrape the scales off the fish, or do it yourself with a regular dinner knife (scrape against the grain)—you want to be able to eat the crispy ham-wrapped skin.

4 individual sea bass (9–12 ounces each), gutted and scales scraped off
Coarse sea salt
Handful of flat-leaf parsley or celery leaves
8 slices of Parma ham, sliced paper thin
⅓ cup unpitted green olives with herbs
½ cup of champagne (or white or rosé wine)

Heat the oven to 400°F.

Rinse the fish thoroughly, removing any stray scales with your fingers. Place the fish in a shallow casserole dish. Sprinkle the inside of each fish with a pinch of sea salt and stuff with a few sprigs of parsley. Wrap each fish with 2 slices of ham, leaving the head exposed. Scatter the green olives on top. Pour a good splash of champagne in the bottom (about ¼ inch) and bake for 30 minutes, until the skin is crispy and the flesh is firm and opaque down to the bone.

Serves 4

Tip: This would work equally well with thick meaty fillets like cod or monkfish; just take down the cooking time a bit.

MENDIANTS

I predict this will soon be an annual holiday project at your house. Put them in glass mason jars, tie with a pretty ribbon, and give as hostess gifts.

1 pound best-quality dark chocolate (you can use milk chocolate if you like . . .)

If you are being traditional, you'll need a generous handful each of:

Dried figs (cut into small pieces)
Dark or golden raisins
Blanched almonds
Whole hazelnuts

If you are feeling fancy (and don't care much for monkish symbolism), you can swap in a handful of:

Dried apricots, cut into small pieces
Candied orange, lemon, or grapefruit peel
Candied ginger
Unsalted pistachios
Macadamia nuts
Walnuts
Dried cranberries or cherries

Place a sheet of parchment paper on a cookie sheet.

Gently melt the chocolate in the microwave oven or a double boiler.

Place a teaspoonful of melted chocolate onto the sheet. Make sure the disks are about 1 inch apart. Make several at a time so that the chocolate does not have time to harden.

Place a piece of fig, a raisin, an almond, and a hazelnut on each disk, and leave in a cool spot to harden. The *mendiants* are ready when the chocolate is solid and they peel off the parchment paper with ease.

Makes about 50 chocolates

CHAPTER 8

Roots

E very once in a while, my agent calls from New York.
"What do you *do* all day?" she asks tentatively, trying to hide
the sound of her carefully manicured nails tapping on the table as
she awaits my next project. I'm loath to explain. There's my morning workout—carrying logs from the cellar, around the corner and
up the steps to the wood-burning stove. There's finding where
Alexandre has hidden his slippers (he can't walk on the freezing tile
without them). Then there's the half hour with the balled-up newspaper and egg cartons to light the smoky fire (thanks to our green,
wet wood). The ten-minute walk to and from Alexandre's babysitter
often takes the better part of an hour. In a village this size, there is
no question of rushing past people in a hurry. I stop for the all-
important *bises* and a brief but solemn evaluation of how this winter's frost will affect the peach trees. The prognosis, *bien sûr,* is grim.
In France, optimism is akin to hubris; better to expect the worst and
be pleasantly surprised. After the weather report is a frantic calculation: butcher or e-mail? The butcher closes at half past noon; the
Internet is always open.

Then, of course, there's lunch.

Our social life has become frantic since we moved to Céreste. Our agenda fills up weeks in advance, like the dance card of a busty cashmere-clad sorority girl. Luncheons, dinners, barbecues, *apéro*—maybe it's the new-kids-on-the-block effect, but we've had more nights out in the eight months that we've been in Céreste than we did in the eight years we lived in Paris. Despite this flurry of kind invitations, there's one of my own I'm having trouble extending. It's Passover this week, and though I'd like to celebrate, I'm not sure we know anyone here well enough to ask them into our home for a religious occasion.

A Passover Seder at my mother's house was thirty-five people—airline seating—once you sat down, you didn't get up till Moses freed the slaves. My mother led the Seder herself, first out of divorcée necessity, and then, when she married Paul, to keep up the tradition. My aunt Debbie was always in the kitchen with a vodka tonic, supervising the soup and giving gefilte-fish juice to the cat. There was always a feminist contingent who wanted to get into an argument about whether we should refer to God as He or She.

Passover was the only meal at our house that required a twenty-pound turkey and a yearly washing of the Lenox china, gold rimmed with tiny enamel flowers. My mother always set the table a few days in advance. I loved to come downstairs in the morning and see the Lalique crystal wineglasses, bought on my mother and father's first trip to Paris, sparkling in the early-spring sun. If I were back in the States this week, everyone around me would be making matzo balls, grating horseradish, and dipping into the freezer for a slice of Grandma Elsie's mandel bread. In Céreste, no one even knows I'm Jewish.

It's not that I've kept it from people on purpose, exactly. But I haven't been screaming it from the rooftops either. This may sound weird, even cowardly, but Judaism in Europe is not something casual, like *Seinfeld* and whitefish salad in New York. It lives in the shadow of the Holocaust, and there are residual fears and cautions.

When I hosted my first Seder in Paris, at the end of the meal I asked each of my guests to sign the inside cover of their Haggadah, the book used for the Passover service. It's a family tradition; I love going back through the signatures. I can trace a whole lifetime of family, friends, colleagues, and lovers. There were two French Jews at the table that night; they both hesitated. "It's no good to leave traces," they said.

Religion is a topic that confused me when I first arrived in France. There are hundreds of churches in Paris, but almost no one we know goes to Mass. Gwendal has a few Jewish friends; they knew I was far from home, but we were never invited for a holiday.

Both France and the United States guarantee freedom of religion, but they go about it in completely different ways, from different starting points and with different consequences. Among America's first settlers were Puritans who came to the New World to escape religious persecution. So America guarantees religious freedom by making sure that all citizens can practice their religions openly, whether it's by wearing a turban in school or swearing on a Bible at a presidential inauguration.

France has a very different history. The French Revolution sought to sever the State from the Catholic Church and the king—God's divinely ordained representative. So the French definition of laïcité— a secular state—means that all signs of religion are absent from public life. Children are not allowed to wear veils, or crosses, or yarmulkes in public school; a French president never mentions God in his speeches. Religion in France is considered a purely private matter, and, as a result, no one knows much about other people's traditions. I understand the historical forces at work; I also think it's a shame. Hidden religion breeds ignorance and sustains stereotypes. I always loved having my Catholic friends at Passover, and I've enjoyed being invited to Persian New Year and Midnight Mass.

When I went into the huge supermarket in Manosque for

matzo, the woman at the customer service desk had never even heard the word *Passover, Pessah,* or *Pâques Juive* (Jewish Easter, as it's sometimes called here). Asking for the kosher aisle didn't help. I finally found a box of *pain azyme,* unleavened bread, in the diet aisle.

I came home in a funny mood, ready to skip the holiday altogether. Gwendal insisted I celebrate it; he knows how lonely I feel when I don't. In the end we invited Angela and Rod for a mini-Seder. I made a lamb and dried-fig tagine and steamed asparagus. Rod was a little suspicious—he has a firm anticlerical streak—but I think he enjoyed my revised version of the holiday, which is less about prayer and more about a universal search for freedom. Angela brought one of her mother's porcelain teacups as a present—such a lovely thought—and Alexandre got to use my mother's silver asparagus tongs, which may have been the point of the whole exercise.

❧

TRANSITION PERIODS ARE never easy for me, which is problematic, since I've basically been in one for the past thirty-five years. Right now, Provence is in transition too. March is that kind of month; Wednesday the fog was so thick you couldn't see the *vieux village* from the parking lot by the chapel. Today the sky is cloudless blue and the bees are hard at work among the blossoms of the apricot tree across the way. It's like the set of a Disney movie: the whole town seems ready to open the shutters and burst into song.

This changeable weather is a perfect parallel for my mood.

Since I got back from the United States in February, something hasn't been right. I'm simply amazed at my body's ability to manifest what's going on in my head. Getting to sleep is a challenge. So is getting up. Pushing the stroller the half mile to the sitter leaves me winded and wishing for a Sherpa. Young mothers are supposed to be tired, right? But this feels different.

I've been trying to focus my attention on small tasks. This week, I've decided to tackle the herb garden. We haven't paid much attention to the garden since our sudden hibernation in late October. We left everything as it was, the hortensia bush cut back to a stub, last season's mint brown and matted. I was afraid to do too much; I didn't want to dig up the lilies of the valley by accident or kill a rosebush with ill-timed pruning. But there is a bare section on the left, separated from the others, maybe five feet long and three feet wide, a small patch of earth that I can make perfect and orderly, beautiful and useful.

I dug a shallow hole in the dirt—not unlike the one I'm trying to crawl out of right now. I'm in what the French call a *creux,* and it happens every time I have to leave one professional project and start another.

I used to think of success in terms of before and after. I had this fantasy that at some point in my life, in my career, I would just *arrive.* I kept waiting to cross the threshold and find my final, complete self on the other side. The self I could settle into for good, the self I wouldn't have to reinvent every time the sun set on a project. Constant reinvention; most people would call that, well...life. But at the moment, I'm finding the whole thing, well...exhausting.

Many writers, artists in general, see misery as the price of creation. Personally, I've never been able to do diddly-squat when I'm miserable. When I was young, I found a book in a secondhand shop called *Impressive Depressives* that was about historical figures—Chopin, among others—who may have suffered from manic depression. As if being depressed might somehow be useful to me.

As someone who grew up with a close personal relationship to mental illness, bathed in its sour stream, I know there's nothing romantic or inspiring about it. My father wasn't an artist, or a genius; he was sick. Like drinking polluted water, I absorbed a tiny bit of his sadness every day—it built up in my brain and my organs. I will carry that sediment around with me for the rest of my life.

Because of my family history, the line separating a bad day or a long winter from something clinical has never been easy for me to judge. Every gray day presses some kind of internal panic button. *What if this is it, the day I never quite recover from?* My thoughts quickly spiral out of control. My husband won't love me anymore, because all I want to do is sleep and I never brush my hair. I condemn my son to watch what I watched: a parent melting into the stone floor like the Wicked Witch of the West. I can't write a word, and because I never leave the house, I have nothing to write about. It's like the chick-lit version of a Paul Auster novel—an upright, Manolo-wearing member of society reduced to a bag lady, padding around in an army surplus coat stuffed with crumpled pages of the Style section, pushing a shopping cart full of empty cans of Coke Zero.

My therapist once told me that if I got through my twenties without a major depressive episode, it probably wouldn't happen. I just don't trust that anymore. I look at the life I have, how full and rich it is, and I think: *If you're not happy every minute of every single day, you must, objectively, be a little crazy.*

The therapy I did after my parents' divorce and during the long years of my father's illness focused on coping mechanisms, small practical things I could do to combat these feelings in the outside world. It still works. If I force myself to get out of the house for an hour, I feel better. If I write, even a few lines, I feel like I've accomplished something. If I stop watching programs about serial killers on YouTube, I feel less afraid in my bed at night. I try to focus on manageable tasks. Hence, the herb garden.

When we lived in Paris I treated myself to a bouquet of fresh herbs every Saturday at the local market, the way some women buy themselves flowers. I put them in an old jam jar full of water on the kitchen counter or on the door of the fridge. I ripped off fresh mint leaves for tea, dill to stuff inside whole fish, flat-leaf parsley and sprigs of thyme for my braised beef, cilantro for my chicken tagine.

In the spring, I waited patiently for slim blades of chive to appear for my swordfish tartare. In the summer, I bought bunches of purple basil for a tomato salad.

When I first arrived in Provence I searched the market in vain for my weekly bouquet. Nowhere to be found. Sometimes, the vegetable man would throw in some free parsley with my salad and leeks. When I asked where I could find some thyme, he looked at me like I'd asked him if he could please bend down and tie my shoelaces: *"Mais ça pousse partout."* It grows everywhere.

He had a point. Thyme grows with wild abandon, anywhere there is a patch of sun between the trees. Up in the hills, you can't walk ten feet in any direction without stepping on a small tuft. The vegetable man's meaning was clear: in Provence, you never buy what you can grow or gather for free.

Taking his advice, on our last walk up the hill at Montjustin, I dug up a bunch of thyme by the root. We'll see if it will grow in captivity.

When we'd arrived in Céreste, our neighbor Arnaud said we should go to the Musée de Salagon, in Mane. In addition to its twelfth-century church and Gallo-Roman ruins, the museum has a wonderful medieval garden. The monks used these herbs to heal as well as to flavor. I've met many people in Provence who use herbal remedies, not because it's trendy, but because it's what their grandmothers taught them. My friend Lynne puts lavender oil on bug bites to reduce the swelling; I recently found Arnaud on his front steps tying small bundles of wild absinthe, which he burns to fumigate the house. Many of the pharmacies in France still sell licorice root for low blood pressure. We drink lemon verbena herbal tea for digestion.

I also like the more poetic symbolism of the herbs. I'm planting sage for wisdom, lavender for tenderness (and, according to French folklore, your forty-sixth wedding anniversary), rosemary for remembrance. Thyme is for courage, but there is also the Greek legend that when Paris kidnapped Helen of Troy, each tear that fell to the ground sprouted a tuft of thyme. All things being equal, I prefer courage to tears in my pot roast.

In addition to the regular sage, I planted *sauge ananas;* when you rub its leaves, it smells exactly like pineapple. I don't know if it has a particular medicinal value, but I can't wait to try it with a pork roast.

I patted the earth around the thyme. Maybe I was the one who needed planting. When I was back in the States, Mom and Paul announced that they'd decided to sell my childhood home in Teaneck, New Jersey, and move to Wilmington, Delaware, to be near my aunt. "I don't want a lawn to mow anymore, or a driveway to shovel. I don't want to worry about replacing the oil burner," said my mom, trying to sound casual. Sell our little Tudor house on the corner, with a turret in the middle that you can access only through a low door in the back of my mother's bedroom closet? It's where we stored extra wrapping paper and scarves and my mom's collection of antique handbags.

I don't know why this should hit me so hard; I've been gone a long time. Maybe that's just it. Without saying a thing, my parents are making plans around the assumption that I'm never coming back. This seems at once obvious and terribly sad. It's my final permission slip. *Go on, pussycat. I'll be fine.* My mother's generosity, not for the first time, humbles me.

I recently started to give English lessons to Julien, the ten-year-old son of Alexandre's old babysitter. We started with adjectives. We made little stickers for the wall. Today is *hot, cold, sunny, cloudy.* I am *happy, sad, smart, funny* (I left out *stupid,* on purpose). I told him to change it every day. When I went by last week I realized that I'd also left out *perfect. Perfect* is a word I use in English all the time. How's one o'clock for lunch? Perfect. Can I get back to you next week? Perfect. How's the tiramisu? Perfect. The French equivalent, *parfait,* is not something you hear very often. No student ever gets 100 percent on a term paper. Perfection is considered prideful, even ridiculous. This is depressing, but also true. I am *perfect*. It's a tall order.

Most people are nostalgic about childhood. Not me. When I was a kid I couldn't wait to be an adult so I could control things. Surely, I thought, this would make life easier. I would have the perfect job. I would meet the perfect man. I would make perfect decisions. There have been moments—I stick to my American guns—that have been downright perfect. But as I get older, my decisions have become more tangled, less perfect, harder to uproot.

Gwendal and I wanted the garden to retain some of its disorder, some of its surprises. He had trimmed the rosebushes in the fall. Jewel-like buds, round and tight, had begun to form on the branches; a bed of tiny violets grew at their base. The new mint, insistent as a hormonal teenage boy, began to poke through in inch-high sprouts. We had never seen the garden at this season before. I rubbed a sage leaf between my fingers; the musky oil stuck to my skin. I'd like to greet the unknown with pleasure. If I could just manage my fear, there might be something wondrous about not knowing what will pop up next.

⌘

MIREILLE'S MOTHER, Marcelle Pons Sidoine, passed away yesterday. I saw the announcement, a simple black-and-white photocopy, posted on the tree in the place des Marronniers.

We'd had the good fortune to meet Marcelle several times when we first came to Céreste. Even at the age of ninety-four, she was a decisive woman—short of sentence and sure of opinion. The first time we met was for a lunchtime aperitif. Mireille brought out her home-made peach wine for the occasion.

Marcelle was seated in the garden when we arrived. She was

petite and wore several layers of sweaters under a blue housecoat. In his poems, Char refers to her as *la Renarde*—the fox. Her quick eyes were hidden now behind large glasses, but her hair still had the pompadourish rise that I recognized from photos of her younger self.

The wine was a deep rose color, infused with the leaves of local white peach trees. When her son-in-law tried to serve her a second time, Marcelle covered the top of her glass with the palm of her hand. *Pas moi,* she said—"one more and I'll dance the Charleston." I had a sudden flash of a girl in sensible brown shoes and an A-line dress secretly practicing the steps in her bedroom.

When we asked about Char, she said: "He was always hanging around, *ce grand,* being nice to my mother. *Il m'agaçait, celui-là.* He annoyed me." I imagined a large bee buzzing around the head of a pretty young woman. I guess love is always the same; when he starts cozying up to your mother, you're in real trouble.

✑

THE FUNERAL SERVICE was held in the local church. The walls were frigid. This is the season in Provence when the locals have stopped spending money on heat; it's often colder inside than out. We sat discreetly on a wooden pew near the back; the crackling of the antiquated sound system blotted out most of the eulogy. Marcelle had been a recognized member of the French Résistance, so there were two men in uniform in attendance, nearly Marcelle's age themselves. Heavy gold epaulettes sagged a bit on their shrunken shoulders.

On foot, we followed the hearse to the local cemetery. After the chill of the church, the sun was warm and welcome. The cemetery is on a hill overlooking the village and the surrounding fields. Not a bad place to spend eternity.

When we got home, the house looked slightly different. The first thing that struck us when we'd visited the house was the danger and, at the same time, the warmth of the memories associated with the war. The following event took place in what is now our living room:

Looking for Char, the Gestapo decided to do an impromptu search of the entire village. They ordered the townsfolk out of their homes, instructing them to leave the doors ajar. There was no way Char could present himself at such a lineup. Even if the soldiers didn't recognize his face, they'd know him because he was a full head taller than any man in Céreste. Marcelle and her mother wrapped a bandage around Char's jaw so he looked like an old woman with a toothache, and they left him in bed, pistol in hand and the covers pulled up to his chin. The room is just a short flight of stairs off the living room.

When the Germans arrived, Marcelle was standing in front of the door, holding the key. "Leave it," said the soldiers. "Go to the square." "I don't trust these people," she said. "There are thieves in this village. If you want to search the house, go ahead, but I will stay here and lock the door behind you."

The Germans came in, looked around the living room, went out into the garden. They got halfway up the stairs—it's only six steps—to Char's room and turned around. "We don't have time for this. There's no one here. Let's go."

It was only after the soldiers left that Marcelle saw the grenade lying carelessly on the table in front of the wood-burning stove. How had she—how had *they*—not noticed it? Possession of any kind of weapon (to say nothing of hiding a Résistance leader with a pistol in the bedroom) would have been enough to get the whole family shot.

It's hard to describe the room where all this happened—how small it is. "I was sick for eight days after that," said Marcelle when she told us the story. As if risking your life were like coming down with the flu.

That afternoon, I went back to my spring cleaning, making the house our own. But we will never forget why we first came to this place, drawn by the good-luck lilies of the valley and an extraordinary history.

It will always be her garden.

෴

SINCE MARCELLE'S FUNERAL, Jean has been looking a bit down; feeling his age, perhaps.

"It's a blow," he said, leaning against the gate. They had been good neighbors but were hardly the best of friends. Mireille used to complain about Jean grilling sardines under the window of her daughter's bedroom all summer. Jean still talks about the 637 empty yogurt pots he had to clean out when he bought the property from the Pons family. No doubt if we stay another forty years, they'll find a story like that about us.

"*Tiens,* if it rains on Wednesday, this weekend there will be mushrooms."

My ears perked up. I'd been waiting for this moment since we arrived. Mushroom hunting in Provence is veiled in secrecy, second only to truffle hunting in the level of dissimulation and suspicion it inspires. If you are lucky enough to find a good spot, you might unearth skinny yellow and black *trompettes de la mort* (trumpets of death) or flat meaty *pleurots* (oyster mushrooms) or even small spongelike black morels. If you are not sure exactly what you've found, you can take your basket to the local pharmacy, and the pharmacist will help you sort the culinary from the potentially deadly—it's part of their training.

"I'll show you *mon coin,*" he said, looking pointedly at Gwendal.

Being taken to a good spot is like Bluebeard drawing you a map leading straight to his buried treasure. Jean and Paulette don't have any children; we were touched that they liked us enough to bestow this legacy.

"I'll go," I piped up in my uniquely American way.

"You'll be home with the baby," responded Jean in a tone that brooked no argument.

I made another attempt to stick my nose into the breach. "Gwendal can stay with the baby."

He waved this notion away with a flick of his hand. Like a gold pocket watch, a mushroom spot was clearly something to be passed down among men.

They started out early on Saturday morning. "You must hide your *sac*. If anyone sees the bags, they will follow us." Jean had a large walking stick in hand, for camouflage. "We need to look like we are just out for *une balade*." I watched them disappear around the corner with a twinge of envy.

They were gone all morning. Alexandre had just woken up from his nap when Gwendal walked in the door.

"Did you find any?"

"No. Someone must have been there before us. But it's a beautiful walk, across the river, up around the edge of the cliff on the rock face.

"He would never say so," said Gwendal, trying to console me, "but I think he wanted me there instead of you because he was afraid he might slip."

Recipes from the Herb Garden

ROSEMARY CAPONATA

By the time the peppers and eggplants are back at the market, my rosemary bush is in need of some judicious pruning. This is a great excuse to do it. Served with sourdough toasts, caponata is perfect for lingering over drinks in the garden. It's a great addition to an omelet or a gourmet sandwich layered with fresh goat cheese and cured ham.

1½ pounds of onions, a mix of red and white, cut into eighths
1½ pounds eggplant, cut into ¼-inch rounds, then into ½-inch
strips
1 pound red bell peppers, cut into 1-inch cubes
1 pound tomatoes, chopped
Small handful pine nuts
3 sprigs of rosemary, about 3 inches each
¾ cup golden raisins
½ cup fruity extra-virgin olive oil
1 tablespoon sugar
Grind of black pepper
1 large handful of flat-leaf parsley, chopped

Preheat oven to 350°F.

In a large mixing bowl, combine all the ingredients except the parsley; toss to coat. Line a large baking sheet with aluminum foil. Spread the mixture evenly on the baking sheet and roast for 2½ to 3 hours, stirring every 45 minutes or so, until the vegetables are tender and slightly caramelized. Remove from the oven, let rest for 10 minutes, then mix in a handful of flat-leaf parsley. When you transfer the caponata to your serving bowl, be sure to get all the yummy juices as well. Serve warm or at room temperature.

Serves 6–8 as an hors d'oeuvre

WHOLE-GRAIN SALAD WITH CHICKPEAS AND HERBS
Salade de Petit Épeautre aux Herbes

Even the French don't do *everything* from scratch. Precooked whole grains are a great thing to have around the house for a quick healthy meal. I buy an organic brand that has cool combinations like kamut, spelt, and cracked wheat, but the supermarket brands are starting to catch up. When I need an impromptu side dish for guests, I dress up the grains with chopped herbs, chickpeas, and preserved lemon. With a sliced tomato salad and some grilled chicken, dinner is done.

3 tablespoons olive oil
Juice of 1 lemon
¼ cup (packed) coriander, chopped
1 cup (packed) flat-leaf parsley, chopped, with stems
1 tablespoon preserved lemon (rind only), diced
1 14-ounce can of chickpeas (or red beans), rinsed
Black pepper to taste
2 cups precooked whole grains (quinoa, bulgur, barley, farro, or wild rice)

In a medium mixing bowl, whisk together the olive oil and lemon juice. Add herbs, preserved lemon, chickpeas, and a good grinding of black pepper; toss to combine.

Heat precooked grains with very little extra water so they remain al dente. Add the warm grains to the herb mixture; stir to combine. Serve the salad warm, cold, or at room temperature.

Serves 4 as a side dish

Tip: Preserved lemons can be found at Middle Eastern groceries and specialty stores. I use only the outer rind (about ¼ inch thick) and discard the inner pulp. I don't add any salt to this recipe, as the precooked grains sometimes have added salt and preserved lemons are pickled in a salt solution. If you can't find the preserved lemons, add the zest of ½ lemon instead.

MINI–ALMOND CAKES WITH APRICOT AND LAVENDER
Financiers aux Abricots et à la Lavande

Just as the first sun-kissed apricots arrive at the market, lavender fields all over Provence are bursting into bloom. They are a perfect pair. These mini–almond cakes are gluten free, a treat for a special summer breakfast or teatime in the garden.

7 tablespoons unsalted butter, at room temperature
½ cup plus 2 tablespoons sugar
2 eggs
½ teaspoon almond extract (or a few drops of real bitter almond essence, if you can find it!)
½ teaspoon vanilla extract
1¾ cups almond meal (ground almond flour)
1 good pinch of coarse sea salt
¼ teaspoon lavender grains, plus a few for garnish
6 small apricots, halved
1 teaspoon light brown sugar or raw cane sugar for garnish

Heat the oven to 400°F.

Whip the butter until light and fluffy. Add the sugar and beat until combined. Add the eggs one at a time, beating well after each addition. Add the almond and vanilla extracts; fold in the ground almonds until thoroughly combined. Add a good pinch of coarse sea salt and the lavender grains to the mix. Stir to combine.

Line a muffin tin with aluminum-foil cupcake wrappers (paper wrappers will stick). Divide the batter evenly into 12 mini-cakes (a heaping tablespoon of batter for each should do it).

Place an apricot half, skin side down, in the center of each mini-cake. Place 1 or 2 lavender grains (resist the urge to add more) on each apricot. Sprinkle the fruit with a pinch of brown sugar. Bake for 20 minutes, until golden brown. Cool on a wire rack. I peel the wrappers off before serving, but you don't have to, especially if you are taking them on a picnic or otherwise transporting them.

Makes 12 mini-cakes

CHAPTER 9

A Cherry on Top

Spring has sprung early this year. Nothing could have prepared me for the magnificent bloom of the irises along the old Roman road or the snap of the first local peas. We discovered the short-lived fields of narcissi sprouting across from the old train station. Once cultivated for perfume production, they now grow wild in the tall grass. For a week or two, everyone stops to gather the small daffodil-like flowers, their scent powerful, almost sickly sweet.

Alexandre is learning to talk; his first sentences are "Weed a book" (you get the general idea) and "I'm a cook" (thanks to Pixar's *Ratatouille*). I always thought we would raise our children in Paris, that I would take Alexandre to the Louvre on Saturday mornings and we would slurp miso ramen at our favorite hole-in-the-wall Japanese restaurant for lunch. But the spectacles are different here. We can spend a whole morning on the steps of the town hall spotting tractors; watching the three guys raising beams for the new roof of the butcher shop is like a night at the ballet.

Now that Gwendal is working from home, he's around a lot more than your average executive. He and Alexandre are so natural together; I am having a harder time. Now that he's out of the baby stage, I've realized that I don't really know how to play.

These past few months, there's been a quiet abdication going on, like a queen gracefully (but begrudgingly) handing over power to her more genial younger brother. I still do the cooking, the bath, and Alexandre and I go to the butcher and the bakery together, but the giggles, the wrestling, the circus acrobatics, even the quiet-time hugs are Gwendal's domain. It's hard, maybe impossible, for a mother to admit that she is not her child's primary parent, that maybe his father is just more fun.

If I don't know how to play, I sure have learned how to squeeze.

For better or worse, my relationship with my son is also a male-female relationship. I've never chased a man in my life (okay, once — very bad outcome). My mother taught me never to wait by the phone. I never made the first move. I knew how to play the game. At least I thought I did. Alexandre is the first boy in a long time — maybe the first boy ever — who makes me feel needy, insecure. So here I am, at the age of thirty-seven, chasing my son around the kitchen table like some crazed lover in a 1930s bedroom farce, grasping in vain after one more smooch.

Where's a good old-fashioned Oedipus complex when you need one?

I discussed it with my friend Keria, the one who gave me such sound advice about who should look where during the actual birth. "They're little men," she said. "Simple as that. Respect the space. The same thing happened to me. I was screaming at Theo one night, trying to get him to go to bed. Marco explained it all.

"'He's a man, Keria,' he told me. 'You don't talk to a man like that, belittling him. He has pride. Accept his innate superiority as a man and he will accept your innate superiority as his mother.'"

Her husband, of course, is half Italian.

❧

TODAY ALEXANDRE WOULDN'T let me sit next to him on the couch. With his full weight pitched forward, he shoved me away, both hands against my invading thigh.

There are days, most days, when I'm unprepared for the fundamental asymmetry of maternal love. The tug of it. I wonder if it's always going to be like this, me asking for more love than he wants to give.

When I talk to Gwendal about these feelings, I end up sounding like a wounded, whiny child myself. "I know you think it's annoying to have him all over you all the time, but he never, never comes to me. Only by default, when you're not around."

"Do you play with him?"

"I don't know," I said honestly, bewildered. "You think I don't play with him enough?" It was half question, half accusation.

"I don't know."

I don't know means "yes."

❧

I'VE BEEN ACCEPTED as an apprentice in Jean's garden, a hidden oasis of plum, pear, cherry, and walnut trees down by the river. This means getting up at dawn and making my way across the Pont Roman, walking along a deeply rutted dirt road, and taking a sometimes smelly left at the sanitation plant. The last thing I grew was a potato on three toothpicks (that was in kindergarten), so we'll see how it goes.

Jean's garden is a secret garden, a square plot surrounded by a thick hedge and a padlocked gate. Even if I were to be shut out forever, like Adam and Eve from the Garden of Eden, I would always remember this place, keep a map of it in my head.

Just beyond the gate is a neat circle of giant irises. My middle name is Iris, and they are among my favorite flowers. The blooms are almost as big as my hand; there are the royal-purple ones, which I knew, but also colors I'd never seen before: bright yellow, white, even burgundy, a deep red with the texture of crushed-velvet.

Behind the irises, in the sunniest spot, are the beds for tomatoes, eggplants, zucchini, parsley, and potatoes. Jean likes to plant small round eggplants and also round zucchini; pale green and the size of softballs, they are the perfect shape to hollow out and stuff with sausage and spices.

To the left is the shade of the walnut tree and just beyond that the shed. The walnuts are already ripening in their fuzzy green pods. In June, Jean soaks the young nuts with *vin de table, eau de vie,* and sugar to make a winter's worth of his own walnut wine. There are two rows of muscat grape vines and two plum trees, one for tiny green *mirabelles* (I like to freeze them and use them as ice cubes in summer drinks) and one for *quetsches,* oval and dusky purple, perfect for making compote. There is a border of rosebushes, pale peach, feathery pink, and lavender, and an apricot tree that hasn't given fruit in several years.

Jean walked me up the central path. Next to the cherry trees, only a few feet from the river, is a concrete *puits,* a well. "A neighbor told me a few years ago, 'You'd better cover it, or someone might put a dead deer in there to poison the water.'" I tried to trace this story back to its origins. Between the Marseillais gift for exaggeration and the *paysan* gift for paranoia, the truth could be a long way off. Maybe one day a rabbit tried to drink from it and fell in. Give it ten years and two more tellers, and it would be a grizzly bear.

Of course, I was not there simply to admire. I was there to work. We made our way back to the shed, where Jean handed me a pair of large canvas gloves. I thought of the white felt gloves I'd once aspired to, the kind used to handle Renaissance manuscripts. As my mother would say: Life leads you to amazing places.

Jean approached his garden the way I imagined he'd approached his engineering work, with precise gestures and all the right tools. In addition to small hand rakes and spades, he had a series of short metal poles he had cut himself to measure between the rows of vegetables. Thirty-two centimeters between each row, eighteen centimeters between each potato. He gave me a bag of spuds he'd saved from the previous winter; they were already sprouting knobbly green buds from the eyes. I soon abandoned the gloves; they only got in my way.

Just short of his eightieth birthday, Jean still squats in the dirt with relative ease. When we finished with the potatoes, he picked up a thicker, longer metal pole that was lying in the grass. "I was wondering what that was for," I said.

"This," he told me with a laugh, implying everything had its purpose, "is to help me get up off the ground."

Jean doesn't like chemical fertilizer. His trinity for a healthy garden is a mixture of sheep shit, pellets of dried cow's blood, and ground goat horn. "When we were first married, Paulette had a cousin that worked at the *abattoir*—the local slaughterhouse. He would send us buckets of blood to pour around the base of the trees." I thought about my pregnant cravings for *boudin noir* and raw steak—maybe the trees feel the same way.

Jean left me a bare patch behind the plum trees to plant beans. It took me a few days to rake it clear; it was covered with the debris: last year's tree trimmings, vine cuttings, and dead leaves. When I was finally ready to turn the earth, I expected a Colonial Williamsburg–style hoe, but instead he brought out a bright red *motoculteur*—a sort of handheld tractor—its undercarriage spattered with mud. It had a narrow head, a spoked wheel underneath, and two handles perpendicular to the earth like pointy ears. It looked like a large red poodle riding a unicycle.

As soon as he turned it on, the poodle began to buck like a calf at a rodeo. I tried to press the rotating head deep into the soil, maintaining a straight line. The sound was deafening.

"*Tiens bien,*" yelled Jean as I veered to the left like a drunk driver. I was dangerously close to the heirloom rosebushes when he finally flicked the switch and the beast came to a halt.

"Here," he said, handing me back my rake.

After Jean finished turning my plot—he controlled the red devil with a grim determination and more upper-arm strength than I possessed—he needed a break. He sat down on a tree stump in a spot of sun near the cherry tree, his stomach settling between his knees. Talking is his way of resting, and sensing that I am more interested in cooking than in nuclear submarines, he often narrates his favorite recipes.

"Do you know *sardines à l'escabèche?*" he began, taking out his handkerchief and wiping his brow.

"You take sardine fillets, or whole sardines with the guts and heads removed, dip them in a bit of flour, fry them, and then let them cool." I wondered if this was the recipe he had been making underneath Mireille's bedroom window all these years.

"Make a sauce with chopped onion and olive oil, add a glass of red wine vinegar and a *cuillère à soupe* of honey." A *cuillère à soupe* is a soupspoon. In France it's not a precise measurement—the size depends on the heft of your great-grandmother's silver service.

"Let it boil a bit. Pour over the sardines, store in the fridge for *un apéritif.*" He looked pleased with himself, as if he wanted to go home and make some right then. "I might chop some parsley," he added, by way of conclusion.

Every day, before we leave the garden, Jean cuts a bouquet of peonies and roses for Paulette, carefully trimming the thorns with a pocketknife. He cut one for me as well, wrapping the stems tightly with kitchen string.

"Do you have a recipe for bouillabaisse?" I asked as we hung the gardening tools back on their hooks in the shed.

"For that you must go to the fish market in Marseille."

"Do you think that one day, when you go"—they still had their apartment in the city—"I could come?"

"*C'est de l'authentique.* This is what you do." For this, like everything else, Jean had his method.

"*Tu arrives de bonne heure.* You must arrive early. I ask, 'How much?'" he said, eyeing the imaginary fish with an air of disdain. "Bah." He threw up his hands at the temerity of the imaginary fishmonger. "'If you want to keep it, keep it.' Then I walk away. Later, about half past twelve, I come back. *Il en reste toujours,* he still has plenty of fish, *et là,* you have it for half price. *Si non, c'est trop cher*—they take you for *un imbécile.*"

I held my bouquet while Jean closed the padlock.

"But if we go," he said, wagging a finger under my nose, "*toi, tu ne parles pas!* You don't say a word. If you do, they'll take me for an Englishman."

His pride would never recover.

⁀ℐ⁀

I'M AN OLD soul. Three going on thirty, as my mother used to say. In this, as in so many things, she's not wrong. Everyone has a natural age, and there's something about my thirties that just fits. When I hit thirty-one, I somehow felt right in my skin. My mental age and my actual age finally merged, like overlapping film negatives synchronized for a perfect Technicolor image. Gwendal has a natural age too—about five and a half. He still approaches the world with a sense of wonder—it's one of the things I love best about him.

He and Alexandre understand each other perfectly; every stick is a sword, every puddle demands to be jumped in. I've tried it, and no matter how hard I concentrate, I still see a stick. I'm kind of a party pooper that way. Gwendal is a much better knight-errant than I.

So how did such an old biddy find herself, this past week, giggling, six feet off the ground in the limbs of a cherry tree? Since the sun came out for good in April, nature seems to be on fast-forward. The lilacs were wilted by the first of May; now the cherry trees are groaning with fruit, several weeks in advance. We've been invited down to Jean's garden this afternoon to help pick the cherries before the crows do.

We arrived with a wooden crate. We barely had to touch the fruit; it almost fell into our hands. Alexandre squealed every time a cherry accidentally hit the ground; he ran around our feet, picking up the strays. Jean sat on his tree stump, pointing us toward branches we had missed. Somewhere in the stretching, tugging, and plucking of the cherries was a childlike sensation that I couldn't remember feeling ever before. Not to mention the forbidden pleasure of staining a perfectly good white T-shirt with fresh cherry juice.

I don't have many childhood memories. In fact, I don't remember anything before the day, just after my seventh birthday, when my parents called me from the den, where I'd been coloring, up to their bedroom and announced they were getting a divorce. It was the first time I'd seen either of my parents cry. My father was packed and a taxi was already waiting outside. I sat on the steps thinking I should do something—scream, kick—but I did not.

When I try to remember anything that came before that, there are only snippets: my mother at the sink pulling the beards off steamers; my father, head propped up on one arm, reading Dr. Seuss on my bed with the Strawberry Shortcake sheets. When Gwendal and I find ourselves kissing in the kitchen (this happens quite a bit), Alexandre will invariably come and insert himself between our knees. He loves this tent of legs; the pillars holding up his universe, I guess. Every time this happens, I feel a lump rising in my throat. I have no memories of my parents in the same room.

Up until now, I would have told you this didn't matter. When I was young, I was proud to be a little adult, serious, precocious, mature, responsible—all the adjectives that grown-ups use to describe children old beyond their years. I took it as a compliment. After my parents split up, my dad's illness took up so much space, the breakup of our family became an ancillary effect, a footnote.

One thing I do remember very clearly: Just after the divorce, my mom wanted me to see a psychologist. She met several, and I was to pick one. We entered an office full of hanging plants and crowded bookshelves. A man stood up and reached out to shake my hand. "I'm Dr. ——. I'm a child psychologist." I remember looking up into his face; he had a short black beard and wire-rimmed glasses. "I don't need a child psychologist," I said. "I don't have child problems." That was the end of the interview.

It's only now that I have a child of my own that I realize what I might have missed. A good childhood is something to cherish and emulate; a bad childhood is something to banish and fix. But no childhood at all? It was not until I had Alexandre that I realized the blank I was facing. In all my travels, childhood is the strangest land I've ever visited.

I always thought I would be a good mother because I have a good mother to look up to. But maybe what really makes a good parent—what I seem to be lacking—is the child I once was to look back on.

Jean's wife, Paulette, and Alexandre were making a pile of bruised cherries to leave for the crows. I reached up into the leaves and popped a final sun-warmed globe into my mouth. If today is the best day I can remember, is that really so bad? Maybe it's cheating, to be creating my own childhood memories at the same time as my son, but I don't think Alexandre will mind me piggybacking on his pleasure. He might even show me a thing or two.

WHEN WE GOT home, there was a brief moment of panic—now I had to figure out what to do with several kilos of ruby ripe cherries. Jean came to the rescue with two recipes he'd copied onto index cards in his neat square hand. The first, a classic *clafoutis*, uses the burst of fresh cherries for a wobbly breakfast flan. The second is for what he called "cherry marmalade." Cherries are too watery for jam, but this is perfect—slightly wrinkled, toothsome cherries in a velvety syrup. Jean does all his own canning, and he has his own method of "insta-sterilization" that involves flipping the sealed jars and storing them upside down. As is often the case with family recipes, the instructions were lacking a few salient details, like the fact that the cherry syrup needs to be boiling hot when you're doing all this. My seals didn't take, so just to be safe, we'll have to eat the whole batch of cherry marmalade for breakfast, lunch, and dinner this month. Come to think of it, that sounds like another thing my childhood self might have enjoyed.

Recipes from Jean's Garden

GRILLED SARDINES WITH VINEGAR AND HONEY
Sardines à l'Escabèche

This recipe is pure Marseille—grilled sardines in a zippy vinegar-and-honey sauce. Jean serves them before dinner with an aperitif. A large glass of pastis, of course.

1 pound small whole sardines or sardine fillets
3 tablespoons olive oil plus ½ tablespoon for grilling
Pinch of coarse sea salt
Handful of chopped flat-leaf parsley, about ¼ cup, loosely packed
½ cup shallots, minced
6 tablespoons red wine or sherry vinegar
1 tablespoon honey

For the sardines: If you are using whole sardines, gut, descale, and rinse them under cold water. If you are using fillets, rinse the fillets to remove any stray scales. Toss with ½ tablespoon of olive oil and a pinch of coarse sea salt. Grill over medium heat. This will be quick: for whole sardines, 3 to 4 minutes on one side, 1 to 2 minutes on the other (even less for fillets). I like my sardines with a bit of char on the outside. You can also do this under the broiler.

Layer the cooked sardines with the chopped parsley in a shallow serving dish. You don't want more than two layers, and if you have room for only a single layer, so much the better—that way, the fish soaks up the sauce evenly.

For the sauce: Heat 3 tablespoons olive oil in a small nonreactive saucepan (stainless steel or enamel). Add the shallots and sauté over low heat for 4 minutes. Add vinegar and honey; simmer over lowest possible heat for 4 minutes. Pour hot sauce over the sardines. Add a last layer of chopped parsley. I think they are super served warm on the day you make them; Jean likes to refrigerate his overnight, to give the flavors time to blend (bring back to room temperature before serving).

Serves 4–6, with drinks

STUFFED TOMATOES AND ZUCCHINI
Légumes d'Été Farçis

This dish instantly transports me back to Jean's garden—big, bright beefsteak tomatoes and croquet-ball-size round zucchini stuffed and baked to sagging perfection. Lovely for a casual dinner in the garden.

2 slices of slightly stale sourdough or dense whole-grain bread
⅓ cup milk
4 perfectly ripe beefsteak tomatoes (10–12 ounces each)
4 round zucchini (7–8 ounces each)
4 tablespoons olive oil
1 large red onion, chopped
1 cup chopped fennel (about ½ bulb), with some fronds
2 large cloves garlic, minced
½ teaspoon herbes de Provence
Black pepper
Handful of flat-leaf parsley, chopped
1 egg
1½ pounds best-quality pork sausages (you can use Toulouse, saucisse
  fraîche, or Italian, sweet or hot)
1 pound ground beef
½ cup white wine

Preheat the oven to 400°F.

Put the bread and milk in a small bowl to soak.

Cut the tops off the tomatoes and hollow out until you have about a ½- to ¾-inch shell. Chop the pulp and reserve with the liquid.

Hollow out the zucchini as you did with the tomatoes. Chop the inside zucchini flesh and reserve in a separate bowl. Place the hollowed-out vegetables in a large ovenproof dish, preferably one pretty enough to bring to the table.

In a medium frying pan, heat 2 tablespoons of olive oil. Sauté onion, fennel, and zucchini pulp for 5 minutes, add garlic, and sauté for 3 minutes more. Add chopped tomato pulp, herbes de Provence, and a grind of black pepper; simmer for 5 minutes. Add parsley and stir. Remove from the heat and let cool.

Squeeze a bit of the excess milk out of the bread, chop into coarse crumbs, set aside. In a small bowl, lightly beat the egg.

Remove sausage meat from its casings and break it up without overworking the meat. Add the beef, bread, and tomato mixture and combine—I use my hands for this part. Then add the egg and give the stuffing a final mix. Divide the stuffing evenly among the vegetables. Drizzle with the additional 2 tablespoons olive oil. Add the white wine to the bottom of the dish.

Cover the dish tightly with tinfoil and bake 1½ hours, until the sausage is cooked through and the vegetables are perfectly tender; the saggier the better, as far as I'm concerned. Remove the foil and pass under the broiler for 3 minutes to brown. There will be quite a bit of yummy sauce at the bottom of the dish.

Serve on a bed of quinoa or wild rice. Pass a bowl of sauce.

Serves 8 as a light dinner

Tip: Round zucchini are sometimes available at farmers' markets and high-end grocers. If you can't find them, buy 1 extra-large zucchini or 2 medium ones, cut them in half lengthwise, and hollow them out like a hot-dog bun. Stuff according to the recipe.

CHERRY CLAFOUTI
Clafoutis aux Cerises

Clafouti is a homey dessert, a wobbly set custard chock-full of summer's first cherries. What it lacks in elegance, it makes up for in comfort and sheer deliciousness, perfect for brunch among friends. I've been fiddling with clafouti recipes for many years. Jean's had too much flour for my taste, more like a Far Breton. This recipe is adapted from *Les Clafoutis de Christophe* by Christophe Felder (Éditions Minerva, 2001). Many traditional clafoutis use unpitted cherries, to get the bitter almond flavor from the pits, but if you don't want to pay for your guests' dental work, I suggest you pit the cherries and add some amaretto instead!

¾ cup sugar

2 eggs

2 egg yolks

⅓ cup flour

1 cup plus 1 tablespoon 2 percent milk

1 cup plus 1 tablespoon light cream (18–20 percent fat)

1 tablespoon amaretto, rum, or kirsch

1 pound cherries, pitted

Preheat your oven to 400°F.

In a medium mixing bowl, whisk together sugar, eggs, and egg yolks until a light lemon yellow. Add flour; whisk to combine. Pour in milk, cream, and amaretto, whisking just to combine—this is like pancake batter; once you add the flour, you don't want to overwork it.

Butter and sugar a 10-inch ceramic tart mold (I sometimes skip this step and just line the dish with a big sheet of parchment paper). Put the cherries in the bottom of the mold. Give the batter a final stir and pour it in. Bake on the middle rack of the oven for 50 to 55 minutes, until well browned and fully set in the middle. Serve slightly warm or at room temperature (though I never say no to the leftovers straight from the fridge the next morning).

Serves 6–8

Tip: You can make clafouti with any kind of seasonal fruit that won't give off too much water; blackberries and apricots immediately come to mind.

CHAPTER 10

Tomatoland

We'd been warned. *Une maison dans le midi, des amis pour la vie.* A house in Provence, friends for life. Like clockwork, or should I say like a sundial, friends started calling on the first of February so they could reserve their train tickets for the long weekends in May.

We were suddenly the proprietors of the shabby-chicest, most disorganized bed-and-breakfast on the planet. I silently thanked my mother for the three extra sets of matching sheets I'd told her not to bring from New Jersey. I posted a calendar on the kitchen wall. There was a brief, guilty rush of relief when someone canceled at the last minute (forty-eight hours to hang my underwear on the line without anyone seeing!). We are booked solid from now until the first of October.

I genuinely love entertaining, but now I know why the locals savor the long, lonely winters. The population of the village has doubled with the warmer weather—and that's without the tourists. Les Marseillais have opened their summer homes for the season. With the Parisians in their convertibles parking every which where, it is easy to get curmudgeony (and easy to forget that a mere twelve months ago, we *were* those Parisians). We've got to get rid of our Paris license plates; we're still getting honked at.

Thanks to the thirty-five-hour workweek and all the built-in religious and civic holidays, summer weekends often begin on a Thursday morning and end on Tuesday. We've perfected the all-inclusive four-day tour of our tiny corner of Provence. It goes something like this: Put on the sheets. Buy haricots verts and sea bass for six, eight, or ten. Open the wine. Sleep in. Have a late breakfast of croissants and *pains au chocolat*. Explore the village. Drive down to Apt market to buy cheese and strawberries; hike up to Montjustin to admire the view of the Alps. Go to Carluc to admire the chapel; go to Pertuis to taste the wine. Check if there's a flea market, sit at the café, play in the garden, grill lamb chops. Strip the sheets. Wash the wineglasses. Repeat.

At least we don't have a swimming pool. Everyone told us it would be worse if we had a swimming pool.

Nicole came to hide chocolate bunnies in the garden with Alexandre for Easter. Paul and Catherine, old friends of Gwendal's from university, came down from Paris with their three boys (five people, two carry-on-size suitcases—French parents are nothing if not efficient packers). Fans of my first book from San Francisco came by for lunch and a cooking lesson—we produced a very successful apricot-almond tart. Bachir, a documentary filmmaker, and his wife, Nicola, a scientist, dear friends living in Canada, stopped by with the kids en route from Montreal to the family's summer place in Brittany. Jessica, a friend of mine from college days, and her husband had just sold all their worldly goods to go on a trip around the world. They were making a pit stop in Europe before heading off to South Korea. My auntie Lynn came from New York. She got stuck in the middle of a herd of sheep while crossing the street; I took a picture and had it framed for posterity. Even my parents are slowly acclimating themselves to the rhythm of village life; once they accepted there was nothing to do, they were quite happy to sit at the café with the *International Herald Tribune.* The reactions to our new life were fairly consistent: This makes no sense. You seem so happy.

✍

THANKFULLY, THE LOCAL ingredients multiply at almost the same rate as the guests.

Summer cooking in Provence does not leave a lot of room for free will. Exceptional ingredients come in tidal waves; no sooner have you finished gorging yourself on cherries in June than you find yourself drowning in melons in July.

My favorite of the recent culinary tsunamis are the zucchini flowers. These bright yellow blooms epitomize the beauty—some might say the urgency—of French seasonal cooking. Picked at dawn, still dripping with dew, by the following day they are practically useless, a wilted, shriveled shadow of their former selves. This is not pragmatic, plan-ahead cooking. This is impulse cooking, fly-by-the-seat-of-your-pants cooking, follow-your-heart cooking. Delicate, with a surprisingly intense flavor, zucchini flowers are often fried and served as beignets. I prefer to stuff them: goat cheese and fresh mint from our garden, wild rice, tomato and feta, *brousse de brebis* (our local sheep's milk ricotta), and green olive tapenade.

The only real problem with all this holidaymaking is that, strictly speaking, Gwendal and I are not on holiday. We are playing house or, rather, playing hotel. It's lovely—and completely unsustainable. He manages to sneak up to his office for a few hours after breakfast, reappears for lunch, disappears again, and magically turns up in the garden just in time to dole out the ice cubes and pour the pastis for the evening *apéritif.* There's an increasing contrast between what goes on up in his office and what goes on down here. I don't know if our guests can feel his frustration. But for the past year, Gwendal's been acting like a nine-to-five French civil servant, deftly steering the conversation away from his career and back to the view.

Gwendal used to love talking about his work. He's been passionate about film since he was a child. Breaking into the industry as an outsider was not just a question of professional development—he'd conquered the stonewallers and the snobs and adopted the American habit of projecting himself into a bright future. He loved shepherding the transition to digital cinema throughout Europe—the biggest shake-up in movies since the introduction of sound. But what five years ago had felt like a revolution was suddenly business as usual. It was time for him to move on.

As for my professional obligations, as I mentioned, I am a master procrastinator. Without an imminent deadline, writing is the easiest work in the world to ignore, especially in favor of my other favorite activity: hostessing. I've always loved the idea of an old-fashioned house party, the kind you see in the movies, with croquet on the lawn and cocktails under the wisteria at dusk. (We're lacking the butler, the maid, the gardener—and, come to think of it, the lawn. I'm happy to fill in for the cook.) It's wonderful to watch our friends relax, squint into the sunshine, shut off their phones, drip melon juice on their trousers, and peel off the chestnut leaves around the Banon to reveal a ripe, gooey goat cheese. This may not be real life—but it's a lovely hiatus.

I fetch my zucchini flowers out of the oven while Gwendal opens a chilled bottle of rosé. There is something about biting into a flower that surprises, then delights, our guests. If they didn't feel like they were on holiday before, they do now.

❧

When I was little, my grandmother kept an old cookie tin of beads in her closet for me to play with. I would spend hours studying the colors and textures, letting the different weights fall through my fingers. That's how I feel when I pick out my cherry tomatoes *chez* Marion.

I met Marion at the small Thursday market in Céreste. It's only a few vendors: Christophe, who sells olives and *saucisson,* and my precious, dedicated fishmonger who makes the one-hundred-and-fifty-kilometer trip from the coast each week. Marion sets up her trestle table next to the couple who make their own goat cheese.

Marion grew up here; she has a small organic farm in the fields below Céreste, in the dimple between the village and the Luberon hills. If you arrive early, her stand is heaped full of colorful beets and slim tapered carrots, Swiss chard, bouquets of purple basil, and chives. In addition to zucchini flowers, she sometimes has pumpkin flowers, slightly larger, slightly sweeter, and completely new to me.

Marion favors colorful sarongs and large mismatched Indian earrings. Her brown hair is often pulled off her face in two loose pigtails. Her appearance is well suited to her métier—she has the full cheeks, ample bust, and beneficent smile of an earth goddess. In fact, she smiles more than any French woman I've ever met.

The mystery of French women is an enduring one. I recently had this conversation—yet again—with an American woman living in France. "What *is* it with French women? Do you have any female friends here? Why don't they like us?"

I considered my answer, the cumulative experience of ten years on the fringes of French female life. "It's not that they don't like us. It's that they don't *need* us." A French woman's life is very full—she has her work, her kids, her family, her childhood friends, her university friends, maybe even a lover. By the time most of us American women arrived, in our late twenties or early thirties, the roster was simply full. Of course, there are the exceptions that prove the rule. But if you're looking for a gaggle of girlfriends to pour your heart out to, you've come to the wrong place.

I had a feeling Marion was different. It started with the dirty carrots. One Thursday morning, I picked up a stubby triple-pronged carrot that bore a striking resemblance to a sex toy.

Reading my mind, she broke into a huge grin. "I have a whole collection." She wrote down my e-mail address on the pad where she adds up her clients' bills. The next day I had three salacious vegetable photos in my inbox.

I knew I was onto something. I also knew I had to bide my time. Americans are used to instantaneous everything, including friendship. We get giddy, a little desperate. Making a friend in France is like training a lion; you have to approach slowly, over time. Pretend you are totally in control of the situation. There's a period of adjustment. You don't get to pet until they're good and ready.

When I arrive at the stand, sometimes Marion is on her own, but often she is chatting with another client, usually about cooking.

"*J'ai fait un gratin,*" said an older woman with chic bobbed hair as she picked out her zucchini. "*C'était super.*"

"Do you put cream in your gratin?" asked Marion.

"Just white wine and onions—and a bit of Gruyère on top at the end. *C'est plus léger.*"

She saw me listening as I filled a paper sack with slim baby eggplants.

"A few years ago," said Marion, "I started putting together a book of recipes from friends and clients. I can print you out a copy if you like." She made another note on her pad.

I began browsing the beets. Marion grows several varieties of beets, some purple-black, some yellow, some a lighter pink. One was striped inside, like a candy cane.

"Do you want them with the greens or without?" she asked, ready to twist off the bunch of long green leaves veined with fuchsia that sprouted from the head of the beet.

"I don't know," I answered honestly. "What do you do with them?"

"I sauté them, like spinach—they are a little sweet."

"Pourquoi pas?" I'll try anything once.

I served the beet greens with tuna steaks for lunch. Wilted with a little olive oil, garlic, and sea salt, they were delicious—slightly bitter at the top, sweeter near the root. The only problem: they cooked down to nothing, and Gwendal was scraping the bottom of the pot with enthusiasm. Next week I'd have to buy double the number of beets, just for the leaves. Maybe dig deep into the Ashkenazi archives and make borscht.

A few weeks later, I rolled up to the market with Alexandre.

"Tu dis bonjour, Alexandre?" I'm trying to get him into the all-important habits of French *politesse,* which in a village this size involves saying *bonjour* and *au revoir* to perfect strangers. We'll have to revise the rules on our visits to New York.

Marion weighed my cherry tomatoes and wrote the sum down on her pad. "Is he named after"—and then she spouted the long title of a book I'd never heard of. "It's one of my favorites. Do you know it?"

Dirty vegetable photos, recipes, and book recommendations. All the things I look for in a friend.

∞

I COULD SAY I've been cooking this summer—but *cooking* would be a distortion. Between the guests and the heat, it's more like arts and crafts, combining, stacking, slicing, and dicing a few essential summer ingredients: tomatoes, melon, *jambon cru,* peaches, plums, figs, tomatoes. And did I mention the tomatoes? I haven't turned on the stove in weeks.

The Provençal tomato is a thing of wonder—it can be as small as a marble, large as a human heart, red like a valentine, yellow like a sunflower, pale green like a brand-new leaf, orange like the sun in a child's drawing. My favorite is the *noire de Crimée,* a tomato that's purply-olive, like seaweed seen through moving water. I take my tomatoes home in a wooden *cagette*, stem-sides down. They are too delicate, too perfectly ripe to be jumbled together like gumballs.

There have been other religious moments in my discovery of French cuisine. I felt a rush of lightning in my veins when I gutted my first fish. The heavens opened and angels sang the first time I tasted homemade mayonnaise. But nothing quite equals the simplicity, the sublime transcendence, of the Provençal tomato.

It helps to understand that I grew up on tomatoes with the texture and taste of wet sawdust. It doesn't matter what you think about organic, locavore, slow food, and so on. To eat a tomato ripened in this relentless sunshine and picked from its stem that very morning is a conversion experience. I'll never again forget that a tomato is actually a fruit.

There's no messing with perfection. (Okay, a little messing, just for fun.) A few crystals of coarse sea salt, a drizzle of local olive oil, and a sprig or two of purple basil. Sliced and layered in a white ceramic dish, the tomatoes often match the hues of the local sunsets—reds and golds, yellows and pinks. If there were such a thing in our house as "too pretty to eat," this would be it. Thankfully, there's not.

If I'm not exactly cooking, I have done some impromptu matchmaking: baby tomatoes with smoked mozzarella, red onion, fennel, and balsamic vinegar. A giant yellow tomato with a local sheep's milk cheese and green basil. Last night I got a little fancy and layered slices of beefsteak tomato with pale green artichoke puree and slivers of Parmesan. I constructed the whole thing to look like the Leaning Tower of Pisa. I love to think of the utterly pretentious name this would be given in a trendy Parisian bistro:

Millefeuille de tomate provençale, tapenade d'artichaut et coppa de parmesan d'Italie (AOC) sur son lit de salade, sauce aigre douce aux abricots.

And of course, since this is a snooty Parisian bistro and half their clientele are Russian businessmen, the English translation would be printed just below:

Tomato napoleon of artichoke tapenade and aged Parmigiano-Reggiano cheese on a bed of mixed greens with sweet-and-sour apricot vinaigrette.

The *sauce abricot* was a happy accident. While making the dressing for the green salad, I mistook a bottle of peach/apricot syrup for the olive oil. Since I didn't realize my mistake until it was at the bottom of the bowl, I decided to try my luck. Mixed with Dijon mustard and some olive oil, it was very nice—much sweeter than a French vinaigrette, more like an American-style honey Dijon. I decided to add it to my pretentious Parisian bistro dish because, believe it or not, Parisian bistros love imitating American food. Anyone who has been in Paris in the past five years will note the rise of le Tchizzberger. (That's bistro for "cheeseburger.")

I'm moderate in my use of social media, but I can't stop taking pictures of the tomatoes. Close up. I've taken to snapping endless photos of the voluptuously rounded globes. I rejoice in the mingling of olive oil and purply-red flesh. Basil leaves rest like the strategically placed tassels of high-end strippers. Crystals of sea salt catch the afternoon sun like rhinestones under the glaring lights of the Folies Bergère. I may have invented a whole new type of food photography: tomato porn.

WE HAD A welcome cancellation for the fourteenth of July.

Each village has its own traditions to celebrate Bastille Day. There are community picnics and fireworks, go-go dancers and karaoke. Alexandre was most interested in the cotton-candy stand and merry-go-round installed in the parking lot near the tourist office. He got behind the wheel of a shiny blue Rolls-Royce. Like any bachelor out for a joyride, he was pleased as punch when two little girls climbed in back.

The main event was up the hill near Angela and Rod, after dark. I've never seen a community theater production of *La Cage aux Folles,* but it must look something like this. There were fishnet stockings, feathered headdresses, and not much else. The choreography was greatly appreciated by a row of elderly men in plastic chairs. There was a dance floor below the stage; kids chased a pair of soccer balls among couples dancing *le rock.* By midnight, Alexandre was a zombie, but there was no question of pulling him away from the music and the flashing lights. When I sat down next to him, he immediately got up and moved farther on, nearer to the smoke machine. *Not in front of the girls, Mom.*

When Gwendal went to the bar to get a Perrier, the butcher blocked his path. "You bring that to your wife and come back for a real drink." I didn't see him for the rest of the evening.

I approached the bar with Alexandre almost asleep on my shoulder at 1:00 a.m. Gwendal was still drinking with the butcher. "I heard the cancan dancer was you," I said. Apparently our butcher, in honor of Bastille Day, has been known to put on a majorette outfit and parade down the main street. "I was disappointed to have missed it."

"Next year," he said.

"We'll be here." A scantily clad butcher is part of the stock French fantasy, like the handsome young doctor or the buff plumber of American daydreams. Or maybe that's just me.

☙

THE NEXT EVENING there was a *fanfare* concert up the hill at the Café du Cours in Reillanne. These roaming brass bands sometimes came to our neighborhood in Paris. People would open their windows and throw coins down into the street, sometimes inside an old sock. It always made my day.

If I owned the Café du Cours, I would be unable to resist the urge to fix it up—light the dark corners, strip the tin ceiling, put the brick pizza oven back to work; in other words, totally ruin it. As it is, the cement tiles with their colorful Liberty pattern are never quite swept clean; the barman empties the espresso grounds into a grimy wooden drawer underneath the machine. The hot chocolate comes with cocoa powder on the bottom and warm milk above—if you want something drinkable, you have to stir it yourself. There are open-mike poetry nights and exhibitions of local photographers. The place is perfect just the way it is.

In contrast to the citizens of Céreste, the residents of Reillanne look laid back, like their shoes have walked from here to St. Jacques de Compostelle and their shirts, in soft and flowing fabrics, have been washed by being beaten against a rock. Reillanne has a reputation as a village of *soixante-huitards* and *néo-ruraux*—old hippies and young neo-rural transplants, both types looking for a life outside the traditional French circuit of *Métro, boulot, dodo* (subway, work, bed). The moms in Reillanne carry their babies in colorful hand-tied slings.

We take a table on the terrace, overlooking the main square. The awning of the Café du Cours is a sheet of corrugated metal. The name is painted in large block letters on the wall. The *f* in *café* has been chipped away, along with a portion of the plaster. There's a single strand of oversize Christmas bulbs above the door.

When the *serveuse* arrives with our drinks, she smiles at Alexandre. *"C'est pour monsieur,"* she says, shaking up his apricot juice before pouring it into the glass. *"C'est des habitués du comptoir."* Alexandre's a regular, you see. Every week, while I'm buying our roast chicken at the Sunday-morning market, he's at the bar with his dad, elbows on the counter.

There's a hum of conversation. I watch the girls in their headbands, striped dresses, and toe rings. A car stops in the middle of the crosswalk, blocking my view; a man gets up from his table and leans into its window, catching up on the news. These are the times and places that make me feel most like writing. At the next table, a little girl does pirouettes with her mom, bumping into several metal chairs.

The band wanders out of the café to begin their first set. There's a French horn, a clarinet, a tuba, and a man with a drum and a cymbal strapped to his chest. The drummer stubs out his hand-rolled cigarette. He is wearing orange chinos and a white version of the pageboy cap Gwendal wore when I first met him.

What are they playing? Is it "Sunrise, Sunset"? Broadway seems a long way from here; not just another time zone, but another galaxy. I watch the shadows of the leaves playing against the facade of the church. A pizza truck is parked in the center of the square; it's too early for dinner; everyone is still outside, enjoying the lingering light.

Time slows down. I'm constantly amazed at the simplicity of our life here. Pleasure completely without irony, detached from the calculations and one-upmanship of my former life. Nights out in New York—an art opening, a bar, a club—were filled with anticipation. Who would we meet? Is this a step in the right direction? Are we the center of attention? My twenties were about being looked at. My thirties are about looking.

Alexandre went inside with his father to the Turkish toilet, leaving me with the serious task of guarding his apricot juice. I still avoid *les toilettes à la turque*—no more than two porcelain footprints and a drain. My thigh muscles are not up to sustained squatting of this kind.

The sound of the tuba resonated, floating over the terrace, beyond the facade of the church, through the square, up into the narrow streets to the tip of the clock tower before dissolving, like smoke, into the night sky.

⁕

MY FIRST EXPERIENCES with French Cuisine (with a capital *C, merci* very much) took place at Babette, a now-defunct restaurant in a brownstone in Manhattan's theater district. The silverware was heavy, the ladies old, and the calf brains sautéed in clarified butter. Even today, a certain formality still hovers over French dining. It's hard to shake the image of starched chefs, maniacal shallot-chopping technique, and maybe a baroque birdcage of spun sugar to enclose your single scoop of grapefruit-champagne sorbet. *Oui*, the French know how to lay out a five-course dinner like no one else, but in Provence, I've discovered a less formal repertoire: the dishes people bring to picnics and serve with evening *apéritifs*, savoring the last of the long summer sun.

It's the end of August and the tourist hordes have begun to thin. Tonight Gwendal and I have organized a neighborhood picnic and outdoor film screening on the terraced stone steps of the lane just behind our house. In the summertime, it's easy to issue invitations; we meet everyone in the street at least twice a day.

The kids are up late; it's the last hurrah before school begins next week. All the guests have brought their mismatched garden chairs, and after setting up the screen at the bottom, we managed to arrange a very respectable, if narrow, amphitheater. Young and old, village natives and city transplants, mingled, drank wine, and ate quinoa tabbouleh salad.

Jean's contribution to the picnic was a savory cousin of the crumbly butter cookies that the French call *sablés*. Pebbled with chopped black olives, rosemary, and freshly grated Parmesan cheese, they are what my British friends would call "moreish"—a succinct way of saying you could eat the whole batch in one sitting. The French, of course, would never do such a thing. Someone had brought a branch of dried dates. Paired with a date and a glass of white wine, the *sablés* were the perfect start to our casual dinner *en plein air*.

It's hard to find a movie that everyone from the age of two and a half to ninety will enjoy. We settled on Jacques Tati's *Les Vacances de Monsieur Hulot*. Tati is a bit like a French Charlie Chaplin; he can make serving a tennis ball or buying an ice cream cone into a comic ballet. Some of our older neighbors had seen the movie when it came out in 1953.

We'd recently gotten friendly with a couple who'd moved into a house up the road. As soon as we got to talking, we realized the husband used to work just a few blocks from our old apartment in Paris. He is from Senegal, and he promised to teach me how to make a proper *maffé*—the traditional West African groundnut stew. We reminisced about the hole-in-the-wall boutique on Faubourg du Temple, owned by a grumpy Chinese guy, that sold all the hard-to-find African ingredients—fiery hot peppers, okra, and broken rice. Our kids get on beautifully. Alexandre is crazy about their little girl, who alternates between playing with him and coyly ignoring him. It starts so early.

I spent the evening doing what I can't help doing, hostessing. I brought drinks to two older women firmly ensconced in their canvas chairs. "So adorable," said Madame X with a smile, patting one of our new friends' kids on the head. "Remind me. Do little black children have the same color blood as the rest of us?" It was said with no animosity, just the blithe, terrifying ignorance of someone who went to elementary school before the Civil War.

I would be morally naive to think that no one holds these opinions, and politically naive to think that no one says this kind of thing out loud anymore. But I wish I hadn't heard her. It left a hairline crack in the lens, a flicker of shadow on an otherwise perfect evening.

We had to wait till sunset to start the film; the kids had run themselves ragged, and they leaned against our knees or slept curled up on our laps. It was cool; we took turns running the fifty feet to our respective houses to get sweaters and stuffed animals and blankets. We laughed all together when Tati served his tennis ball.

Recipes to Welcome Friends

ZUCCHINI BLOSSOMS STUFFED WITH GOAT CHEESE, MINT, AND ANISE SEEDS

Fleurs de Courgettes Farcies au Chèvre, à la Menthe, et Graines de Anis

This is a wonderful—and easy—welcome for summer guests. Buy your zucchini flowers at the farmers' market in the morning, and store them in the fridge like a bouquet—with the stems in a glass of cold water—until you are ready to use them.

1 egg
6 ounces goat cheese, cut into small cubes
1 teaspoon whole anise seeds
1½ tablespoons chopped fresh mint
Pinch of coarse sea salt
Black pepper
12 large zucchini blossoms
1 tablespoon olive oil

Preheat the oven to 350°F.

In a small bowl, lightly beat the egg. Add the cheese, anise seeds, mint, salt, and pepper and mash/mix with a fork to combine. Carefully hold open each flower (no need to remove the stamen) and stuff with a heaping teaspoon of filling. (Depending on the size of your zucchini blossoms, you may have a bit of stuffing left over.) Twist the ends of the flowers to close. Place the olive oil in a 9-by-13-inch casserole dish and shake it around so it coats the entire bottom of the dish. Gently roll each zucchini flower in the oil and retwist the ends to close.

Bake for 20 minutes, until fragrant and golden. Serve immediately. I usually serve these before dinner with drinks. They are not quite finger food; you'll need a small plate and a fork to eat them.

Serves 4 as an hors d'oeuvre or light appetizer

TOMATO NAPOLEON WITH ARTICHOKE PUREE

Millefeuille de Tomate à la Tapenade d'Artichaut

For the artichoke puree

8 ounces artichoke hearts packed in olive oil, drained (save the olive oil)
1 tablespoon (packed) basil
¼ of a small clove garlic
About ¼ cup extra-virgin olive oil (use as much as you can from the jar of artichokes)
Freshly ground black pepper
4 beefsteak tomatoes
Parmesan or aged sheep's milk cheese, sliced paper thin

For the apricot vinaigrette

1 tablespoon olive oil
½ teaspoon sherry or red wine vinegar
1 level teaspoon apricot jam
Pinch of coarse sea salt
Small grind of black pepper

Drain the artichokes, reserving the oil. Blend artichokes, basil, and garlic in a food processor. Measure out the olive oil, using as much as you can from the artichoke jar; make up the difference with plain extra-virgin olive oil. Pour in the olive oil with the food processor running, blend until smooth. Add black pepper. Blend again.

Think of this as making a tomato layer cake. Slice the tomatoes from top to bottom about 1 inch thick; put a tablespoon of tapenade and a few ultra-thin slices of Parmesan between each slice of tomato, and pile them on top of one another. Put the little tomato cap back on. Whisk together the ingredients for the apricot vinaigrette and drizzle around the edge of the plate à la snooty Parisian bistro.

Serves 4

Tip: The artichoke puree is great on its own with crudités or pita chips.

JEAN'S ROSEMARY, OLIVE, AND PARMESAN SABLÉS
Sablés aux Olives, Romarin, et Parmesan

I have a real affection for the sandy-textured cookies called *biscuits sablés*. Here is the savory version that Jean brought to our neighborhood cinema evening. They are extremely easy to make, provided your butter really is at room temperature when you start. Serve them with a glass of white wine and some plump dates; I can't think of a better beginning to an evening *en plein air*.

10½ tablespoons unsalted butter
1¼ cups flour
2 scant teaspoons fresh rosemary, finely chopped
1 cup finely grated Parmesan cheese
Black pepper
12 cured black olives, pitted and finely chopped

An hour or two before you want to bake, take the butter out of the fridge. It needs to be really soft.

Preheat the oven to 350°F. Line a large cookie sheet with parchment paper.

In a medium mixing bowl, combine flour, rosemary, Parmesan, and a grinding of black pepper. Add the olives and the softened butter cut into three or four chunks. Knead the butter into the flour mixture with your hands until the ingredients are evenly distributed and a ball of dough has formed. Do not overwork the dough.

Put the dough in the fridge for 10 minutes. Roll out the dough on a piece of parchment paper to a thickness of about ¼ inch. Using a 2½-inch biscuit cutter (the top of a glass will do just fine), cut 16 rounds. Bake on a sheet of parchment paper until fragrant and highly colored, 15 to 17 minutes. Cool on a wire rack. Store in an airtight container; they keep nicely for 2 to 3 days.

Makes 16 cookies

CHAPTER 11

The Quiet Diet

I checked the fridge twice. I want everything to be beautiful. Tomatoes, a whole shelf of fresh peaches, peach compote, ginger root, lemons, red onions, and a ripening melon.

My dear friend Courtney is arriving today. We've known each other since college; she is a fellow writer and journalist, my mentor, really. She's worn a burka in Afghanistan, covered the haute couture shows in Paris, and been embedded with the Singapore army after the tsunami. After several years in London, she's just moved to New York to take up her rightful place in the elevator of the Condé Nast building. She's done all of this while managing binge eating and bulimia that have sent her weight zigzagging wildly over the past twenty years. She's in a good place with food right now, so for this trip, we made a little pact. She wants to learn more about cooking. I want to learn more about dieting. Since I had the baby, since I wrote a cookbook, there's a stubborn ten pounds that refuses to go on its merry way.

Last time I went back to the States, I had lunch with another friend from college who was five months pregnant. "God, you look great," I said, patting the baby bump. "It's so much better not to gain it in the first place, because, wow, I'm finding it really hard to lose." She looked at me with the disdain of a hardened war veteran lecturing a weekend reservist. "Of course it's hard," she snapped. "You have no skills." Yikes. Apparently dieting, like scuba diving or a plumbing license, requires some kind of special training. I spent thirty-five years feeling pretty comfortable with my body. I was never model-thin or Madonna-toned, but being embarrassed to prance around in my underwear is a new feeling for me. I know I'm a little late to the party—but here I am.

No matter how long it's been since Courtney and I have seen each other, it always feels like we're picking up in the middle of a conversation. She is curious about the contents of my cabinets. "I swear, I never do this at anyone else's house." I think she feels safe here, which I'm really glad about. I'm her private chef for the next two weeks, so she knows she'll be eating fresh, whole foods. We just found a Provençal kitchen armoire at a flea market. It's open on the top with wire netting over the cabinets, so you can see my glass jars of lentils, quinoa, *riz rond* for rice pudding, several bars of dark chocolate, a big jar of raisins. I have a passion for dried fruit, particularly dried apricots, cherries, and—since I've been in France—figs.

"A hundred calories! Are you kidding me?" I was holding one of my favorite dried figs from the market. Courtney is full of these fun facts—stuff that I've blithely ignored all these years. "That means two figs is basically the same number of calories as a box of Dots."

"The fiber will probably keep you full longer, but yeah."

Huh.

❧

"THESE ARE BEAUTIFUL," said Courtney as she helped me set the table in the garden. The right plate is the oldest diet trick in the book. I recently bought a whole service of Limoges dishes at a local flea market. They are white with small blue flowers, the gold rim faded by years of use. Like the French baby clothes, these old French plates are a good inch smaller in circumference than the modern set I bought at Ikea.

Today for lunch I'm making monkfish with a quick pan sauce of tomatoes, white wine, and fresh peas. Monkfish is meaty, as fish goes; if it's not overcooked, its texture resembles lobster.

"Why do you put peas into the sauce?"

"It just looks nice—and it's a nice contrast of textures." I throw in the peas at the last minute so they don't lose their crunch and their bright green color. I get the feeling that thinking about the aesthetics of food is something new to Courtney. She knows everything there is to know about the chemistry—the building blocks of food—calories, fat, carbs, protein. But a holistic approach, putting together a pretty plate, is not something she's focused on before.

This morning she picked up the box of Alexandre's chocolate LU *petit déjeuner* cookies.

"They're not very good," I said, in case she was thinking of wasting one of her allotted snacks on them. "But he used to like them."

"No wonder—they're almost two-thirds sugar," Courtney said, studying the nutrition panel.

"How can you tell?"

"There are a little more than eight grams of sugar, which is four calories a gram. So thirty-two calories' worth of sugar, and there are fifty-eight calories in a biscuit. The rest of the calories are fat, pretty much—there are two grams, so that's eighteen calories. What's not to like about sugar and fat?"

Courtney is a lot more laid back than she used to be about the timing of meals, but waiting to eat past a certain hour will bring out the gremlin in anyone. I still have a hard time convincing friends that fish is fast food in our house, but with precooked organic quinoa out of the bag (even the French don't make everything from scratch) and steamed broccoli, this is no more than a fifteen-minute operation.

Above all, I want the food to be relaxing for her. Eating outside in the garden is a good start. I know that serving—judging a reasonable portion—is a problem area for Courtney. The French have an excellent solution to this: they never buy more than one piece of protein per person. Meat and fish are expensive.

⁂

I GET A lot of work done when Courtney is around. We sit at the kitchen table, our computers back to back, trading sentences like baseball cards. We talk about future projects. She just started a novel. I think her life is a novel, if she would just sit down and write it.

And then there's nap time. I have to admit, I still feel pretty sluggish. This winter's fatigue has not subsided. I work around it. Gwendal makes no comment when I go to sleep in the middle of the afternoon, knowing that mine is not likely to be a twenty-minute power nap, like his, but a full-scale two-hour siesta, after which I often wake up—head aching, mouth dry—feeling worse.

Just like Courtney is trying not to binge in front of me, I'm trying not to sleep in front of her. She's succeeding. I'm failing. There's always an excuse: period, migraine, we stayed out late at a concert, maybe I caught a cold. The fact is I'm just bone tired. I spent my birthday weekend hiding the rash from a case of shingles. Correct me if I'm wrong, but I thought people my age aren't supposed to *get* shingles.

My new doctor in Reillanne thinks it might be my thyroid. The numbers on my blood tests are not off the charts, just on the low end of normal, which, come to think of it, is exactly how I've been feeling for the past two years. When I look at the list of symptoms for hypothyroidism—fatigue, weight gain, depression, loss of concentration—I'm shocked by how spot-on it is, and also how similar it is to the clinical depression I've always feared. The doctor started me on an infinitesimal dose of thyroid hormone. The first day I took it, I felt a buzzing through my whole body—a double espresso that lasted all day. He might be onto something.

We all have habits we'd like to change, but staying up late talking about them in the dorm room and doing it on the other side of thirty-five are two different things. We are no longer "going through a phase"; there are now firmly ensconced bad habits, official patterns, not to mention a toddler, to work around.

Having Courtney here this week inspires me. It also comforts me. We all hide things. We want to show only our best selves to the world.

Upstairs, looking through the dresses in my closet one afternoon, I feel like I need to show Courtney the baby fat. She is one of my very few go-to girls; we stay up all night talking because we look to each other for solutions. She asks me why I put raw tomato on top of the ravioli; I marvel at her ability to meet us at the market by *running* to Reillanne—ten kilometers, uphill all the way. I remember hearing about a sorority in college whose members made their pledges strip down to their underwear and then circled all their cellulite with a permanent marker. This is the friendly version of that twisted ritual—full disclosure.

"It would probably come off if you exercised," said Courtney, examining a necklace on my dresser. "Of course, that would be breaking your rule: 'I reserve sweating for sex.'" She's been quoting that line back to me for fifteen years. She knows me way too well.

The problem is, I'm surrounded by women who look the same way they did when they were twenty, and *they're* not going to the gym. They may go bike riding on a Saturday afternoon or on a walking vacation in the mountains with the kids. They are taking tango lessons and going on yoga retreats, not running marathons.

Here's an example. The other day I spotted my friend Virginie at the market. I hadn't seen her for two weeks, so I came up from behind and gave her a little squeeze. Except it wasn't her.

It was her mother. From the back, they look exactly the same. Same skinny jeans, same ballerina flats, same oversize Indian scarf, denim jacket, and sunglasses perched above a low ponytail. I apologized profusely and everyone had a good laugh. But I was mortified. France is not a country where you just wander down the street squeezing women you've never met.

I saw Virginie a few days later at the café. I apologized again. "Your mom just looks incredible."

"Oh," said Virginie casually, "but she was quite young when she had me." I did some quick math. That still put her over sixty. When I'm sixty, I fully expect to have a turkey wattle.

Growing up, I was told that women gain an average of two pounds a year every year after they graduate from high school, which is about where I am right now. That may be true in the States, but it's simply impossible that the French women around me are forty pounds heavier than they were in high school. If that were the case, there would be entire *lycées* full of girls with the protruding ribs of famine victims. There's just no way.

Without lingering on the topic, I brought it up with French friends who were here over the summer. Unlike most French women, our friend Catherine is a low-maintenance gal. Her dark curly hair is usually pulled back in a ponytail; she favors painter's pants and Birkenstocks and T-shirts that don't necessarily show off her figure. But she has a figure.

Catherine spent the weekend toting around her six-month-old son, her third little boy. "There's no reason to gain weight after you have a child." Catherine is a scientist, and she expresses herself with empirical certainty. "Maybe you go up one size after your third. Size forty by age forty." I did a quick conversion in my head: that's an American size 8 at age forty. The national message is clear: there is no earthly reason why I shouldn't look exactly like I did before I had this baby, or better.

"What do you guys eat for dinner on the weeknights?" I asked as Catherine and I snapped the ends of haricots verts in front of the sink. *"Les enfants mangent à la cantine,"* replied Catherine. Her kids eat a four-course lunch in the school cafeteria, and she and Paul both go out to lunch with their colleagues, so dinner at home is consistently the lighter meal. "Often I make soup at night, with bread and cheese. Yogurt for dessert. Or pasta. Sometimes I make crepes." Naturally. Catherine is from Brittany; she has the pro equipment at home.

When I add up these tidbits of conversation, it's clear that in France, the American equation of a quick salad for lunch and then steak and a baked potato for dinner is entirely reversed. What emerges is a smaller, simpler meal, even a kind of de facto evening vegetarianism. Soup is a recurring theme. I've never met a French person who does not extol the virtues of soup.

SPEAKING OF SOUP. We've been invited to La Roulotte this evening for a *soupe au pistou* party.

Alain and Evelyne, who helped us with the tiles, have a brightly painted circus wagon (a *roulotte*) that they park outside of Céreste in a quiet corner of one of Marion's fields. Since they don't have a proper garden attached to their house, they go out there on summer afternoons to read and relax, and sometimes they have evening *fêtes*—simple picnics, or concerts with musician friends.

Soupe au pistou is the quintessential Provençal dish—economical, full of seasonal ingredients, easy to stretch for a crowd. At its basic level, it's a vegetable bouillon packed with white and cranberry beans, cubes of zucchini and potatoes, chopped green beans, yellow beans, and elbow macaroni. Like Italian minestrone, there is a different—and definitive—recipe for *soupe au pistou* in every family. Some people add chopped tomato or a piece of slab bacon to the broth; some add sliced broad beans in addition to the haricots verts. *Soupe au pistou* is served warm, rather than hot, which works out great. There is no electricity at La Roulotte.

I'd been asked to bring a dessert, so Courtney and I decided to make oatmeal raisin cookies.

"How many calories are in an oatmeal raisin cookie anyway?"

Courtney stood up, holding her hand out like a stop sign, shaking her head to toss the thought away. "I just. Can't. I'm having one of those moments. I just can't stop thinking about all the things I want to eat, all at once. I can't talk about calories." We'd been holed up in the kitchen for the last hour, mixing butter and brown sugar and raisins. What was I thinking? The smell alone—it's like asking an alcoholic to spend all day working in a bar.

✑

WE ARRIVED JUST after dusk. You can drive only three-quarters of the way to La Roulotte. We parked behind the other cars on the side of the dirt track and then followed a deeply rutted path through the juniper bushes. Wooden picnic tables were arranged in the field. They were set with colorful striped bowls and lanterns to light after dark. Alain and Evelyne arrived just after we did, lugging an industrial-size soup pot between them.

We drank wine from plastic cups and ate sliced *saucisson* for the *apéritif*. When the soup was served, the cranberry beans bobbed to the surface. I love their dense texture, their pink and white spots. We passed around bowls of grated cheese to stir into the soup. It makes the broth just a bit saltier, a bit thicker—a little *richesse* in a peasant dish. It would never occur to me to call this diet food, but packed with vegetables, beans for protein, and just a soupçon of fat from the cheese to give it body, this isn't food that Courtney would object to.

Alain and Evelyne live next door to a musicologist and internationally known bagpipe player. In a village of thirteen hundred, what are the chances? We sprawled out on the grass as he began his plaintive melodies. The stars feel closer out here.

∽

JUST BACK FROM a run, Courtney put her iPod on the kitchen table and sat down with a glass of water. "I guess you can't walk around with your headphones here." True enough. I now know half of the village by sight, a quarter by name. There's no question of rushing past in a hurry. Every person on the street merits a nod and a *bonjour;* every neighbor a quick chat. I need to ask about Laura's broken ankle, Helen's roses, Thierry's roof repairs. These are small conversations, but over time, they build up into genuine *liens* — links that hold the village together, like the almost invisible layer of cement between the stones of the château. I've grown attached to this aspect of village life. For someone like me, a young mother and a writer with no formal office to go to, these encounters are a welcome part of my day. I'm positive I speak to more people on a daily basis here than I did in Paris.

This level of social interaction also has a real effect on my eating habits. Courtney once talked to me about the secrecy of binges. "I would go to three different stores," she said. "Because I was too embarrassed to buy everything in one place." What strikes me is the anonymity of the process, the solitude of it.

I tried to imagine myself staging a similar raid in Céreste. First of all, there aren't three different stores. Even if I wanted to buy ten croissants at five o'clock in the afternoon every day for six weeks, what would I tell the baker's wife? I bought a donkey? I'm harboring refugees? What would *she* tell everyone else? Even if I could think that fast on my feet, the system of lies would quickly become so elaborate that I'd be unable to keep up.

In France in general, and in Provence in particular, there is *nothing* anonymous about my food. Every week, the chicken man makes it a point to greet me by my first name. The cheese monger wants to know when I'm going to get started on my driver's license. The fishmonger knows better than immigration how much time I spend in the United States; if he doesn't see me for two weeks, he gets worried. I've traded dirty carrot photos with the woman who grows my tomatoes. This intimacy makes you accountable. Food involves so much human connection here, there's almost no way to sneak it. I don't shop alone; I don't eat alone. Every gesture involving food is woven so tightly into the social fabric that it is very hard to rip—to tear off on a bender.

I SET A bowl of sausages and lentils in front of Courtney. This is her favorite French meal, and I make it at least once every time she comes. What surprises me, now that I'm privy to the logic of how Courtney eats, is how closely her carefully controlled diet resembles traditional French eating habits, particularly those of my mother-in-law.

Like Nicole, Courtney doesn't eat between meals. When she's done, she's done. She eats a full plate of food (and, at our house, cheese), but she skips the hors d'oeuvres and doesn't pick. For her, picking spells disaster, the start of a binge. For me, it's a family tradition.

Because my mother is diabetic, she is denied a lot of what she considers "real food." She is always hunting around for something good to eat. That's the refrain I heard my entire childhood. I would watch when she came home after work, shifting around the containers and the plastic bags: "I'm looking for something good to eat."

She ate sugar-free biscotti, sometimes an entire extra meal of leftover pork roast or Muenster cheese at four or five o'clock. If she wanted something sweet, she would settle for a diet chocolate-cream soda with ice cubes and milk—her version of a milk shake. When I go home, I always find Weight Watchers raspberry-swirl pops in the freezer. They're not bad; they're not good either.

This is perhaps the biggest difference between my eating habits in the States and in France. When I am in France, I don't eat fake food.

I grew up in the United States in the 1970s and '80s, so I spent a lot of time around fake food. I remember Kraft macaroni and cheese, Devil Dogs, and Oodles of Noodles with great affection. The sex, drugs, and rock 'n' roll of my adolescence was studying for my finals doped up on Pillsbury vanilla frosting mainlined with a plastic spoon.

I suspect one reason why fake food plays no part in my life in France is that I don't own a microwave. I buy very little prepared food, and because I cook mostly one meal at a time, there are not a lot of leftovers to reheat.

When I serve cheese after dinner, I see Courtney avoiding the bread, neatly cutting cubes of cheese and eating them delicately with her fingers. My mother-in-law does the same thing. When I first arrived in France, Nicole showed me a diet book from the late 1980s that she used. It's called—a riff on Descartes—*Je mange, donc je maigris (I Eat, Therefore I Lose Weight)*. You must avoid bread with cheese, not because bread is bad, says the author, but because, *traditionnellement*, that's not the proper way to eat cheese. Looking back to move ahead—it's classic French. That's the way I feel about fake food versus real food. Sometimes progress isn't really progress. Sometimes you have to look back to move ahead.

☙

"I'm *SO* HUNGRY."

"Me too."

On this, Courtney and I are in perfect agreement.

We like to be hungry.

Maybe it's our collective immigrant past, maybe it's the undying ethos of bigger and better, land of plenty, but Americans can't stand the idea of being hungry. It's the fear that leads us to keep power bars in our purses, juice boxes and bags of Cheerios in kids' strollers, jumbo cup holders in cars. God forbid anyone, anytime, anywhere, should actually experience hunger.

Courtney has a fraught relationship with hunger. "It used to scare me, because I was always on a diet and I just felt like I'd never be full. But now, for me, being hungry—not starving, but hungry—is a good thing. It lets me know my body is functioning normally, that I've eaten the right amount and now it's time to eat again."

"I think it makes the food taste better."

Because the French don't snack, one is likely to arrive at meal-time genuinely famished. There might be an *apéritif* before dinner but no opportunity to stuff yourself; your hostess will probably put out a small cereal bowl of potato chips for eight people. You are forced to pace yourself.

For me, being genuinely hungry can make the simplest meal taste like something special. This works particularly well for foods I'm convinced I don't like—chunky *pâté de campagne* or the classic French rice salad with tuna and chopped tomatoes.

When you're hungry, textures take on a particular pleasure. Cold rice moistened with the juice from the tomatoes and a bit of olive oil feels summery yet substantial. The crackle of a fresh baguette is suddenly the perfect partner for toothsome bits of ground pork; even the slippery bits of fat find their place. It tastes even better if you've spent the morning walking uphill.

Tonight we are making pasta.

That's one thing that's great about Courtney's approach. She's been through enough crazy diet fads to know that there's nothing she should outlaw—it's all about moderation.

I do things slightly differently when Courtney is around. I measure the pasta servings. I find that if I do that, I concentrate on the mouthfeel, on chewing each piece and putting enough good stuff on top to make it a real meal.

Thankfully, the end of August is an avalanche of tomatoes, zucchini, eggplants, and peppers. There's simply too many of them. There's only so many times a week a girl can make ratatouille, so in the afterglow of fresh tomato everything comes (what's a girl to do) *roasted* tomato everything.

There's something a little greedy about roasted tomatoes. Slick with olive oil and mellowed with garlic, pulpy like a supermarket romance novel, they are my attempt at pleasure hoarding. I want to be able to peek into the freezer in December and know I can use this spark of sunshine to light up a winter pasta sauce or guarantee a sensational base for braised veal shank or white beans. Of course, the nature of greed means that I couldn't wait until December to explore my pasta fantasies.

For tonight's dinner, I used a tablespoon or two of the roasted tomato oil to sauté some eggplant until tender, then added some raw shrimp, the roasted tomatoes, a splash of white wine, and a pinch of cayenne pepper at the end. I divided the pasta among my favorite shallow bowls. They have relatively small interiors with large white rims. Just like paintings on the wall of a gallery, food looks better if there's lots of white space around it.

I prepared everyone's plate individually in the kitchen, like a chef in a restaurant, piling the vegetables and shrimp artfully on the pasta. (I would count this as another diet trick: everyone gets his or her full portion up front; no one expects seconds in a restaurant.) I garnished each plate with ripped fresh basil. I was pretty pleased with the result. It looked like something you might order at a luxury resort. The blue-plate special at Canyon Ranch.

THE FACT IS, there is no way to be on a real hard-core diet in France. It's simply impolite. You need a diet that allows you to eat with enthusiasm at five-course luncheons. Unless you are in danger of going into anaphylactic shock at the table, it's unheard of to call the hostess to ask what she is serving or, heaven forbid, mention what you will or won't deign to eat. A French diet is a balancing act. If you eat a little extra dessert at dinner, you have a bowl of soup or a plate of steamed vegetables the next day for lunch.

I call it the quiet diet. It's nobody's business but mine.

By the time Courtney packed her bags, I had a rough idea of what I needed to do to lose the extra weight. That's the fact of most diets. We know what we are supposed to do; we just don't do it. It's my leftover American habits that get me into trouble: making too much food, eating when I'm not hungry, nibbling at night. I know when I'm doing something counterproductive, but I didn't grow up with a French superego to rap me on the knuckles every time I broke the rules. My id grew up in a place where a pint of Ben and Jerry's was a single serving.

Still, my friend in the States is wrong: I do have some skills. What most Americans call dieting—no snacking, smaller portions, single servings, lots of fresh seasonal vegetables, yogurt or fruit for dessert, nothing but 70 percent cacao dark chocolate in the house—the French call *eating*. There are times when the structure, the rigidity, the tradition-bound aspects of French life are a drag. But where healthy eating is concerned, it's actually very helpful.

I'll just have to keep doing what I'm doing. Cut down on the dried figs. Cross my fingers about the thyroid pills. I'll take the exercise question under consideration.

Recipes for a Quiet Diet

MONKFISH FILLETS WITH TOMATOES AND FRESH PEAS

Filets de Lotte aux Tomates et aux Petits Pois

This is quick to make and lovely to look at.

2 tablespoons olive oil

1 small red onion, diced

3 medium vine-ripened tomatoes, chopped

½ teaspoon sugar

2 large pinches of dried Spanish ñora pepper or good paprika

⅓ cup white or rosé wine

Sea salt and black pepper to taste

4 monkfish fillets, 6–7 ounces each

1 teaspoon fresh lemon thyme or lemon basil (regular fresh thyme with a bit of lemon zest would do)

1 cup fresh peas

Heat the olive oil in a good-size frying pan. Sauté the onion until translucent, 4 to 5 minutes. Add the chopped tomatoes, sugar, and ñora pepper; simmer 5 minutes. Add wine; simmer 3 minutes more. Taste the sauce, add a pinch of salt and a grind of pepper, stir to combine. Add fish fillets and thyme. Cover and simmer on medium-low for 8 to 10 minutes, turning the fillets once midway through. Cooking time will depend on the size of your fillets; start checking early. Be gentle. Monkfish, when properly cooked, has a nice firm texture like lobster. You don't want to boil it to mush.

When the monkfish look nearly done (opaque to the center), turn off the heat and stir in the peas. Cover and let rest for 5 minutes.

The peas don't really need to be cooked, just heated through so they retain their color and crunch. Serve with quinoa or crusty bread to soak up the sauce.

Serves 4

Tip: You can also make this recipe with thick cod fillets.

SOUPE AU PISTOU

This is a great informal meal for a crowd. It's meant to be served warm rather than hot, so there are fewer worries about timing. Start with some *saucisse sèche* for your guests to nibble on. Then serve the soup and pass the *pistou* (make sure your significant other eats some of the pungent garlic basil paste as well). Add some sourdough bread and a well-chosen cheese plate to complete your meal.

For the soup

3 quarts of water
2 teaspoons coarse sea salt or 1 teaspoon fine sea salt
1 pound tomatoes (2–3 medium)
1½ pounds unshelled fresh cranberry beans (12 ounces shelled), about 2 cups
1½ pounds unshelled fresh white beans (12 ounces shelled), about 2 cups
½ pound of broad beans, cut into 1-inch pieces
14 ounces green beans, cut into 1-inch pieces
1½ pounds zucchini (3 medium), cut into bite-size cubes
¾ pound (3 small) potatoes, cut into bite-size cubes
1 cup of small elbow macaroni (optional)

For the pistou

7 large garlic cloves
1 cup (packed) basil leaves
¼ teaspoon coarse sea salt
¼ cup olive oil
To serve: Grated Parmesan or Red Mimolette cheese

In a large stockpot, bring 3 quarts of water to a boil with the salt. Add the whole tomatoes and blanch for 3 minutes. (This makes it easier to remove the skin.) Remove the tomatoes and rinse under cold water until cool enough to handle. Peel, seed, and chop the tomatoes. Add the tomatoes and other vegetables to the pot, simmer for 1 hour or a bit longer, until the beans are perfectly tender. If using, add the macaroni about 20 minutes before the end.

While the soup is cooking, get out your food processor. Whiz together the garlic, basil leaves, and salt until finely chopped. Scrape down the sides, and then, with the motor running, slowly pour in ¼ cup olive oil and mix until well blended (it will look like store-bought pesto).

Ladle a good portion of vegetables and broth into each person's bowl, then pass the *pistou*—I usually add a teaspoon (it's strong) and stir it in. Pass the grated cheese and enjoy. Serve with a light red wine.

This recipe can easily be doubled, and the leftovers freeze well. If I think I'm going to get two meals out of this, I don't add the elbow macaroni the first time around, because the pasta gets a bit soggy when reheated.

Serves 6

WHOLE-WHEAT PASTA WITH ROASTED TOMATOES, SHRIMP, AND EGGPLANT

Pâtes Intégrales aux Tomates Confites

The oven-roasted tomatoes used in this recipe are the basis for many of my pasta sauces and braises. They make a wonderful addition to a warm white bean salad, or they can be the star attraction in a tomato tarte tatin. I make them all summer and freeze as many batches as I can manage so I'll have them for the winter months.

For the slow-roasted tomatoes

4 pounds of perfect heirloom tomatoes, sliced 1 inch thick
1 head of garlic
A few sprigs of fresh thyme (optional)
⅓ cup extra-virgin olive oil
Coarse sea salt to taste
1 teaspoon sugar

Heat the oven to 325°F.

Line your largest baking sheet with aluminum foil. Arrange the sliced tomatoes in a single layer, tuck the cloves of garlic (unpeeled) and the thyme, if using, between them, and pour the olive oil over all. Sprinkle with a pinch or two of sea salt and the sugar. Leave in the oven for 1½ to 2 hours, until the garlic is tender and the tomatoes are soft and a bit wrinkly. When everything has cooled a bit, remove the garlic from its peel; this should be easy to do with your fingers. If not using immediately, carefully layer the tomatoes and garlic in a shallow container, keeping as many whole as you can. Don't forget to pour in every last drop of that tomato liquid. (For the last slick of oil, try wiping your cookie sheet with a slice of bread. Yum.)

Store in the fridge (cover with additional olive oil to keep longer) or freeze for a snowy day.

For the pasta

2 very small eggplants, slim and dark
2–3 tablespoons of your tomato–olive oil liquid
1 pound raw frozen shrimp (I don't recommend using frozen cooked shrimp—in my experience, they are limp and watery)
2 cups (give or take) roasted tomatoes, with a bit of the liquid
A pinch or two of cayenne pepper
A splash of white wine
½ teaspoon sugar (optional)
Small handful of basil leaves, ripped by hand

Slice the eggplant into thin strips (¼ inch thick and 2 inches long); you want it to cook through in a reasonable amount of time. In a large sauté pan, heat 2 to 3 tablespoons of your tomato–olive oil liquid. Over medium heat, sauté the eggplant until really tender (there's nothing worse than eggplant that bites back). Add frozen shrimp, tomatoes, cayenne, wine, and sugar, if using. Cook until shrimp turn pink, about 5 minutes. Turn off the heat and stir in the basil, leaving aside a few leaves for garnish.

Serve over whole-wheat spaghetti.

Serves 4

CHAPTER 12

The Golden Parachute

Every Sunday at the Reillanne market, I buy my raspberry jam, tomatoes, and salad (and the occasional excellent rum-flavored *chouquette*) from Martine and Didier Caron at the small stand next to the church. When I'm feeling flush, I also take a gram of their home-grown saffron, a tangle of deep orange threads in a glass jar the size of a pot of expensive eye cream. Saffron grows plentifully in Provence, and like chickpeas and spelt, it is a local ingredient I have quickly incorporated into my everyday cuisine. Okay, not my *everyday* cuisine—I'd be bankrupt if I did that.

Saffron first entered my kitchen through our friend Marie, a teacher, poet, film buff, and classicist who lives in the *other* South of France, across the mountains at the foot of the Pyrenees. It was Marie who taught me to add a cube of sugar and a pinch of saffron to my ratatouille in case the vegetables lacked sun. The description is a good one—saffron's reddish-golden glow is very much my idea of sunshine in a bottle. Good saffron is sweet and spicy at the same time; Didier and Martine's smells faintly of dried peaches and cedarwood.

Although I've been using it for years, saffron is one of the few products in my French kitchen whose origins remain mysterious to me. Over my decade in France, I've become intimately acquainted with the hairy knobs of a celery root; I now buy my beets with greens and my chickens with heads. Though I have no problem identifying saffron in a jar, I have no idea what it looks like when it pops out of the ground.

France has made me a bit shy about asking people for things, so it took me over a year to work up the courage to inquire if I could come and see the saffron harvest. I gave Didier my cell phone number and hoped he would call.

Meanwhile, another call came in this week. From Warner Brothers. They are looking for a technical director for Europe, the Middle East, and Africa, and Gwendal's name came up. After a year of relative peace and quiet in our Provençal backwater, we were all aflutter. I don't have much experience in the business world, but when someone starts throwing around job titles with whole continents attached, I sit up and take notice. It would be a prestigious next step, from the start-up world of digital cinema to the cushy establishment of a Hollywood studio. It was flattering, and no doubt well paid. And like almost all important jobs with American companies in Europe, it was based in London.

I could see Gwendal's excitement, and also his confusion. Because no one ever gives them any positive reinforcement, the French are very bad at judging what level they play at in the outside world, their true value on the open market. This was a gold star, a rubber stamp with the word *Approved*. I immediately went into supportive-spouse mode. Without thinking, the American in me grabbed instinctively at the next rung on the ladder.

"No problem," I said, mentally throwing our whole life up into the air like a handful of confetti. "If that's what you want, we will find a way to make it work." I silently rearranged my life: *I'll just have to go back to my nineteenth-century-literature roots. I'll spend my days in the British Library writing a potboiler set in a Victorian insane asy-*

lum. I wondered if Gwendal would be paid enough for us to rent a nice flat in central London and what it would be like to take Alexandre to school on a red double-decker bus and eat lemon curd on pre-fab squares of whole-wheat toast on rainy afternoons.

We spent the next few evenings updating Gwendal's résumé—putting all the right American-style active verbs in place. He was focused on the task, but he also wondered why he'd never heard of or met the last guy who'd done this job. Was it a new position, or was it some kind of golden broom closet where they stuck talented middle managers, never to be heard from again?

He talked to his team in Paris. Most of them were ten years his junior and could hardly contain their excitement. "*Écoute,* it's perfect. It makes perfect sense. You do this, and then you move to LA, and, and—I didn't want to say it, man. But you gotta get the hell out of Céreste."

My parents were pleased, impressed. It was so logical, such a nice acknowledgment of his rise in the industry. The compass that had been turning without direction for two years suddenly seemed to be pointing, well, up.

Despite the general enthusiasm, there were small but persistent forces tugging in the other direction. Sitting like Jiminy Cricket on everyone's shoulder was the spirit of Steve Jobs, who died this past week, at the age of fifty-six. Gwendal kept replaying a YouTube video of the graduation address Jobs gave at Stanford: "If this were the last day of your life, would you want to be doing what you are about to do right now?"

∽

My afternoon walk along the path to the babysitter gives me a few moments each day alone with my thoughts. Walking through the *vieux village* in the early fall, you can tell which houses have children in them: smooth brown chestnuts are piled carefully on the front steps. They are the local kiddie currency this time of year, hoarded like pennies. This morning, Alexandre showed his collection to Jean. "You put that in your *poche,*" said the old man, patting the pocket of Alexandre's sweatshirt. "It keeps away the rheumatism."

How? I was about to ask, but then I stopped myself. Better to keep these city-girl interrogations to myself. That's what the Internet is for.

They say Provence is a cold country warmed by the sun. Seasons bump into one another, a botanical pileup. Along the side of the main road, the still-green stems of the irises poke out from beneath a layer of brittle brown leaves. Small branches from the plane trees litter the path, waiting to be gathered for winter kindling.

Ever since Gwendal got the call, I've been walking around with a tiny knot in the pit of my stomach. Could I leave France, my new life, my career, my cheese monger? I've gotten spoiled; I like it when Gwendal makes crepes on Sunday afternoon. Could he do that and still supervise satellite transmissions to Dubai?

My instinct is to be supportive, but if I'm honest with myself, London was often a lonely place for me. I understood the books, not the people. I am too straightforward, too sincere. Irony whipped past me like a cricket ball; I'm pretty sure they were aiming for my head.

But this wasn't just any job, I told myself, this was Warner Brothers. It was as if Bugs Bunny himself had picked up the phone and said, *Wass up, Gwendal?*

If I have a knot in my gut, I also have an American in my gut. A reflex, a mental knee-jerk leftover from my twenties in New York—the era of big plans and sour cherry martinis. "Onward and upward"—that's the phrase, isn't it? For the American in me, moving on always meant moving up. Staring up into the hills, I feel, perhaps for the first time, how far I am from that young woman. Her priorities are no longer my own. The checklist in my twenty-two-year-old head—status, money, unending acquisition—has been utterly transformed by my years in France. This may be the hardest thing in the world for an American to admit: There is such a thing as *enough*. Gwendal and I have a perfectly lovely quality of life, a lot of debt, a little savings, all based on a fraction of what my friends in the States bring home every month. It isn't exactly a golden parachute, but we are doing okay. I love my job, and that's a privilege in itself, but a career in France is not what makes a person whole, or valuable. Success has a different meaning here; it's more about the quality of my fig tart than the size of my paycheck. I literally can't remember the last time someone asked me what I do for a living.

What I really enjoy about being in Céreste is the length of the days, the way time rolls out smoothly in front of us, like the gentle rise of the fields. Don't get me wrong—I'm still greedy, but now I am greedy for time. I crave it like big bowls of *soupe d'épeautre* padding my rib cage and warming my organs. I am getting used to having Gwendal home for lunch, tickling Alexandre after his bath, the occasional power nap that turns into an afternoon tryst.

Alexandre and I walk home from the nanny, the stroller bumping along the uneven path. Alexandre drags a stick across the ground, squinting into the sun. As we turn past the village fig tree, past the clean sheets flapping on the medieval ramparts and the narrow streets free of cars, I realize what we would be giving up. All my life I've resisted living in the moment, shoved aside the present in favor of the next big thing. For the first time, I am confronted with a situation where everything—*everything*—I want is right here. Right now.

⁓

To my surprise, Didier did call, on Tuesday afternoon after lunch. The saffron harvest is quick, two or three weeks in September or

October before the first frost. We decided to make it a family outing. Didier's directions to La Ferme de la Charité were a little sketchy, something about two tall cypress trees and a sign with a black goat. Alexandre fell asleep as we drove through the backcountry of Forcalquier, past battalions of knotted pines standing at attention, their trunks notched with short spikes like the rungs on a ladder. We got lost a few times on the back roads around Les Tourrettes. The signs, when there were signs, began to indicate *hameaux*, hamlets, rather than villages or towns.

Didier met us at the bottom of the drive, waved us over to park next to a rusting tractor in front of the house. He's so tall and thin he looks sketched by a cartoonist—all lean lines with a beard that comes to a furry point in the middle of his chest.

Martine came out of the kitchen onto the porch, wiping her hair out of her eyes with the back of her wrist. She is tan and rugged, her body hidden under a pile of shapeless woolly sweaters. Her arms were red up to the elbows, her apron dripping. It looked like she'd been chopping up bodies in the back room, but I'd been in Provence just long enough to realize that she was probably just sticky from pitting cherries. I took a quick peek behind her into the kitchen. A batch of jam boiled furiously on the stove; the KitchenAid was covered with a light dusting of flour—all the signs of a kitchen at work. The yellow tiles were the color of a good saffron risotto.

When we arrived, the wooden picnic table on the porch was already covered with crates of delicate purple crocuses, the remains of yesterday's haul. So this is where my saffron comes from; the spice is actually the stigma (the pollen trap) of the flower. "There are three threads per flower," said Didier. "Occasionally you come across a flower with six stigma, a lucky one, like a four-leaf clover." Saffron is one of the world's most expensive spices. When I asked why, he nodded toward the baskets of spent flowers on the table. *"Le main d'oeuvre*—the labor, he said. "There's no way to mechanize it. It all has to be done by hand."

To give you an idea: Didier and Martine harvested 90 grams of saffron last year from 17,000 flowers. To make a kilogram (2.2 pounds) takes roughly 225,000 flowers, all plucked and sorted by hand. A kilo of saffron sells for about 30,000 euros. Yesterday's pickings—more saffron than I had ever seen at once—lined a white ceramic dish on the table. A slight breeze swept over us. Nature has a cruel sense of humor. One good gust of wind, and several thousand euros would end up scattered all over the front lawn. Martine must have been thinking the same thing, because she carefully lifted the dish and brought it inside.

I stood there with a ready smile, trying not to look too useless. Didier pointed the way toward the field below the house. In these situations, I find it's best to tell people up front that I'm a New Yorker; it gives me the liberty to ask one or two really dumb questions. As we walked out into the field, Martine issued a warning. "Just be sure not to step on the flowers," she said, looking at the soles of my conspicuously white sneakers.

I walked gingerly around some pellet-size droppings. "Do you spread the rabbit dung, or do they just come themselves?"

"Les moutons," said Martine. "Those are sheep droppings."

Ah. Provence is a country where a girl had better know her dung.

"Where are the sheep?" I asked, looking around.

"In the freezer," answered Didier. "They make less noise."

In less than an hour, we had emptied the field of the open blooms. Other flowers, their purple tips just poking out of the ground this afternoon, would be ready tomorrow. *"Ça va, les reins?"* Martine seemed concerned about my kidneys (the French are very protective of digestive organs), squished up as they were by my jackknifed position as I bent forward to grab the final flowers. Gwendal stood at the edge of the field taking photos. He never tires of sending them to my family and friends in the States: Elizabeth discovers manual labor, comic relief, or simply proof that I not only owned sneakers but occasionally found some reason to wear them.

There was a stiff wind, the beginning of a fall chill, as we headed up to the porch. We sat down at the table and began gently removing the precious threads with the press of a fingernail. My thumb was soon stained with a bright orange smudge—the vegetal equivalent of the Midas touch. The new harvest would be spread out on a cookie sheet and dried at a low heat for about a half hour. Then Martine would leave it overnight in the oven to dry out before weighing and preparing bottles of ½ or 1 gram each.

After a few minutes of silent plucking—Didier and Martine would finish later—Didier walked us around the farm. We looked out over the field that until very recently had held hundreds of tomato plants to provide company for our summer mozzarella. We had to forcibly remove Alexandre from the seat of the tractor—he would happily have slept there. The geese scattered at the approach of an energetic toddler. We passed the goats, a majestic black bull, and a nine-hundred-pound pig I wouldn't want to meet in a dark alley. He eyed us with suspicion, one long, belligerent tooth hanging out of the left side of his mouth.

"He'd chew your leg off, given the chance," mused Didier.

"Hmm," I smiled, backing Alexandre away from the pen.

Gwendal didn't say much as we drove the tight turns back to Forcalquier. He was due to talk to the headhunter later this week. The sun flashed through the rows of pines like a hypnotist's coin at the end of a chain.

THE NEXT DAY after lunch, I wandered up to Gwendal's office. He was sitting at his desk, the detritus of our administrative life strewn around him on the floor, the extra bed for guests without its sheets. Our decorating efforts had not quite extended to this part of the house. The English wicker colonial couch didn't match the Moroccan rug, and the mirrored door of the art deco armoire we found at the *dépôt-vente* was in danger of falling off. True, it wasn't the most glamorous workplace for a man of his abilities. I sat down on the edge of the bed.

I've given Gwendal many American-style pep talks over the past few years, and he's risen to every occasion. This time he just needed to be let off the hook. "You never wanted to work for a Hollywood studio," I said softly, "to be a cog in the wheel. You don't like office politics. There are some people who are good at it, made for it. But that's not you." Gwendal swiveled slightly in his chair. "Your honesty, your integrity, your unlimited capacity for work, *these* are the things that make you great, that force people to take you at your word. You're an entrepreneur. You should be in a place where who you are is the greatest asset you have. I don't think we should try to stick a round peg in a square hole just because it's a nice next line on your résumé."

I saw his relief. I forget sometimes that he needs me to say these things aloud, that he's afraid to disappoint me.

"I think we both underestimated the toll these last two years have taken. It's been bad for a long time. Look how starved you are for this tiny bit of validation of what you've done. That doesn't mean it's right."

I know my husband. He has a bit of an Atlas complex—if there's no one else to do it, he'll hold up the whole world. He's so invested. He treats every job he's ever had like he owns the company.

He took both my hands, rubbed his thumb gently over my wrist.

"I'm never doing this again," he said quietly. "I just don't have it in me. If I'm going to put in those kind of hours, that energy, time away from my family, it has to be mine."

I WANTED TO find a way to say thank you to Didier and Martine. I debated carrot-saffron muffins but decided to go with the old standby no French person can resist—Toll House chocolate chip cookies. I brought the plastic-wrapped paper plate of goodies to the market on Sunday.

Martine wasn't there, but there was Didier, leaning against the truck, the stub of a hand-rolled cigarette between his lips. *"Mais, il fallait pas"*—you shouldn't have.

Mais, si.

By way of response, he handed me a small jar of saffron; the threads caught the morning light, glowing slightly around the edges.

"Mille quatre cent soixante quatorze," he said, looking at the collection of jars laid out on his checkerboard cloth. Translating numbers is one of the last lags in my French vocabulary, along with driving directions and tax jargon. (Come to think of it, maybe it has nothing to do with my French.) I slowly worked it out, repeating every syllable in an attempt to visualize the accompanying number in my head. "One thousand four hundred and seventy-four flowers last Thursday," he repeated with a certain satisfaction, as if to say, *Not bad for a New Yorker who doesn't know a sheep turd when she sees one.*

I tucked the jar into my bag and gave Didier *bises* on both cheeks. For the time being, this is the only golden parachute I need.

Recipes for the Saffron Harvest

SAFFRON SUMMER COMPOTE
Compote de Pêches aux Safran

A few threads of saffron add depth—maybe even a little fancy-pants—to this summer compote. I make mine with a mix of white and yellow peaches and juicy nectarines, whatever I have on hand. Top your morning yogurt, layer in a parfait, or serve with a slice of pound cake and a dollop of crème fraîche. When I get my canning act together, this is what I'm going to make, jars and jars of golden days to last me through the chill of winter.

2 pounds of slightly overripe fruit (a mix of peaches, nectarines, and
  apricots)
1 tablespoon of raw sugar
2 good pinches of saffron

Cut the fruit into 1-inch cubes. I don't especially feel the need to peel. In a heavy-bottomed saucepan, combine the fruit and sugar. Bring to a boil, stir in the saffron, and let simmer over low heat until thickened and slightly reduced; mine took about 40 minutes. Serve warm or cold.

Serves 6–8

CLAMS WITH SAFFRON-FENNEL TOMATO SAUCE
Palourdes au Safran

Saffron and seafood have a natural affinity for each other. This is quite simply among the best things I've ever eaten—elegant enough for a dinner party, but happy to be family finger food as well.

¼ cup olive oil

½ cup shallots, minced

3 large cloves garlic, minced

*1½ cups fennel, about half a medium bulb, chopped (save the fronds for
    garnish)*

14 ounces cherry tomatoes, halved

1 teaspoon sugar

*Scant ¼ teaspoon best-quality saffron—I use whole threads that I crush
    with a pestle and mortar*

Black pepper

1½ cups white wine

2¼ pounds fresh clams

Heat the olive oil in a large sauté pan or Dutch oven. Sauté shallots, garlic, and fennel over medium-low heat until softened, about 10 minutes.
Add the tomatoes, sugar, saffron, and a grind of black pepper; simmer
for 5 minutes. Add the white wine, simmer 5 minutes more. Add the
clams and stir to coat with sauce. Cover tightly. Cook 10 minutes, until
clams are fully opened. Serve immediately, or you can turn off the heat
and let them rest for 10 minutes or so—it won't do any harm.

Serve as an appetizer over arugula with lots of fresh bread to
soak up the sauce. Or serve over linguine as a main course. Garnish
with chopped fennel fronds.

Serves 4

*Tip: No need to add salt to a dish like this—the water released from the
clams will take care of that.*

CARROT-SAFFRON CUPCAKES

In my opinion, almost nothing improves a good carrot cupcake, but this recipe
changed my mind. I tasted something similar at a small farmers' market; a

young woman was selling dense carrot muffins along with her homemade saffron syrup and apricot-saffron jam. Her secret: infuse the eggs with the saffron the night before you want to bake. I don't usually organize my baking twenty-four hours in advance, so I tried adding the saffron on the day and it still works wonders—the subtle perfume infuses the cupcakes perfectly. These are terrific without the icing for breakfast or a lunchbox, but I have a love affair with cream-cheese frosting, so why not gild the lily.

For the cupcakes

3 eggs
1 generous pinch saffron threads, crushed (or ⅛ teaspoon ground saffron)
2 cups sugar
½ cup vegetable oil
½ cup olive oil
1 cup whole-wheat flour
1 cup all-purpose flour
¾ teaspoon salt
2 teaspoons baking soda
½ cup walnuts, chopped
½ cup golden raisins
3 cups (packed) grated carrots (approximately 5 carrots)

For the icing

1 small pinch saffron threads, crushed
1 teaspoon boiling water
½ stick butter, at room temperature
3 ounces Philadelphia cream cheese, at room temperature
2 cups powdered sugar

Preheat the oven to 375°F.

In a large mixing bowl, lightly beat the eggs together with the saffron; add sugar and whisk to a light lemon yellow. Add oils; whisk thoroughly to combine.

In a small bowl, combine flours, salt, and baking soda.

In a medium bowl, toss the walnuts and raisins with the grated carrots; set aside.

Whisk the flour mixture into the egg mixture until evenly combined; don't overwork. Fold in walnuts, raisins, and carrots with a spatula.

Line metal muffin tins with paper or foil wrappers (enough for 24 cupcakes). Divide the batter evenly. Bake for 22 to 25 minutes, until golden brown and a toothpick comes out clean. Cool for 5 minutes on a baking rack, then turn out and cool completely.

To make the icing: Dissolve the saffron in 1 teaspoon boiling water; let cool. Beat together the butter, cream cheese, and saffron water until smooth (don't worry if there are some flecks of saffron thread). Add the sugar and beat until smooth. Slather your cupcakes at will. Once the cupcakes have been iced, store in an airtight container in the fridge.

Makes 24 cupcakes

CHAPTER 13

Home

Holy Empire State Building, Batman. I've just been taken for a tourist in the city of my birth.

After I'd spent a week at my parents' new place in Delaware, Gwendal flew in. We headed up to New York together and walked out of Penn Station onto the sunshine-soaked concrete. I sucked in the noise and the car exhaust like the air at the top of Everest. Gwendal started to veer toward the forty-person taxi line.

"Uh-uh," I said. I walked twenty-five feet up the block and did what any native New Yorker would: I flagged one down in the middle of moving traffic. One has better things to do with one's time than wait in the taxi line at Penn Station.

We hoisted our suitcase and two large shopping bags of French liqueurs (samples for a friend) into the back.

"A hundred and forty-nine West Tenth Street."

I must have been distracted by a fly or something, because it was nearly twenty blocks before I noticed what was going on.

"Excuse me, sir. Why are we going uptown?"

"I thought you said Tenth Avenue and Amsterdam." (Never mind that this is geographically impossible.)

"Tenth Street," I screeched. "Tenth Street. Sir, I'm not a tourist, and you heard me perfectly well. Please reset the meter to zero and take us downtown."

And that's exactly what he did—but not before my pride was wounded, an identity crisis ignited, and a half hour that I could have spent in my favorite hat shop in SoHo wasted.

When we got out of the cab, Gwendal looked at me like I had just peeled off my face. "Do you think he was really trying to cheat us or he just didn't speak English very well?"

"Doesn't matter," I snapped. And it didn't. The damage was done. Sometime during my ten years in France, I'd crossed a line. New York is in my blood, but somewhere else is in my voice, my hair, my clothes, and the fact that I now have to carry a suitcase out of Penn Station. *Merde.*

GOING HOME, BACK, back home—*whatever*—to the United States is getting confusing. It's hard to explain to Gwendal what happens to me when I land in the States. He's supposed to be disoriented; I'm not.

The first sign we'd left Europe was the little girl in her pajamas. The plane was late and it took Alexandre and me an hour to get through customs. When we finally rounded the bend into arrivals, there were only four people left in the room: my parents, a young mother, and a five-year-old. It was four thirty in the afternoon, and the little girl was rolling on the couch in a pair of pastel cupcake pajamas. It was a tiny thing, but as a cultural signifier, it was as clear as the banner-size American flag in immigration—*Welcome to the Land of Anything Goes.* Just as you'd never see a French woman on a plane in sweatpants, you would never see a French child out in public in her pj's.

Surely most people are not this porous about their environments. The first thing that goes out the window when I return to the States is my carefully cultivated sense of moderation, patience, and, dare I say, order. There's a change of frequency, like a slight twist of the knob on one of those old-fashioned radios, when I start speaking English full-time. I become impatient. I look for opportunities to have a little rant. *This is unacceptable. I'd like to speak to a manager.* Just for the sheer pleasure of knowing it might work.

Like that little girl at the airport, my schedule gets all mixed up. (Truth be told, I always thought it was a shame that the French have no word for "spend the day in your bathrobe eating leftover Chinese food and watching reruns of *Law and Order*.") Food has no specific time or place, it's just abundantly, constantly *there*. I get overwhelmed by all my options. I order blueberry pancakes and bacon for dinner at the diner. I heat up leftover stuffed cabbage for a four o'clock lunch. I'm forever eating and never hungry. I inhale Dots, boxes and boxes of fluorescent-colored, high-fructose-corn-syrup, Antichrist-of-your-orthodontist Dots. These foods are at once wildly satisfying and a reenactment of *Invasion of the Body Snatchers*. Forty-eight hours after my arrival, I can usually be found in the bathroom nursing a sugar-induced migraine and throwing up a stray package of Twizzlers.

⚬

THE WEEK I arrive, my mother always buys a celebratory bone-in pork roast—for eight. It takes three hours to cook, and what with talking and unpacking and my usual digging through my mother's jewelry drawer, we never seem to remember to turn on the oven before six o'clock. I rarely have time to marinate the roast, and there's always a dead peach and a half-frozen Granny Smith apple lingering in the back of the fruit drawer that my mom insists we throw in the pot. At eight thirty, well past the American dinner hour, the roast is still raw in the center. We give up and cut it into eight thick pork chops dangling from the bone and blast it under the broiler. Sometimes we *really* give up and order pizza.

As I prepare the pork roast, I can hear my mother at the table with Alexandre. "Where does the purple one go? No," she says gently. "Which one's the purple? There it is. Bravo. Can you show me where this goes? How many spots are there? One, two, three. That's *right!*" She hasn't seen him in four months—a lifetime at this age. Maybe it's the way she uses her high-pitched teacher's voice, but to me, this kind of play seems so... directed. I feel like she's testing him.

My mother is a wonderful teacher. She spent the first part of her career teaching teenagers with disabilities and the second half in an administrative role, making sure kids got the appropriate therapeutic services. This means she has a checklist in her head—occupational hazard—of things Alexandre's *supposed* to be doing. You will never—ever—hear a French teacher trying to evaluate a child's skill set at age two and a half.

Alexandre recently started taking a kiddie music class in Reillanne. For the moment this is his only formal activity (unless you count watching tractors). No one in France seems terribly concerned with programming kids with lots of activities. On the contrary, scheduling too many activities for them is seen as negative—an imposition on their time to play. Claire, our next-door neighbor in Céreste, has recently gone back to her work as a speech therapist. "Sometimes a little *ennui*—boredom—is good for the kids. It obliges them to invent things—develop their imaginations."

The music class for the two- and three-year-olds is called *Éveil Musical*—Musical Awakening. Unlike Mommy and Me, parents are not invited to stay. I don't think they are practicing scales or learning to identify Mozart. When we come to pick him up, he usually refuses to put down the flute. The phrases I hear tossed around translate to "awaken the senses" and "take pleasure"—*prendre plaisir*. The theory goes, if you instill a sense of pleasure, learning will follow. I feel like American kids—including myself—were raised with the equation reversed: If you learn something, you will have the pleasure of accomplishment. Pleasure, for the American child—and, I have a sneaking suspicion, for the parent—comes not just from doing, but from doing better than everyone else. I want my child to be successful and happy; I don't think there is a parent the world over who doesn't wish for the same thing. It's the cause and effect that differs between cultures: Does success make you happy, or is being happy a success?

⁓

"'Are You Mom Enough?'"

Are you kidding?

My mom likes to save articles for me. She leaves them on my night table so when I go back to the States, I learn all about the latest eye cream for my dark circles, the hot new chef who opened a restaurant fifty yards from our old apartment in Paris, and the success of the charter-school movement. This trip, there's a cover article from *Time* magazine with a picture of a slim, ballerina-like blonde nursing her three-year-old son. The headline "Are You Mom Enough?" confirms some of what I've come to suspect: Parenting in the United States has become an extreme sport.

I have conversations that I never expected to have.

"I'm obsessed with car seats," says a friend in North Carolina who decided to leave her PhD program in psychology to stay home with her three kids.

"Why?" I blurted out before I could stop myself. I hope I didn't sound arch. I'm sure I did.

"Because it's really important."

Well, yes. But.

She wasn't alone. When I called Maya, an economics professor in LA, she repeated a version of the exact same thing. "We're looking for a new car seat for Serge. Did you know a car seat can expire? The plastic becomes brittle, and therefore less crash-resistant, so you have to replace it." Maybe I've been in France too long, but if one of those flimsy blue plastic bags can sit unchanged in a landfill for thirty thousand years, how is your car seat going to expire before your kid is out of diapers?

It's not that I was hearing opposing arguments in France. I simply wasn't having these conversations at all. The best word I can find for the moms around me in France is *décomplexées*. It means "relaxed," but also "uncomplicated," "anti-neurotic," if you will. French parents don't seem to worry that they are screwing up all the time, sickening their kids with dirt or stifling their kids' creativity with discipline. It has nothing to do with competition and a lot to do with common sense. There is no peer-reviewed study you could brandish that would convince them that throwing spaghetti is a form of self-expression.

My own family was not immune to these "Mom Enough" insecurities.

One morning, Aunt Joyce, my mother's younger sister, walked in the door, keys jangling.

"Hi, shortcake," she said to Alexandre. "High five." She is teaching him some local lingo.

Aunt Joyce is a great favorite with Alexandre. She has a Big Wheel in her driveway and, often, a pack of peanut M&M's in her bag.

She poured herself a diet Coke, no ice, which she drinks at all hours of the day and night. "You're not going to make us take Grandma Classes, are you?"

"Grandma Classes?"

"I have a friend in Pittsburgh, and before her daughter would let her babysit the kids, she had to take Grandma Classes."

"You raised us, and we're all still here. I think we can skip the diploma."

THERE WAS ANOTHER reason I went to New York: to see Linda. I hadn't seen her since my father's funeral. I meant to keep in touch, but years, and soon oceans, got in the way. Linda was my father's last girlfriend, but she was also the little sister of his best childhood friend. She had had a crush on him when she was barely a teenager. Thirty years and two divorces later, they found each other again. If my father hadn't been ill, I'm sure she would have been my stepmother.

Manic depression, like all mental illness, is insidious. Though it's physiological, like diabetes, instead of restricting your access to cheesecake, it changes your personality. Sometimes it made my father silent, unable to muster the energy to trim the hairs in his ears. Sometimes it made him loud, irrational, delusional. He would scream at waitresses, sue his doctors. In the end, he drove Linda away, as he did most people. Everyone, really, except me. He died of a heart attack, alone in his apartment, a few months before I turned twenty-four. When the police called me at work, I asked the sergeant if there were any pills, gas. When he said no, a tiny part of my sadness turned to relief.

I've felt better these past few months. The thyroid pills are making a difference, and my doctor and I are gradually upping the dose. But after the hole I fell into this past winter, I'm still scared, tired of waiting for the other shoe to drop. Alexandre gives these questions of heredity a new sense of urgency—I don't want to pass on this weight, this fear.

Linda agreed to meet me at a coffee shop near her apartment on the Upper West Side. I spotted her as she walked up the street in a tracksuit, with a cane. She was older, and blonder, than I remembered.

"Oh, honey, it's so good to see you." She gave me a big hug. "Sorry about the sweats. I just came from physical therapy."

Inside, I slipped into the faux-leather banquette. The tables were close together; the man to our left, eating a bowl of oatmeal, nearly brushed me with his *New York Times* whenever he turned the page. Linda told me about her daughter, her twin grandsons.

"I guess I just want to know..." I was surprised at how hard it was to get this sentence out. "What I wanted to know is...was he always like this, even when he was young? Did anyone know?" Behind these questions were others. Did I miss the window? Will this happen to me?

I've heard about this phenomenon. As children approach the age when a parent got sick or died, they wait to pass the threshold, the magic number, like kids on a road trip holding their breath when they pass a cemetery.

I stared into my coffee, biting my lip to keep back the tears.

"Oh, honey, you're not...you always...he was so proud of you."

"I just wonder if it was always there or if he woke up one day and felt like this. Was there something that set it off?"

"Honestly, if he was sick, I don't think we would have recognized it. He tried to tell me, later on. And I said, 'Oh, everyone gets depressed sometimes.' I didn't really know what it was. For the families of alcoholics, there's Al-Anon. But for us, there was nothing."

She paused, taking a sip of her herbal tea. "I feel like I was robbed of something."

I'd never heard anyone put it quite that way, but so did I. The early childhood I didn't remember, the fragility I felt when Alexandre gripped my knees, all this was wrapped up in that empty space, something stolen.

"I'm sorry I haven't been in touch," I said. "I thought about it, and then all this time went by. I always thought we should have been family."

"Your father was a warm soul," she said, staring over my shoulder into another life. "He was terrific. Such a wonderful dancer. When we were kids, we used to dance in the basement. He would turn me upside down and sweep the floor with my hair."

I inspected the bottom of my coffee cup. "Did you know that my grandmother, Dad's mom, had shock treatments? In the late sixties, right after my parents got engaged."

"No," said Linda, "I don't think I did know that."

"I read something recently. Apparently, it's coming back into fashion."

The woman at the table just behind us stood up and zipped her coat. "It's true," she said, leaning in to collect her bag. "It's much safer now. Very effective."

I smiled in spite of myself. Gotta love this town. Innate one-up-manship coupled with a complete lack of personal space. In a way, it was touching. Only in New York would a total stranger butt into your private conversation just to let you know there's somebody out there who's a tiny bit crazier than you.

I said good-bye to Linda, promised to send her a copy of my book, and walked across the park. When I need to talk to my father, I go to the Metropolitan Museum of Art. After the funeral, I'd never gone back to the cemetery. I can't imagine he's there. For me, he's buried in the Egyptian wing, under the Temple of Dendur, a small sanctuary they took apart stone by stone in Egypt, carried across the ocean, and rebuilt under a glass atrium on East Eighty-First Street.

My father and I came here nearly every weekend from the time I outgrew the Museum of Natural History to when I left for boarding school. The admission fee was "suggested," which meant he could hand over just a few singles without comment and then help me clip the shiny metal tag with the capital M to the neck of my sweater. There's still no mandatory fee for admission, but since my dad died, I always make a point to pay the full price so that some other parent, short of funds, can give his or her daughter what my father gave me. I carry one of those metal tags in my wallet. My talisman, my good-luck charm.

I still love the ritual of visiting my favorite objects, the clever feeling of knowing my way around. I walk past the Roman-era mummy in the foyer, past the seated jackals, and go into the temple, look at the Napoleonic-era graffiti carved into the stones.

If I wasn't mentally ill, to anyone watching, I must have been doing a pretty good imitation: sitting on a granite bench, tears streaming down my face, counting the pennies and nickels in the fountain. Any high-school student who has read Machiavelli can tell you: fear binds as well as, maybe better, than love. My fear of getting sick is my last link to my father. I miss him. If I stop being afraid to be like him, I will have to let him go.

I cut through the back doors, made a left at the Chippendale chairs, went past the Tiffany stained-glass windows, and hung a right to the Regency dining room. Such a comfort, this house full of beautiful things where nothing ever moves. As much as my childhood bedroom, these rooms feel like home. I feel so unmoored sometimes, never more so than when I come back to somewhere safe, somewhere knowable. So many places are inside me now; I feel spread a little thin. Who knows what will feel like home to Alexandre. The narrow paved streets of Céreste? The smell of the wood smoke from the chimney and the croissants from the *boulangerie*? What will be our special place? Where will he go to think of me?

There are moments I want to wrap Alexandre up like a mummy and keep him close, and moments I want nothing to do with him. I know I am missing a piece of his childhood, but how can I be fully present for something I never experienced? *I feel like I was robbed of something.* Where did she go, that little girl, and why does she only show up—fragile and hurting—when Alexandre pushes me away? Am I protecting myself? Leaving him before he leaves me?

ON SUNDAY AFTERNOON I took the train up to Connecticut to visit my friend Kim. Her daughter is already six months old and I haven't met her. I am looking forward to lunch. After three weeks in the States, my palate is completely exhausted. All I can taste is sugar, salt, and fat. A few more days of this and I'm in danger of turning into a cranberry streusel muffin.

Kim is one of the best cooks I know. We met in college, and during our single days in New York she taught me how to make super-easy chocolate fudge and a very reassuring chicken potpie. She has a recipe for carrot cake with cream cheese frosting that ought to be carved on stone tablets and stored in an ark. She supervised my first béchamel in Paris, and she always has the right tools at hand, including a heavy sloped cookbook stand and one of those flat metal spatulas for even icing.

Kim's husband is Hungarian, and she has tackled intercultural marriage in much the same way I have—through pastry. When she and Mark got engaged, Kim invited her future in-laws for dinner and served her famed carrot cake for dessert. It elicited a strangely muted response; no doubt it was too sweet for their European palates. So Kim did what any smart daughter-in-law-to-be would do—she immediately went out and bought several Hungarian cookbooks.

"They are very hard to find," she said. "I love this one." She handed me a thick volume. The cover was old-fashioned, an older man in a three-piece suit standing behind a buffet laden with layer cakes, grapes dangling from a raised brass stand, and a whole fish in aspic.

"It's by George Lang, who used to run Café des Artistes. He died recently; his obituary was in the *Times*."

"I love reading the obituaries."

"It's an amazing story," she continued, searching for serving pieces in the silverware drawer. "His parents died in Auschwitz, and when the Russians took over after the war he escaped to Austria hidden in a coffin. The recipes are very precise—most of the Hungarian cookbooks are grandma-style, with directions like 'stir until it looks done,' which is not very helpful if you've never seen it, let alone eaten it."

The result of Kim and Lang's joint efforts was already sitting on the counter when I arrived. A simple yellow cake, dotted with slightly sunken cherries and topped with crystallized sugar. "Instead of baking powder," she said, bending to take the salmon out of the oven, "you lighten it by folding in beaten egg whites."

Lunch was served at lunchtime, which felt like a treat after my haphazard eating schedule these past few weeks. Along with the oven-roasted salmon, Kim tossed a salad of peppery rocket leaves with roasted red onions, cubes of butternut squash, toasted walnuts, and lumps of snow-white goat cheese. The dressing was nothing but oil and vinegar, maybe a pinch of sea salt. The textures and tastes were perfectly balanced—no elbowing of flavors, no spice shouting for attention. She set the table with her wedding china laid on a thick white cloth. It made me feel pampered, like a special guest. Flora played in her playpen. After lunch, Mark made me an espresso; he smiled unabashedly when Kim brought over the cake. It was moist, not terribly sweet. A cherry escaped my fork and rolled to the center of the plate. I picked up a golden crumb from the tablecloth with the tip of my index finger. The longer I'm away the clearer it becomes: Home can be something as vast as a country, as holy as a temple, or as simple as a cake.

Recipes for Lunch Among Friends

ARUGULA SALAD WITH ROASTED RED ONIONS, BUTTERNUT SQUASH, WALNUTS, AND FRESH GOAT CHEESE

Salade de Roquette au Chèvre, aux Noix aux Oignons Rouge, et à la Courge Butternut

Simple, balanced, and satisfying, this makes a wonderful appetizer—particularly when your palate is exhausted from too much heavy food. I go very light on the dressing—barely there—so all the flavors really come through.

½ of a medium butternut squash
1 red onion
2 tablespoons olive oil
Coarse sea salt
1 small individual goat cheese (2–3 ounces)
1 medium bag of arugula or other peppery or slightly bitter salad
½ teaspoon sherry or red wine vinegar
¼ cup walnut pieces

Preheat the oven to 350°F.

Wash the squash and cut it into cubes, about 1 inch by ½ inch (I see no need to peel). Cut the red onion in half and slice into half-moons. Line a baking sheet with aluminum foil. Toss the squash and onion with 1 tablespoon of olive oil; spread in a single layer on the baking sheet. Sprinkle with coarse sea salt.

Bake for 30 to 35 minutes, until squash is tender. Allow to cool.

Cut the goat cheese into small cubes. Just before serving, dress the salad with the remaining 1 tablespoon of olive oil, the vinegar, and a good pinch of coarse sea salt. Toss to combine. Top the salad with the squash, onion, goat cheese, and walnuts.

Serve immediately.

Serves 4 as a light appetizer

SIMPLE SALMON IN FOIL
Saumon en Papillote

When I want simple, moist fish fillets, I tend to cook them *en papillote*—in a foil or parchment pouch.

2 pounds salmon fillet, about 1 inch thick
1 tablespoon of olive oil
Half a lemon
Coarse sea salt
Freshly ground black pepper

Preheat the oven to 400°F. Cut the fish into individual portions. Lay a large sheet of aluminum foil on a cookie sheet—the foil should hang over both edges by several inches. Lay the fish fillets close together, but not touching, on the foil. Drizzle with olive oil, squeeze the lemon on top, and season with coarse sea salt and pepper. Place another equally large piece of aluminum foil over the fish and carefully fold the edges together on all four sides to seal.

Bake for 25 minutes if you like your salmon slightly rare, 30 minutes for fully opaque.

Serves 6

HUNGARIAN CHERRY CAKE
Anyám Cseresznyés Lepénye

This recipe is adapted from George Lang's *Cuisine of Hungary* (Wings, 1994). Kim writes: "This recipe is typically Hungarian in that it calls for the eggs to be separated and then the whites whipped until stiff to lighten the cake, rather than using a chemical leavener like baking soda. It is also much less sweet than American desserts, which my husband prefers."

1 ½ sticks unsalted butter
¾ cup granulated sugar
3 eggs, separated
1 cup flour
Pinch of salt
Bread crumbs
1 pound fresh cherries, pitted (or 1 jar Trader Joe's Morello Cherries, well
    drained)
Vanilla sugar for garnish

Preheat oven to 375°F.

Cream the butter with half the sugar. After a few minutes of vigorous whipping, add egg yolks and then continue whipping. Finally, add flour and salt. Combine.

Beat egg whites with remaining granulated sugar until the mixture holds stiff peaks. With a rubber spatula, gently fold the egg whites into the butter mixture.

Butter a 9-inch round cake pan and sprinkle it with bread crumbs. Pour batter into the pan and distribute the cherries evenly on top (they should basically cover it).

Bake for 30 to 40 minutes. Cool 5 to 10 minutes on a wire rack, run a knife around the pan edge, and then turn out to cool completely. Sprinkle with vanilla sugar.

Serves 8

Tip: You can make your own vanilla sugar by splitting a vanilla bean and burying it in a pound of sugar. It will keep for months. You can also dust the cake with confectioners' sugar, but I'm partial to the slight crunch of granulated sugar.

CHAPTER 14

The Emperor of Ice Cream

What would you say if you caught your husband? Caught him red-handed. Caught him at midnight, up to his elbows in juicy, sticky, yellow cherries. Would you say your marriage had turned a corner? Might medication, or at least an extended yoga retreat, be in order?

☙

I WOULDN'T SAY the idea for an artisanal ice cream business came to us overnight, but almost. It had been a long winter. Sometime between the saffron harvest and Christmas, Gwendal negotiated his way out of his job. It felt dangerous to give up a well-paying position in the middle of a recession, and I suppose it was. It also felt necessary. He was forty-one years old and thoroughly demoralized—it was either start his own business or buy a Porsche, pick up a nineteen-year-old, and take that one-way street straight to the corner of Crazy and Unfulfilled. We had his severance, some savings, a small inheritance from his grandparents, and French unemployment benefits for the next eighteen months. Never one to sit idle, he'd spent the dark afternoons editing a book of contemporary Afghan poetry for a friend who lives in Kabul, sourcing alcohols made from protected mountain herbs for a friend on the cocktail-bar scene in New York, and organizing a screening of an American documentary for the local anti-fracking campaign.

⁀

THINGS REALLY STARTED to take shape when Angela and Rod, our original Céreste B&B hosts and dear friends, offered us their cellar. A vaulted stone cellar with a big picture window looking out onto the main street. When Gwendal and I first met, he'd often talked about having a space of his own, maybe an art-house cinema with a café, maybe an old-fashioned cabaret with spicy rum punch and contemporary circus performers spinning from the ceiling. At the moment, the cellar was nothing but a fluorescent-lit storage area smelling faintly of damp, filled with forgotten furniture and cases of wine. But it was there; an empty space, open to our imaginations.

As the weeks wore on and winter hibernation turned into spring thinking, some themes began to crystallize: The new business had to be something that shared the extraordinary flavors we'd discovered here in Provence. Something that would be fun for us and good for the village. We talked about a cocktail bar; we talked about handmade chocolates spiked with lavender liqueur. One night, Gwendal said, "You know what this place really needs—a great local ice cream parlor."

I took it in stride. My husband likes to think out loud—try things out, try things on. I figured this was just one of many slightly wacky ideas that would wander through the front room before one settled in by the fire for good.

I was trying to focus on my writing, to make sure we had something to live on during this entrepreneurial adventure. There I was, perfecting my recipe for sausage with braised red cabbage, and before I'd looked up from my computer he had finished a business plan and was making appointments with bankers. Of course, this was the part that he knew how to do. He had pried twenty million euros for a project out of a banker in the fall of 2008—two months after Lehman Brothers collapsed into dust and worldwide credit was frozen hard as an orange Popsicle. "You have to tell bankers a story," he said, handing me the first printout, a logo in the corner of an ice cream cone stacked with five colorful scoops. "In cinema it was easy. They want to be part of something fun, glamorous." Sometimes he sounds so American, it freaks me out.

I didn't know quite what to say. A thought flashed through my head: *Is this why I went to college?* It sounded romantic, but would he, would we, really enjoy washing dishes all day?

This may be an odd way to put it: I'm a child of divorce, so when I married Gwendal, I promised myself I would be his first wife and his second—the one he fell in love (and into bed) with, and the one he was able to grow and change with. I promised myself that I would support his happiness instead of burying him under a pile of mortgages and responsibilities.

In a sense, by coming to Provence, by learning to love the life we share here, the decision had already been made. Giving up the suits, the title, and the salary was just the final snip of a cord that had been fraying since we arrived. It's a very different life choice than any I'd imagined for myself, for my family—for my shoe closet—but at the same time, it is a perfectly logical extension of the leap of faith that brought us here.

A second thought came rushing in to replace the first: *Fresh fig sorbet.*

I thought about those first weekends Gwendal and I spent together in Paris—full of passion and discovery. About our last first date, two cones at sunset on the Île Saint-Louis. It comes down to this: I love my husband, and I trust him. And if we are going to be knee-deep in bitter chocolate sorbet, we'd best do it together. Welcome to the family business.

AND THAT, DEAR READER, is how I found myself standing in a field making small talk with skinny cows.

It was the beginning of April. Now that the cows and I had been properly introduced, it was time to talk to their owner. Damien stood in the doorway of the white laboratory building wearing a paper shower cap. He didn't look me or Gwendal in the eye; his gaze rested somewhere just to the left of my knees. Though I'd chosen my outfit that morning with an eye toward "girl who spends time around livestock," it was clear this guy thought I was a fraud. Whatever the rural version of street cred was, I needed some, and fast.

"We are making the yogurt," he said. "I'm just changing flavors. Go have a look around the farm."

Just as well I hadn't worn my new boots. As Gwendal and I walked through the half-open barn, my feet sank into the mud around the corrals. I was reminded of my mother's first trip to the French countryside; she'd spent a good portion of the afternoon trying to pet a chicken.

When Damien came out of the lab, we regrouped around a few stacked bales of hay. A new calf had been separated from the others. She stretched her neck, trying to peek over the edge of her pen.

"Céreste, *oui*," he said dismissively. "So you know Madame Gibert?"

"*Oui, bien sûr*, Madame Gibert. Her cousin took care of our son just after we arrived."

"We've heard of you throughout the region," I continued, perhaps a bit too eagerly. "Martine and Didier Caron gave us your name. We did the saffron harvest with them last year."

His face softened a bit. He finally looked me directly in the eye.

Not at the swishiest Christie's auction in New York or the poshest garden party in London had I felt the need to do what I was doing right now: name-dropping. I was desperate to prove that we weren't total newcomers, pretentious Parisians just passing through, that we were beginning to have roots in the community.

Damien walked us to the gate. "This is just a tease," he said, handing Gwendal a small container of pale yellow cream. It was so thick I was tempted to turn it upside down just to see if it would hold its shape. "I don't have enough to sell you. I use it for my own ice cream."

Just as we were walking out, he finally muttered the price to Gwendal. If we came to pick it up ourselves, his raw milk, straight from the farm, life's work of those haughty Jersey cows, would cost one *centime* less per liter than industrial long-life UHT.

❦

OF COURSE, TO start this new business, the cows and I were not the only ones Gwendal needed to convince.

"You have to make them understand this isn't a *crise de la quarantaine*"—the French equivalent of a midlife crisis—said Geneviève, who runs a local agency that provides interest-free loans to promising small-business owners. Gwendal was sitting in her office, dressed in a button-down shirt and a not-quite-pressed pair of khakis (Céreste doesn't have a dry cleaner and I don't iron).

"You need to make sure they don't think you are"—she paused with a certain gravity—"the goat-cheese man."

We'd all heard the stories. "The goat-cheese man" was obviously code for a much-feared archetype: The city slicker who comes to Provence and, eager to liberate himself from the tyranny of his cuff links, buys a hulking great farmhouse with a half a roof and a beautiful view (on a clear day, you can see the Alps). He dreams of starting a charming boutique hotel with footed bathtubs and Bellinis made from his favorite champagne (he's already sent down several cases) and the local peach nectar. He will mix them himself every morning as he chats with his worldly yet undemanding clientele, who compliment him on the Egyptian cotton sheets and ask for advice about local hiking trails. After two years of infinitesimal progress with local contractors, there is still no electricity for the hot tub, so he gives up and moves into the barn, which is too run down to insulate and too large to heat. At the local *boulangerie* (where he walks on his morning constitutional) he meets a picturesque goatherd and decides his true calling is to produce organic goat cheese for Alain Ducasse. After six months of lonely hilltop apprenticeship and the sour smell of whey clinging to his cashmere, he realizes that he hates goats, hates cheese, hates farms, hates Bellinis, and hates Provence. He sells the house at a loss to a retired English couple (who are used to living without heat) and flees, a penniless wreck, back to Paris, to grace, once again, the world of international finance.

If we didn't rise to quite this level of naïveté, it's true that Gwendal and I had both spent the better part of our careers, well, typing. And if our research thus far was correct, ice cream seemed to be more about chemistry than cooking, which meant I would be no help at all.

THE SUNDIAL IS pointing our way again; our friends Isabelle and Grégoire and their three children arrived for the first of May. Everyone should have a pair of friends he or she introduced who are now happily married. Gwendal and Isabelle met during his military service in Australia. Grégoire is a friend of his from engineering school. When I met Gwendal, he and Grégoire were working on a short film about a clown named Max who rides around Paris on a bicycle getting into all sorts of mischief.

This summer would not be quite as carefree as the summer before. We'd been looking at the numbers and it was clear belts needed to be tightened. I wore a corset for a couple of weeks in high school for a production of *The Importance of Being Earnest;* it gave me black-and-blue marks. The fact of the matter was, Gwendal and I had been living rather high on the hog these past few years. With his executive salary, we didn't worry about daily expenses, and when I finally started making a living from my writing, we were able to pay off some of our loans. The majority of the people we know and love in France are living on much less and they still manage to eat fresh food, go on holiday, and celebrate important occasions.

I stayed home with Alexandre while Gwendal took our guests on a hike and a picnic. Their five-year-old made it the whole way up the hill to Montjustin. It's a good two and a half hours at that pace. "You should have seen Nicolas," said Gwendal as they came through the door. "He walked the whole way."

"How do you do it?"

"We give the children little goals," said Grégoire. "Games to play along the way. Otherwise, every five minutes it's 'Are we there yet, Papa Smurf?'"

The next morning we went to the market in Reillanne; Isabelle was in charge of lunch. When I have guests, the American in me still tends to overbuy, overcook. For four adults and four kids, I would have bought two roast chickens from the rotisserie (my mother would have bought three, they're small), a heap of roast potatoes, salad, bread, cheese, and at least two kilos of the year's first strawberries for dessert. But I let Isabelle take over. She decided on a *salade de chèvre chaud*—a salad with warm goat-cheese toasts and lardons.

When we got home Isabelle filled up the sink and washed a huge head of frisée lettuce. She browned the bacon cubes in my biggest sauté pan and took them out with a slotted spoon. Then—and this is a stroke of genius—she put each of the slices of bread into the pan to soak up some of the salty fat. She let them steam a bit, so the bread wouldn't dry out in the oven while we were heating the cheese. I never thought of that.

She cut each round of goat cheese in half lengthwise and laid them on top of the toasts with just a drip of honey. While the toasts were heating in the oven, she made a simple vinaigrette in the bottom of my largest salad bowl.

When we sat down, I did a quick calculation in my head. For perhaps eighteen euros, we had made an incredibly satisfying meal for eight people. It's a shame the proverbial goat-cheese man couldn't join us for lunch. He might have stuck around.

✍

"IT'S YOUR BIRTHDAY tomorrow?" said Isabelle. "We'll bake a cake!" She sounded genuinely excited. Gwendal and I are not so great with celebrations. Our birthdays are ten days apart in May and we've been so busy these past few years that the day itself sometimes passes almost without mention. I can't remember the last time I really celebrated my birthday. When I turned thirty in Paris I didn't have enough friends to throw a party. We went for a quiet dinner with my parents, which I remember thinking at the time was vaguely depressing.

I have a friend who recently turned forty. "We decided to go away to this super-fancy hotel in Cabo for two days," she told me. "I thought about having a party, but then I realized we were going to spend exactly the same amount of money and I was going to do all the work." It was a reminder that whether it's making the canapés or securing a reservation at the "right" restaurant, we've made celebrating expensive—and stressful. There's got to be another way.

On the morning of my birthday, I was banished from the kitchen. Gwendal came back from a walk—alone.

"Where are Grégoire and the girls?"

"They took the long way home."

When I was finally allowed back into the kitchen, the whole family was gathered around the kitchen table. There was a cake—a simple sponge layered with raspberry jam and topped with a melted chocolate glaze that slid down the side in appealing drips. There was a bouquet of flowers from the field across from the chapel: yellow mustard grass, purple flowering sage, and delicate white canopies that Marion told me were actually the flowers of wild carrots.

Tears sprang to my eyes. "So that's what you meant by taking the long way home."

This wasn't even a big birthday, just part of the late thirties' countdown to the big four-oh. It's the nicest I can remember.

⁓

BOB AND JANE, a British couple who retired to the region, live up a winding road on the outskirts of Céreste. It's the kind of dirt track that turns to tire-spinning mud with the first rainfall, quickly becomes impassable in the winter snow, and dries into deep ruts in the spring. By now, tufts of early-summer grass had appeared in the center of the road. It was cherry season (how did it sneak up so quickly *again*) and Bob and Jane had invited us, as part of our first ice cream experiments, to come and pluck their tree.

Bob and Jane's cherry tree is a beauty. It sits at the bottom of the garden, just beyond the pool by the old wooden shed. Branches of waxy leaves shade neat bunches of yellow cherries touched with the merest blush of red. It would make a wonderful children's story: a gossamer fairy, her wings glowing in the Provençal twilight, assigned to paint each one by hand.

We brought three buckets, the largest ones we could find. Our plan was to pick fast, rush back to the blender, puree the cherries, and freeze them to make sorbet. Up the ladder, I couldn't help tasting—the cherries were tart; the sweetness followed behind, like a baby sister trying to keep up with the boys. If we could get this taste, this sunny glow, into a bowl, we might be onto something.

Let me say in my own defense: Nature hates amateurs. Amateurs are disrespectful. Amateurs die trying. It's worth noting that all the books written by castaways washed up on a desert island are written by *survivors*. The people who suck dew off the leaves and know which berries will kill you and which ones will make a nice pie. If you and I were shipwrecked together, I could do you a very fine rendition of *Paradise Lost*. Someone else will have to reinvent the telephone.

I'd had fair warning. When we picked cherries in Jean's garden last summer, he made sure we picked them with the stems attached, carefully turning just below the burr-like knob that held them to the branch so a bunch would grow back in the same spot the next year. But as we were going directly back to the kitchen, we decided to take a shortcut, ripping the ripe cherries straight off the stem and dropping them into the plastic buckets below. When I realized our error, it was too late. A ripe cherry is like a water balloon; our unceremonious plucking had bruised the delicate skin and created a leak. As we finished filling the first bucket, the cherries were already slick with sugary juice, the top layers pressing the ones underneath as surely as if I'd been crushing them with my bare feet, like the episode of *I Love Lucy* where Lucille Ball makes wine with her toes.

It seemed a shame, if not downright impolite, to leave without accepting Bob's offer of a white wine spritzer by the pool. The whole time we were there, the juice was slowly seeping from our precious cherries. The flies, at least, seemed to approve of our method, buzzing excitedly around the buckets, rubbing their stick legs together in delight. As we strapped Alexandre into his car seat, I was overwhelmed with the heady perfume of oxidation, the slightly regurgitated smell of warm sugar.

The rest of the evening was a race against time. We weren't equipped for such an operation. A single cherry pitter is fine for Jean's *clafoutis,* but when you've got a whole tree to de-stone, it's something like emptying the ocean with a thimble. Some of the juice made it into the ceramic dish on the kitchen table; most of it ran down the blue veins on the inside of my wrist straight to the bend of my elbow. On contact with the air, the sunny color of the cherry pulp quickly turned a mustardy brown, the color of my childhood corduroys. By midnight, Gwendal and I, not to mention the blender, the table, and the floor were slick with cherry juice. My engagement ring was glued in place by bits of pulp caught between the pale sapphire and the tiny diamonds. The kitchen smelled like an overboiled hard candy, a cherry compost heap. I wiped my nose on the shoulder of my T-shirt; the juice had made it only as far as my biceps.

I licked some juice off my palm. It tasted like a cherry soda someone had spilled in a parking lot—three days ago. "I think we should go to bed," I said, trying to maintain an optimistic tone.

By the time we shut the freezer and turned out the light, the entire contents of that lovely cherry tree had been reduced to three plastic containers of pale brown slurry that resembled nothing so much as...diarrhea.

The next day was a Sunday; I called Maya in LA.

"Sorry," I said, yawning into the phone. "I was up half the night making cherry sorbet."

"Are you pregnant?"

"No." I tried to think how to explain. "We're just starting an ice cream company."

Recipes for a Simple Celebration

WARM GOAT CHEESE SALAD
Salade de Chèvre Chaud

This is a favorite family lunch—light, yet totally satisfying. That Sunday with Isabelle, we served strawberries and cream for dessert. The kids ignored the cream; they just poured a little white sugar onto their plates and, holding the strawberries by the stems, rolled them around to coat.

1 large head frisée lettuce
3 tomatoes, cut into eighths or sixteenths
1 tablespoon olive oil
14 ounces lardons (pork belly, pancetta, or slab bacon cut into ¼-inch-by-1-inch cubes)
6 slices of whole-grain bread, each about ½ inch thick
6 individual goat cheeses, 3 ounces each
Drizzle of honey

For the dressing

½ cup olive oil
1 tablespoon plus 2 teaspoons red wine or sherry vinegar
1 level teaspoon Dijon mustard
1 good pinch of coarse sea salt
A grind of black pepper

Preheat the oven to 400°F.

Wash and dry the lettuce; set aside. Place tomatoes in a small bowl.

In a large frying pan, heat 1 tablespoon olive oil and brown the lardons. Turn off the heat, remove the lardons with a slotted spoon, and mix them with the tomatoes. Take each slice of bread and press into the bacon fat, coating both sides. Leave the slices of bread in the pan, cover, and let rest for a few minutes; this lets the bread steam a bit, so it's less likely to dry out when you put it in the oven with the cheese.

Meanwhile, in a small jar or airtight container, mix the ingredients for the dressing and give it a good shake to combine. This recipe makes enough for several salads—no worries, it keeps in the fridge for weeks.

Line a cookie sheet with aluminum foil. Cut the rounds of goat cheese in half horizontally, into 2 disks. Lay 2 disks of cheese on each piece of bread; drizzle with honey.

Bake on the center rack for 12 to 15 minutes, until the goat cheese is heated through.

While the toasts are in the oven, put the lettuce in a large bowl, add 2 tablespoons of dressing, toss to coat, taste. Add a bit more if you like, but don't drown things. Mix in the tomatoes and lardons. Divide the salad among six plates. Put the goat-cheese toasts on top. Serve immediately.

Serves 6

A SIMPLE BIRTHDAY CAKE
Gâteau au Yaourt

My impromptu birthday cake was in fact a yogurt cake—still one of my favorite things ever to come out of a French kitchen. This is the first cake most French children learn to bake; it's incredibly fast and easy.

1½ cups flour
A pinch of fine sea salt
1 teaspoon baking powder

1 teaspoon baking soda
1 cup plain whole-milk yogurt
1 cup sugar
½ cup vegetable oil
Zest of one lemon
3 eggs

Preheat your oven to 350°F. Line a 10-inch cake pan with a sheet of parchment paper.

In a small bowl, sift together flour, salt, baking powder, and baking soda.

In a medium bowl, whisk together yogurt, sugar, oil, and lemon zest until sugar is dissolved. Add the eggs one by one and whisk to incorporate. Add the flour mixture and stir to combine.

Bake for 40 minutes, until firm and golden. Cool on a rack, then unmold and cool completely. It's terrific plain, but to make it birthday-festive, cut the cake in half horizontally, into 2 equal-size disks. Spread the bottom half with ½ cup raspberry jam, then gently replace the top layer. Dust with powdered sugar and get out the candles.

Tip: If you want to make a super-simple chocolate glaze like Isabelle did with the kids: Melt together 5 ounces of dark chocolate with 4 tablespoons each of light cream and water. Pour evenly over the cake, letting some dribble down the sides.

Serves 8; store wrapped in aluminum foil

CHAPTER 15

Uphill Battle

This wall needs to come down," said Rod, patting the door frame above his head. Never mind that it is directly under their fireplace upstairs; the beam is probably holding up their living-room floor.

Gwendal, Rod, and I are standing in the soon-to-be ice cream shop. The project is taking shape. Like a team of bank robbers, everyone has a job: Gwendal is in charge of production, Rod in charge of construction, and I am in charge of cookies—and aesthetics. When we get through with it, the vaulted ceiling and exposed stone walls of Rod and Angela's cellar will be very cozy—and, in the summertime, very cool. When Mom gets here, she and I can roam the flea markets looking for mismatched teapots and maybe a three-tiered cake stand. We'll need some marble-top tables. Kitchen space is limited, but I'd love to find a glass-fronted buffet to store the ice cream dishes.

Looks like we are going to get those interest-free loans after all. One of the masons working on the shop is on the jury. He keeps walking in while Gwendal is covered head to toe in plaster dust from clearing the old joints in the rough stone walls. I think this helped our chances. It reassured them he's not afraid to get his hands dirty and counters the more dilettante aspects of his résumé. I guess the dreaded goat-cheese man never got plaster dust in his hair.

We still don't have a name. I can never seem to get going with my writing until I have a great first sentence, and that's how I feel about this; it's hard to imagine what we want our ice cream company to be without first knowing what it will be called. Lots of artisans in France use their own names for their brands, but the only famous Gwendal in France is an Olympic figure-skating champion—not exactly what we're going for. I was up in the office looking for the checkbook when I noticed it, a folded paper hanging off the top of the art deco armoire, the one with the mirrored door hanging by a thread (the décor in here hasn't improved). It was a six-by-four-foot poster for one of Gwendal's favorite childhood films, a swashbuckling Technicolor adventure from the 1950s. He had named his consulting company Avanti!, after a Billy Wilder film from the 1970s; why not continue the tradition? I brought the un-furled poster downstairs, holding it over my head so it wouldn't drag on the floor. It was perfect—just weird enough for people to remember: Scaramouche—Adventures in Ice Cream.

So THIS IS why I pay my taxes. Today I took Alexandre to have his *goûter*—that's French for afternoon snack—at the new village crèche he will attend as of next week. I've decided that state-subsidized day care (from the age of eight weeks) and the right to full-day preschool (for every potty-trained child over the age of three) are the funda-mental secrets of low-stress French parenting. Simply put, the kids are out of the house a lot longer, and a lot earlier, than in the States. Funny, I think I was just starting to get the hang of being a mom (now that Alexandre and I can have a conversation about Dr. Seuss), and now he's going to forge his own way in the plastic playhouse—as he should.

My mom remembers my first day of school very clearly. Me walking down the flagstone path, Mary Janes on my feet, plastic lunchbox in hand. Now I know why. Alexandre is out in the world now. If we do our job right—if he spreads his wings, as I hope he will—except for rice pudding, laundry, and, hopefully, the occasional bit of advice, he's never coming back.

After filling Alexandre's cup with water, I tried to steer him away from the food table. Thoughts of his future girlfriends and career in extreme sports aside, my immediate concern is to keep my son from giving his American roots a bad name by eating too much cake. He actually gets his love of cake from his French father, but where cultural stereotypes are concerned, you can never be too careful.

⁓

IT'S A PRESIDENTIAL election year—both in France and in the United States. I'm feeling the cultural dissonance. François Hollande, the French Socialist candidate, is proposing a 70 percent tax rate on salary after the first million euros, which makes the capitalist in me want to flee to Ohio. But when I describe the services available to working mothers in France, my American friends are incredulous, then furious. My son goes to a brand-new facility with a fully qualified staff and a five-to-one child/adult ratio. He goes from 9:00 a.m. to 6:00 p.m., five days a week. It costs a whopping 2.80 euros an hour—on a sliding scale. We are at the very top.

They say all politics is personal. I hate to sound trivial, but the thing that impresses me most about the crèche is the lunch menu. They post it in the foyer at the beginning of every week, right next to the box of plastic foot covers they ask us to wear to keep the floor clean. I feel like I'm looking at one of the founding documents of

French society—the culinary equivalent of the Declaration of the Rights of Man. So this is how they make little French people—they start with the lentil salad and work up from there.

I'm sure there's a method to all this. I went down the list: Wednesday was *macèdoine mayo* (a salad of carrots, turnips, green beans, and green peas in mayonnaise), followed by roast beef with mashed potatoes, cheese, and fruit compote for dessert. Many of the vegetables seem to be up front. Do they introduce new foods in the appetizer course, when the kids are hungriest? In my general enthusiasm, I asked to come in and observe a meal for research. The director smiled the way she does at the kids. Then I was politely, but mysteriously, put off.

"They didn't say no," I explained to Gwendal that evening. "But they didn't say yes either."

"Of course they don't want you to visit during the day. Not when Alexandre is there. It's not fair to the other kids. It's about equality. The crèche is a place where parents are not. They get all the kids to accept this—then you walk in, and suddenly everyone wants to know where their mommy is, why she can't come to lunch."

Sometimes I forget: Liberté, Égalité, Fraternité. Égalité is right there in the middle, flattening things out, while at the same time holding things together.

When I talk to my American friends about the crèche, half of them think I'm making it up, half of them want to emigrate. On my last trip back to the States, I had lunch with a friend, a fellow writer. She and I lead sort of parallel lives. She is married to a French artist, and they have a son who is exactly Alexandre's age. But they live in Brooklyn, and she has just started filling out preschool applications. "It's a nightmare," she said, taking a bite of her salmon sashimi. (When I'm back in New York, I try to make sure as many outings as possible involve sushi.)

"We are looking at three schools; one is twelve thousand dollars, and one is eighteen thousand." I almost spit miso soup all over the table. "For a half day. There's only six spots and they have this sibling policy, where brothers and sisters of current students get priority. And that's if he gets in." He didn't.

I've also had this conversation with American friends in France. "There's no way we could afford to go back to the States now," said Michelle, who has a French husband, two kids, and a nice tax-exempt salary with a Paris-based NGO. "How would we pay for college?" This kind of educational calculus goes on between every international couple we know. The math is intimidating. Tuition at my college alma mater is now just over $47,000 a year. Add in room, board, books, and beer, and that's nearly a quarter of a million dollars for an undergraduate degree—God knows what it will cost in fifteen years. The average salary in France is between 25,000 and 30,000 euros. Even when Gwendal was earning what the French consider hefty executive pay, he wasn't bringing in what a Goldman Sachs analyst makes the first year out of business school in the States. We couldn't have saved for college if we'd wanted to. There's no such thing as a college IRA in France.

Once again, this is a conversation that French parents just aren't having—at least, not at this level. Tuition at the Sorbonne this year costs between two hundred and five hundred euros, plus an obligatory two hundred euros for health insurance. Gwendal earned a full-time employee's salary while he was getting his PhD. The super-competitive Grandes Écoles—France's Ivy League—are absolutely free.

Of course, my son is just at the beginning of his schooling in France. But I've heard the talk—the French teach to the middle, stifle creativity, and reward conformity. If I'm being honest with myself, I'd like Alexandre to spend a portion of his education in the States. I'd like his classics to be Shakespeare and Steinbeck as well as Racine and Proust. I'd like him to be able to write a term paper on

King Lear, not just a quick e-mail, in English. I want Alexandre to believe that his opinions are valuable, work can be passionate, and that his very best effort will get him somewhere in life. I don't want his American-ness to be some kind of recessive trait, a dangling modifier. It feels like my job to promote these things, and my job alone. I start with the little things. He likes raw cookie dough, so there must be an American in there somewhere.

And if we can't pay for Stanford? (A mom has to dream.) What if Alexandre is two hundred thousand dollars in debt when he turns twenty-one? What kind of life choices does that really give him: doctor, lawyer, banker, Internet millionaire? He certainly won't be able to work in a museum or a cinema archive like we did.

In an election year, these questions seem particularly urgent. What kind of options do we want for our children, and what are we willing to pay for them?

"Eighteen point five percent. That's terrifying." We were in the kitchen listening to the radio. The French have two rounds in their presidential elections. Everyone gets equal airtime during the monthlong campaign, and the two candidates with the largest percentages in the *premier tour* run against each other in the final election. The Front National, the extreme-right party, came in third, only a few percentage points behind the Socialist Party and the centerish-right UMP. Immigration is a soapbox issue with the Front National—they have a sinister way of equating immigration and security issues, deliberately lumping together illegal immigrants and anyone of North African, African, and Roma origins—even if they were born in France.

"I better get on that citizenship application," I said to Gwendal as I spread raspberry jam on my toast. "You forget—I'm still an immigrant. If Marine Le Pen has her way, soon no one will have the right to become French."

Asking for French citizenship is not a formality; it's an admission. Acceptance of a worldview. The truth is, I'd been putting it off. Though I've been living in France for ten years, paying taxes and making homemade mayonnaise, I still don't quite exist here under my own steam.

My legal status, my work permit, my health insurance—my very presence in France is entirely dependent on my being married to Gwendal. I pay into a retirement account, but I can't vote. I have the right to work in France—but not in the rest of the European Union. Alexandre has been a dual citizen since birth, but if tomorrow Gwendal wanted to accept a job in London, or Krakow, or Rome, I would be transformed into one of those "trailing spouses." What a terrible term—it makes your life partner sound like a piece of toilet paper stuck to the bottom of your shoe.

Applying for citizenship now requires a French-language test, and a woman I know in the village heard they were thinking of adding a cultural part to the exam. What would that look like? Should I memorize the names of French presidents or the lyrics to Edith Piaf songs? This is the myth of culture, that there is a set of facts or opinions everyone shares that somehow make up a country. Do you call what happened in Algeria from 1954 to 1962 a war or a police action? The questions say as much as the answers.

Americans are lucky; we can maintain dual citizenship. I won't be forced to choose. As much as I love my life in France, I can't imagine renouncing the country of my birth. The longer I spend outside the United States, the more attached I become to the American Dream. Europe is great at celebrating the past and enjoying the present, but at hurling itself into the future—not so much. That said, it's all well and good to say that the French hate risk and discourage entrepreneurship, but without the security of Gwendal's eighteen months of unemployment benefits—at 50 percent of his old salary—there is no way we could take the leap into our new ice cream business.

If I want to put in my application before the end of the year, there's a mountain of papers to be gathered: fingerprints, criminal background check, marriage certificates, official translations. But it's time—past time. My life is here, my family is here. I should share a passport with my son and husband. In the event of a biblical apocalypse, we should all be running for the same embassy. That, and it would be nice to be in the same line at the airport.

I WAS WALKING back from the butcher at noon and ran into our neighbor Josette with her straw basket of errands tucked under her arm.

"How is Alexandre settling in at the crèche?"

"He loves it. *Merci.*"

"*Alors, c'est pour quand la princesse.* So, when are you going to have a little girl?"

I don't get it. The French never ask personal questions. It could take months of preliminary small talk to find out what someone does for a living, if his parents are alive or dead. But now that Alexandre is firmly ensconced at the crèche, people keep coming up to me on the street and asking when we are having another baby. The state makes it so easy, they can't imagine anyone would have one child by choice. Or does my American tummy already look pregnant to them? Ugh.

A Meal Inspired by the Village Crèche

GRATED CARROT SALAD
Salade de Carottes Râpées

The crèche works magic. I didn't even know this had entered my son's diet until he asked me to buy a version of it at the airport on our way back to the States. This salad uses the French trick of serving vegetables as an appetizer, when the kids are hungriest and therefore most open to new tastes. Our family likes lemon juice, but if your kids don't, you can easily make it with just the olive oil.

2 cups grated carrots
Squeeze of lemon juice
1 tablespoon olive oil
Small pinch of coarse sea salt
⅛ cup golden raisins

Grate the carrots (one of my least favorite kitchen tasks—I buy pre-grated). Toss with the other ingredients.

Serves 4 as an appetizer. It's also great with lettuce on a roast pork sandwich.

SAUSAGE WITH FLAGEOLET BEANS AND ZUCCHINI
Saucisses aux Flageolets et Courgettes Fondues

Beans are a staple of the traditional French table, so, naturally, they trickle down to the crèche. Delicate light green flageolets are often served with lamb, but I prefer to cook them slowly with sausage and zucchini so the salty goodness of the meat has time to permeate the beans. This is family comfort food—great after a hike or a day of skiing. I normally like my zucchini al dente, but in this recipe they are meant to be soft—baby-food soft.

1 tablespoon olive oil

6 saucisse fraîche, *best-quality pork sausages*

1 onion, chopped

1 pound frozen or dried flageolet beans

¼ cup sherry or brandy

½ teaspoon herbes de Provence

2 pinches cinnamon

Good grind of black pepper

1 bay leaf

4 cups boiling water

3 small zucchini, cut into 2-inch chunks

In your largest sauté pan or Dutch oven, heat the olive oil and brown the sausages on one side. Flip the sausages and add the onion. Let the onion sauté while the sausage browns on the other side. When the sausages are browned and the onion is beginning to color, add the frozen beans (or dried beans that you have soaked overnight). Stir to coat with oil. Add the sherry or brandy and the spices, stir to combine. Cover with 4 cups boiling water.

Tuck the zucchini pieces among the beans. Bring to a boil, then lower the heat and simmer over a low flame, with the cover slightly ajar, for 40 minutes. Turn off the heat and leave to rest for a half hour if you can. The beans and zucchini will continue to soak up the liquid. Reheat gently and serve with Dijon mustard and parsley.

Serves 6

Tip: If you can't find frozen flageolet beans, use dried ones. You'll need to soak them overnight in a large quantity of cold water, then rinse. If you are starting with presoaked beans, the cooking time will probably be more than 40 minutes; more like 1 hour or even 90 minutes until they're tender. If you are using presoaked beans you may need more boiling water. The beans should be covered by about 1 inch when you begin; you can top up if it gets low. I can't, in good conscience, recommend canned beans for this recipe—they just get mushy.

DARK CHOCOLATE MOUSSE
Mousse au Chocolat

Dessert at the crèche is often fresh fruit, yogurt, or fruit compote, but occasionally there will be a hint of chocolate. French children start on dark chocolate from the beginning—think of the gorgeous melty bit in the center of a *pain au chocolat*. This is a decadent after-dinner mousse, the one Gwendal's mom makes every year for Christmas. It's so good, it was years before I found out that it's actually from her favorite diet book, *Je mange, donc je maigris,* by Michel Montignac (Editions J'ai Lu, 1994). If this is diet food, sign me up!

8 free-range eggs
14 ounces best-quality dark chocolate, 65–70 percent cacao (I use Lindt 70 percent cacao specialty cooking chocolate)
⅓ cup strong coffee or espresso
1 tablespoon good dark rum
Pinch of table salt

In two good-size mixing bowls, separate your eggs. Put the whites in the fridge. Chop the chocolate. Combine coffee, rum, and chocolate in the top of a double boiler. Melt *very* gently over just simmering water—you don't want to risk burning the chocolate. I turn the flame off once the water is heated; the steam is usually enough to get the job done.

Lightly whisk the egg yolks. Add slightly cooled chocolate mixture to the egg yolks and whisk immediately to combine (otherwise you end up with chocolate scrambled eggs). Remove the egg whites from the fridge and beat with a pinch of salt until stiff. Fold a third of the beaten egg whites into the chocolate mixture to lighten it. Add the rest of the egg whites and gently fold together until evenly combined.

Spoon into individual ramekins or a pretty glass bowl; cover with plastic wrap. Refrigerate for 6 hours, preferably overnight. The mousse is very rich, but not terribly sweet. Serve with a delicate butter cookie like *langue de chat* or almond *tuiles*.

Serves 8–10

Tip: As with any recipe that leans on a few essential ingredients, buy the best you can afford.

CHAPTER 16

Green-Bean Hour

It began with a piece of cake. Or maybe it began earlier. Much earlier.

When Gwendal and I picked Alexandre up from the crèche today, he ran straight past me and threw himself into his father's arms. Same old, same old. I tried to grab a hug as he ran by, but it was clear my arm was some kind of roadblock to him, a barrier he needed to get through.

The kid was famished, his 3:30 *goûter* at the crèche a distant memory. But 6:00 p.m. is a funny time in France. Too late for a snack, too early for a family dinner. We hadn't yet found a consistent solution.

When we got home Alexandre found the remains of my *palmier* on the kitchen table. A *palmier* is the French version of an elephant's ear, puff pastry doused with just enough butter and sugar to give it a caramelized crackle. I broke off a piece and gave him the rest. But then I came back, and as one of Alexandre's favorite Dr. Seuss stories might say, "That's where my troubles began." I chipped off a tiny bit of his half, a burned edge, and put it in my mouth.

Alexandre looked up at me in horror. "No broken, *pas* broken," he said, staring at the crumbs on the table. Bright hot tears spilled over onto his cheeks. He's almost three, and he understands both English and French, but he doesn't say *mine* yet—when he's feeling possessive, he uses the French: *à moi*.

"*Gâteau à moi. À moi,*" he wailed. He pointed to my mouth, then lurched at me and tried to stick his finger down my throat, as if he could extract the not-quite-digested bite from my stomach. "*À moi. À moi!*"

"I'm sorry, Alexandre, I thought it was to share." In truth, I was just being greedy—I knew it annoyed him if I broke the crust off his toast or took a bit of broccoli off his plate. The volume increased; he scratched at my lips, still searching for his lost bit of cake. "*Gâteau à moi! Gâteau à moi!*"

Alexandre is not a screamer. I can count on the fingers of one hand the tantrums he's had since he was born, usually the product of hunger or extreme fatigue. But he was inconsolable. We did what we normally do in these situations: took him upstairs to his room to cry it out. Over the next fifteen minutes, I made three trips up the stairs. He wouldn't let me past the baby gate. He worked himself into a fit, a kind of gasping, irrational rage that made his whole body tremble.

I came down again and stood with my back against the wall. I felt so weak. *How could I have this effect on him? Why is he so angry with me?*

When Gwendal finally went up, Alexandre clung to his father like a baby monkey, blond head glued to his shoulder. I watched from the doorway. Gwendal spoke to him softly, their foreheads pressed together. I heard the *sniff-sniff-sniff* that marks the end of a crisis.

Five minutes later, we were at the table. He started to smile and asked for his own plate, then speared chunks of pork roast and couscous and squash. Somewhere in between, he ate the rest of the *palmier*. I hadn't dared touch it. I decided this was not the time to make a fuss about eating dessert before dinner.

I picked up an asparagus—from my plate. "Would you like

one?" He opened his mouth like a baby bird and gingerly bit off the tip. I crunched a bite and gave it back to him. We ate the rest of the asparagus this way, one bite for him, one for me. "See," I said, a bit sheepishly, "sharing isn't so bad."

By bedtime, I was sure the worst was over. I loaded the dishwasher and wiped down the table while Gwendal read him a story. My limbs felt heavy. Somehow this had become our routine. Me down here, them up there.

When Gwendal came down, I decided to try my luck. I went up to Alexandre's room, smoothed his hair back from his forehead.

"I'm sorry we had a disagreement about the cake. Can we make up and have a hug?"

He looked at me and nodded, so solemnly. This fascinates me. I often wonder how his little bilingual brain knows what it means to "make up." How has he figured out these abstract emotional concepts when he sometimes looks at me blankly when I ask him to do something concrete, like put on his socks?

I wrapped him in my arms and stuck my nose into his neck. But instead of throwing his arms around me and laying his head on my shoulder, he kind of gingerly patted my back, the way he does when he comforts a younger child, and pulled away. I sucked in my breath. *Holy hell. I just got a pity hug from my son.*

When I met Gwendal, I thought I was living the last great love story of my life. That all the hurt, the rejection, the insecurity was past. But there are moments when Alexandre simply…dissolves me. I remember my first broken heart. I never thought anyone would make me feel this way again.

❧

ALEXANDRE WAS FINALLY asleep. I gently rearranged the covers over his bare feet. One arm was thrown carelessly over his head; his other hand clung to the trunk of the stuffed elephant he uses as a pillow. Over the past few months his baby fat has vanished; his knees are sharp and skinned, his blond hair hangs in uneven wisps, growing out from a bad haircut. I sat down on the edge of the bed. His toys and books were scattered at my feet: *The Sneetches,* and a pop-up dollhouse of Goldilocks and the Three Bears, the cardboard bears and their tiny bowls of oatmeal long since lost at the bottom of the toy chest. There was a miniature plastic sword and, a few inches away, a knight in full battle regalia. I've always loved to watch Alexandre sleep. It's the only time my relationship with my son is exactly the way I imagined it would be. The only time he lets me run my hand over his cheek without batting me away. When I can steal a kiss without a squirm.

Gwendal found me sitting on the edge of the bed. When he came in to give me his hand, I started to sniffle. He led me wordlessly out of the room and up the four or five creaky wooden stairs to our bed. After what seemed like hours of listening to Alexandre wail, it was my turn now. I started to sob, great heaving things, like a toddler myself. Tears rolled out of the corners of my eyes into the well of my ears. It took me almost as long as Alexandre to calm down. "He only ever wants to sit on your lap. And soon, he won't want to sit on anyone's lap at all." I couldn't speak, my voice was trapped somewhere in the pit of my stomach, and all that came out was a whispery croak. I barely know if I said it aloud: *And I'll have missed everything.*

∿

GOD KNOWS I didn't want to discuss this with my mother. But I did it anyway, reflexively, instinctively. I figure she's the only person who has to love me when I fail, and this one was a whopper. I was confused, mortified. I didn't want to admit to her that I had somehow tanked at something so basic, so important. Worse, that I had done it almost without noticing. Worse yet, that she had called it, called it from the beginning. I had spent a good portion of my son's early years standing on the outside looking in, not quite sure how to participate.

My mom hemmed and hawed, which she doesn't do unless she is about to say something she knows I'm not going to like. "I'm just trying to find a way to say this." *Great.* "I think you are finally realizing that you are going to have to put some time into this." *Here it comes.* "Let's be honest: you'd rather sit in your bed and read for an hour."

I was silent on the other end of the phone. *And what if that's true. Where is our other self—our selfish self—supposed to go when we have a baby? Does everyone else become a completely different person overnight? I can't be the only one who's having a hard time. Is everybody lying, or is nobody talking?* I was going to start crying again if I tried to say anything.

"Find an activity," she said. "One every day. Maybe you can cook with him. Do you still have those cookie cutters?" I did. "Roll out some dough. Make meat loaf; I don't care if you put parsley in the belly button." I hadn't thought about this in years. When I was little, even not so little, my mother and I would make meat loaf in the shape of a gingerbread man. She would give me slices of carrots for the eyes, black raisins for the buttons, and curly parsley for the hair. "But you have to enjoy it," she continued, gathering momentum, "not feel like you're putting in hard time. I don't know what I would do if it didn't come naturally to me, but I would do it. Whatever it was, I would do it."

"I think I'm going to go talk to someone," I said.

"I think that's great," she answered, sounding relieved. "You'll find someone to help you. Maybe a play therapist."

For him or for me? That's my mother, always looking for practical solutions. But what if it's deeper than that? I was not about to tell her that while she was giving me cheery coping strategies for today, any French psychoanalyst worth his salt would probably go hunting around for what went wrong in my own childhood.

"Don't worry," she said.

"I'm not worried," I blurted out. "I'm hurt. I feel so rejected. I don't even know how to describe this feeling. It's almost physical. Like getting slapped. It's like I'm failing at this bond that everyone in the world says is completely natural. I just think I want something from him that I'm never going to have."

When I express these anxieties to those around me, everyone has a different opinion. My husband tells me to go see an analyst; my mother says I have to work harder; and the lovely lady who runs the crèche simply says, "You are who you are." What's the answer? A? B? C? All of the above?

"Please don't give up," my mother said softly. "If you give up now, you're saying it's his fault. You're the adult. You're the one who can fix it." Suddenly, I felt a thud of recognition. She's right: I don't react like an adult in these situations. Alexandre has found a way to bring out the kid in me—she's scared and selfish, and so much more fragile than I'd like to admit.

When I got off the phone I resented my mother so badly. The only person I resented more than my mother was my son. How could I possibly have to work at this? My mom was a natural. My husband was a natural. Why not me?

I went downstairs and sat at the kitchen table, the marble cool under my hands. I thought about my own mother. How much did I really know about the person she was before she became my mom? I've seen photos of a toothy toddler; a buxom teen in a blue taffeta prom dress; a beautiful young married woman in a red evening gown, her jet-black hair tumbling over her shoulders. But I don't know what that woman was thinking, feeling. All I know is what she was to me. Everything. Alexandre doesn't care if I'm fulfilled, or depressed, or confused. All he knows about me is what I am to him, and what I am at the moment is unavailable.

My whole life, I've run from anything that didn't come easy. Anything I wasn't naturally gifted at—adding fractions, reading music, driving a car—I just walked away. I have a whole life, a lovely life, built around sidestepping everything I'm not good at. It's a crappy strategy—and you'd be surprised how long you can get away with it. But I couldn't, I wouldn't, sidestep my son.

❧

I NEEDED A plan.

The first thing we decided to do was shorten his day at the crèche. Nine to six was too much. He was exhausted, starving, the time between school and bedtime too compressed. I would pick him up at five, and that hour would be ours to fill however he wanted.

How to fill an hour, just the two of us? I realized now how few tools I had at my disposal. Maybe I should have read some books after all. I didn't know what was going on in my son's head. The only thing I could think of was to ask him to make dinner with me.

"Want me to go with you?" Gwendal asked on the first day. My love, my gentle enabler. "No," I said emphatically. "I'll go."

When I arrived at the crèche Alexandre was sitting on a tricycle reading a book about bananas. When I finally got him to look up at me, the first thing he did was ask for his father. "Papa?" he said. I took a deep breath.

"Papa's working," I answered. Gwendal and Rod were clearing the cellar, setting up a test lab where the wine bottles used to be.

"Papa?"

"Alexandre, would you like to go to the *boulangerie* and buy some bread?" Distraction was my friend.

"*Oui.*"

He took my hand as we walked through the parking lot and across the street to the bakery.

Inside, I lifted him up to scan the cases. "What would you like for your *goûter?*" He pointed to a *brioche au sucre*. He left clutching the end of the white waxed-paper bag in one hand. He seemed relaxed; the early hour made him calmer, less hysterical to eat.

We had a little talk on the way back from the crèche. "Alexandre," I said, working up my courage. "Would you like it if Mommy picked you up early from the crèche every day, and we went home and cooked together? Would you like to help Mommy cook?"

"Yah," he said with a smile. *Yah* was the Germanesque combo of "yes" and "yeah" that he was using lately to express casual enthusiasm when something pleased him. Encouraged, I continued. "Mommy's writing a whole new book and there are lots of recipes to try. Will you be my assistant chef"—I stopped, searching, struggling to locate the fun, preschool word—"will you be my little helper?"

Behind the post office, Alexandre bent to examine the gravel at the foot of the public fig tree. Even after two years of village life, I found it difficult to slow my pace. *We have nowhere to be,* I said slowly to myself, flexing my fingers, *nowhere to be.* We walked slowly up the hill. He hid himself around the corner; I tiptoed up behind him and then popped out with a giant "Boo!"

These were the longest days of the year. The sun was still high, and five o'clock felt like noon. "Would you like to sit outside?" I asked, perching myself on the stone steps in front of the house. I went inside to get Alexandre a napkin, and when I got back, it looked like little mice had been at the brioche. He'd nibbled all the sugar off the top in tiny bites and was just starting in on the sides. I smiled, thinking of my special childhood method for unscrewing an Oreo cookie. Why had I never noticed these details before?

For dinner, we snapped the tips off the slender haricots verts. He broke a few in half before he got the hang of it. Me *goûter*. Me taste. We counted as he marched the beans, like toy soldiers, across the table. One, two, three, four. *Un, deux, trois, quatre.*

I gave him the fork and let him stab the sweet potatoes, guiding his way when he came too close to my hand.

I admit it, it was a long hour. Before I left for the crèche, I had put a cake in the oven, and I checked it three times. Once at 5:23, once at 5:44, and again at 5:50.

Dinner was normal that night, uneventful.

∽

MONDAY AFTER SCHOOL, I picked up where I'd left off. When I entered the crèche he said, "Mama," with a big smile and ran to me. He let me pick him up before he asked where Daddy was. "Papa's working, sweet boy," I said. "We'll see him later."

Today, I promised him we would make a cake together. He took a little red basket outside the superette and dropped the yogurts to the bottom with a thud. I tried to avoid the same treatment with the eggs. Alexandre wanted to carry the bag. "Too heavy, *Maman*." He took one handle, I took the other.

We walked home through the tall grass of the public laundry lines to the mulberry tree (public, like the fig tree). The lavender field below was just beginning to color, the neat rows of violet rounded like powder puffs. "Want to go see if there are any berries on the mulberry tree?" *Wow, there's a sentence I never imagined coming out of my urban mouth.* "See, look, you can only take the dark ones."

Squashed berries littered the ground. "We're a little late, Boo."

"What a waste," I said. "Wasst," he repeated as he jumped over a pile of fallen mulberries.

He climbed to the medieval garden, threw gravel, climbed the steps, walked along the wall. Then did it again. And again. We marched like the elephants in *The Jungle Book*. I cupped my hand to make the sound of a trumpet: "Charge!"

It took us an hour to get home. A hundred yards as the crow flies. But when I had nothing to do but be with him, instead of being annoying, it was kind of nice.

Because of our leisurely walk, we were a little late getting started with the cake. He cackled every time we broke an egg. He has this great Wile E. Coyote cartoon laugh. I wish I could bottle it, the best medicine, the fountain of youth itself.

"Me *tourne*. Me *tourne*," he said proudly.

"Yes, sweet boy, you stir."

Every time I tried to remove the spatula from his hand, he started a low growl. So each time I needed the implement, I had to make an exchange, one spatula for a lemon and a grater.

I took some apricots, smooth and ripe, out of the fridge. "Let's make a face," I said, thinking back to my mother's meat-loaf man. "*Pas abricots,* no apricots." He changed his mind when he bit into one.

In the end, the cake with the apricot face made it into the oven. The batter looked a little lumpy. I think I used the wrong flour. I definitely took it out too early; there were soggy bits around the fruit. "This is the best cake I've ever had," I said, as I cut him a second slice. And it was.

At dinner that night, Alexandre kept putting his forehead to mine. Petting my shoulder. "Gâteau, Maman, gâteau, Maman. Me *tourne*."

Yes, sweet boy, you stirred all by yourself.

I felt so much better. He was the same happy boy, but suddenly, almost magically, I was a part of that happiness. I felt so thankful I could have cried all over again. I marveled at his easy forgiveness, his willingness to leap into something better. He let me in, as if I were the new girl at school, without fanfare or recrimination. He let me in, I suppose, because I finally took the time to knock.

That night I let Gwendal load the dishwasher while I went upstairs to read Alexandre a bedtime story. He pointed to the big book of Dr. Seuss. I picked it up. He pushed it out of my hand and reached over my legs, grabbed my shoulder. I couldn't figure out what he was doing. *Oh, sweet boy.*

He was trying to get up on my lap.

Three Recipes That Start to Make Things Better

PUFF-PASTRY "BUTTERFLY" COOKIES
Palmiers

In the States, we call these elephant ears, but I think they look more like butterflies. *Palmiers* are a great after-school project. After you cut the strips of dough, the kids can help you roll them into butterfly wings.

2 tablespoons butter
1 sheet puff pastry
⅔ cup sugar
Good pinch of coarse sea salt

Preheat your oven to 450°F. In a small saucepan or the microwave, melt the butter.

Place two large sheets of parchment paper one on top of the other. Place the puff pastry on top and sprinkle evenly with ⅓ cup sugar. Lightly press the sugar into the dough with a rolling pin. Puff pastry in France is round, and in the States it comes in rectangles, but either way, you want to roll out the dough so it is closer to a square.

Lift the top sheet of parchment paper and gently flip the dough onto the bottom one. Sprinkle the other side of the dough with ⅓ cup sugar, pressing it in lightly with the rolling pin. Cut the dough in ½-inch strips. Take a strip of dough and roll both ends toward the middle. Turn the cookie on its side. You'll end with something that looks like a child's drawing of butterfly wings.

Transfer the rolled cookies to a baking sheet lined with your first piece of parchment paper. Space them at least 1½ inches apart. Using a pastry brush, dab the tops of the cookies with the melted butter. Sprinkle on the salt and some of the sugar that's left on the other sheet of parchment paper. Bake for 10 to 11 minutes on one side, until lightly browned underneath. Turn and bake 4 to 5 minutes more. Watch them carefully—you want the *palmiers* to caramelize but not burn once the buttered side is down. Leave them on the baking sheet for 5 minutes, then transfer to a cooling rack.

Serve with espresso or ice cream (or both)!

Makes about 25 cookies

MIDNIGHT PEAR QUICK BREAD
Gâteau Maman

Along with the traditional yogurt cake (see page 235), this is our most frequent mother-son baking project. He calls it "mommy cake," and I can't help but be flattered that I have a dessert named in my honor, like a raspberry pavlova. This recipe was created by the collision of desire and constraint. Desire: Zucchini bread at 10:00 on a Thursday night. Constraint(s): No zucchini, only a half a cup of canola oil, and a village with nary a store open past 7:30. The result was a pear-and-olive-oil quick bread that surpassed my original intentions in every way. It's great for packed lunches, teatime, or breakfast the next morning with a spoonful of *fromage frais* (try Greek yogurt or whipped cream cheese in the U.S.) and some apple-kiwi jam.

3 cups whole-wheat flour
2½ teaspoons pumpkin pie spice (ginger, clove, cinnamon, nutmeg)
⅛ teaspoon fresh ground nutmeg
½ teaspoon baking powder
1 teaspoon baking soda
½ teaspoon table salt
1 large handful golden raisins
3 eggs
½ cup vegetable oil
½ cup olive oil

½ *cup white sugar*
½ *cup brown sugar (or raw sugar)*
2 *cups grated pear (very ripe)*
2 *teaspoons vanilla extract (or 1 teaspoon of ground vanilla powder)*

Preheat oven to 350°F.

Combine dry ingredients in a medium mixing bowl.

In a large mixing bowl, beat eggs, add oils and sugars, whisk to combine. Add pear and vanilla; combine.

Add the flour mixture to the wet ingredients in two additions; stir just enough to combine.

Grease two loaf pans. Divide the batter between the two. Bake for 45 minutes or until skewer comes out clean. Cool for 10 minutes. Turn out on a wire rack to cool completely. Serve warm or at room temperature. Also great toasted with plain yogurt and jam.

Makes 2 loaves, each serves 6. I usually freeze the second loaf and bake it straight from the freezer. Start checking at 50 minutes.

Tip: Vanilla powder is just that, a powder made from ground vanilla beans. It gives you a straight-up vanilla flavor, and the nice visual effect of little black dots is similar to using the seeds of a vanilla bean. Make sure you buy pure unsweetened vanilla powder—without added sugar. You may have to go to an upscale supermarket to find it, or order it online. It will be more costly than vanilla extract, but I use less. I typically substitute 1 teaspoon of vanilla powder for 2 teaspoons of vanilla extract.

GREENS BEANS WITH BACON
Haricots Verts aux Lardons

This is beyond a shadow of a doubt Alexandre's favorite dinner. And what's not to like: bright colors, sweet and salty contrasts, and, of course, bacon. I serve the sweet potatoes cut in two with a dollop of plain yogurt. Alexandre likes using my mother's silver asparagus tongs to serve the green beans himself.

4 medium sweet potatoes (I prefer long, relatively skinny ones)
1½ pounds skinny haricots verts (use regular green beans in a pinch)
2 tablespoons olive oil
7 ounces lardons (cubes of smoked slab bacon or pork belly); if your brand
   is super-salty, you may want to use less
A generous grinding of black pepper

Preheat your oven to 350°F.

Rinse the sweet potatoes and make a shallow 2-inch slice in the top of each. Roast in the oven for 60 to 90 minutes, until perfectly tender.

Wash the haricots verts; leave them in the strainer with a bit of water clinging to them. (If you are using thicker American-style green beans, you'll want to blanch them in boiling water for 1 minute, then rinse with cold water and proceed. If you are using the thinner French haricots verts, there's no need.)

In your largest sauté pan, heat olive oil. Add lardons and sauté until they are well browned and have released most of their fat, about 5 minutes. Remove the bacon with a slotted spoon; drain on a paper towel. Add the beans to the hot fat, stir to coat. Cover and leave over medium-high heat for 5 minutes. Open the lid and toss the beans. Cover and cook 3 minutes more. Open the lid and toss again; by this point some of the beans will have started to char—which I love. Close the lid and cook for 3 minutes more. Add a generous grinding of black pepper. Transfer to a serving dish and top with the lardons. Serve with the sweet potatoes. I sometimes add a whole-grain and chickpea salad (see page 138) if I'm in the mood for a more substantial meal.

Serves 2 adults and 2 very happy kids

CHAPTER 17

The Vanilla Diaries

This summer I am looking at the market—at everything, really—with new eyes. All my favorite things are back in bloom. Maybe Alexandre and I can bake a raspberry tart this weekend. We should definitely test a tomato sorbet for the ice cream shop. One of the restaurants in town asked if we'd be making a tomato-basil sorbet, but that sounds kind of icky to me, like eating frozen spaghetti sauce.

My relationship with Alexandre has blossomed as well. It sounds crazy, but with the extra effort, in a matter of weeks, our relationship feels transformed. Every step forward I take, he takes two. I have finally found a place for myself in our little family. I no longer feel like an outsider.

Alexandre and I have continued our cooking time together. I love the proximity; he loves the cookies. He loves shelling white beans and peas and slicing zucchini. (For a kid on the cusp of his third birthday, he's not bad with a knife.) I taught him the proper way to walk while holding scissors, which is just as well, because yesterday he almost tripped over his toy fire engine on the way to the herb garden to cut some thyme. While I was chopping a shallot, I asked him to transfer the beans from a plastic bag to the bowl, thinking it would take the better part of an hour. But Alexandre's no fool; he emptied the whole lot in one go, scattering only three on the floor. He still uses beans for counting practice, curving them like snakes around the cutting board.

There's a new stand in the Reillanne market; the man sells a mix of salad greens with edible flowers: marigolds, borage, nasturtium. They would look beautiful on top of an ice cream sundae.

Gwendal and I have been talking a lot about what we want the shop to be. We'd like it to reflect our personalities, be a positive addition to the community—and, of course, share all of the fabulous local products within arm's reach. Alexandre's music teacher in Reillanne had to stop her classes; it was too expensive to hire an employee to help her oversee the little kids. I wonder if there's enough room for her to do it at Scaramouche. We could get a commitment from the parents, one extra adult every week to help.

In the town where I grew up there's an ice cream parlor called Bischoff's, family-owned since 1934. It's where we went in our tutus after ballet recitals, where we bought Easter jelly beans and celebrated elementary-school graduations. The employees, young and old, wore small paper hats like upside-down rowboats. They still make wonderful cherry vanilla ice cream and their own wet walnuts. I've been working on a recipe for homemade hot fudge.

Instead of Bischoff's brown Formica booths, I'd like wrought-iron garden chairs and a marble-top bar with a glass candy jar. I don't know what we would do without Rod; he's not just our business partner, he's like our very own village Leonardo, finding quirky solutions to problems as they arise. At the moment he's designing a curved bench that hugs the back wall of the cellar so we can hide the necessary water pump—and so a couple can sit side by side *en amoureux,* sharing a banana split. Though it's not very French, we've decided to put a banana split on the menu. I used to share one with my dad at the local Dairy Queen.

I picked out a pint of strawberries. Of course, to supply the shop we'll need greater quantities than we can find at the Sunday market. We want our sorbets to showcase the very best of the local farms. For that, we need Marion.

⁓

MARION LIVES IN a yurt; it gives her easy access to her fields. For those of you who have never had a friend who lives in a yurt, it's like visiting a mini–circus tent, with an elevated wooden floor and a sky-light in the center for light and ventilation. The canvas walls roll up and down depending on how much air you want—and how many forest creatures you are willing to sleep with. Marion has an out-door shower with juniper bushes for privacy; she piggybacks onto her mother's WiFi access from the main house using a metal post, a piece of wire, and an empty coffee can.

We sit down at the picnic table outside while Marion makes tea with thick local honey. Alexandre loves it out here. It's the wilder-ness. He thinks we've come to hunt bears.

Marion had to glance only once at the list. She's currently the president of the agricultural collective in the Parc du Luberon—and she knows everyone. I doubt she would appreciate the comparison, but she has the networking instincts of a Fortune 500 executive.

Listening to her talk about where we could find wild licorice root or the sweetest apricots was equivalent to having an imaginary map of Provence spread out on the table in front of us. Like Churchill moving miniature warships, she could pinpoint the best producers for each fruit—sometimes right down to the tree.

For the sour cherries: "I'll give you his cell number. Tell him you want the last two trees on the left—just those. They're the very best."

For the lavender: "My neighbor has a field—it's the size of a handkerchief, really, but he doesn't use chemicals. Everyone else does—I don't care what they tell you."

For the lemon verbena: "You should go up the hill to Saint-Martin-de-Castillon. How is it you've never met Manon? Her mother's American, you know."

⚬

"I HOPE YOU are going to move on to the chocolate soon," said Paul, putting down his spoon with a sigh.

Mom and Paul are back in Céreste, and they've been the victims (if you can call it that) of our endless vanilla ice cream testing. Before we can dazzle anyone with carrot-orange-cardamom sorbet, the classics need to be impeccable, the best possible versions of themselves.

A great vanilla ice cream is like the Holy Grail—simple, impossible, and largely in the eyes of the beholder. We scraped the vanilla beans and boiled them, infused the milk for one day, two days, three days. We tried vanilla powder, which includes the ground-up pods as well as the interior seeds. I liked the coarser taste; I was quickly outvoted. Every day Gwendal came home with a new tub of ice cream for us to test—too thick, too thin, tastes like butter, tastes like water, sandy, icy, not quite up to snuff.

If I thought going into the ice cream business was going to stifle the intellectual in my husband, I was wrong. Gwendal spent the spring reading everything he could get his hands on about recipes, technique. This way of attacking a learning curve seems to run in the family. Gwendal's father was a sailor; he learned his navigation skills out of a book before he ever took to the water.

Tonight, Gwendal has his nose in a tome from the Culinary Institute of America that could easily substitute for a season's worth of weight lifting.

"No wonder it's good," he said. "They put sixty grams of vanilla beans in one liter of ice cream. That's huge. We could never afford it."

The recipes vary wildly, not only between chefs, but between cultures. Last week we tried a recipe from a hip American company that called for a whole teaspoon of salt—it was inedible. I was reading an article in *Bon Appétit* about another artisanal ice cream maker, and as proof of the ice cream's quality, the magazine cited the product's 19 percent butterfat. French ice cream is 8 or 9 percent butterfat, max. The American recipes are two-thirds cream, the French recipes two-thirds milk. We can't figure out why. Does that mean we should tell the tourists our ice cream is low-fat?

MY MOTHER USED to joke that she'd love to own an antiques shop but she'd never have the heart to sell anything. Now we have a whole ice cream parlor to decorate on a very limited budget—my mother's favorite kind of shopping.

There are multiple flea markets every summer weekend in Provence. Some are big, with established dealers and tourist prices, but the best ones are in the small villages where anyone can rent a spot for six euros and clean out the contents of her grandmother's attic. Of course you have to like what's coming out of Grandma's attic—stuff from eighty to ninety years ago. Right now that means art deco soup tureens and pink Depression-glass decanters with tiny glasses for after-dinner liqueurs.

It was a successful morning. We found six frosted-glass ice cream coupes (three euros for the lot), eight gold-rimmed saucers with illustrations of vintage cars (one euro), plus a vintage handbag (not a professional expense). We found an old children's chalkboard with an abacus—we could put it outside to announce specials or new flavors. We barely had room in the trunk, but I couldn't resist the two metal milk cans; if Rod drilled some holes in the bottom, we could use them as flowerpots. The real find of the day was a group of porcelain jars for kitchen staples in descending-size order—flour, sugar, coffee, tea, salt, pepper. It's rare to find a complete set with all the covers intact. I don't know quite where we'll put them, but they spoke to me—so I'll find a spot.

⟜

I THINK MOM and Paul are finally getting the hang of village life. After the Sunday flea market in Mane, we found ourselves in Revest-des-Brousses eating an unseasonal but delicious *blanquette de veau*.

"What is this again?" asked my mom, sopping up the sauce with a piece of bread.

"Veal."

"You could put cardboard under this sauce and it would taste good. Can you ask them how to make it?"

"I think I'll have to come back for a few more years before I do that."

"Why? Can't you say we're going back to the States and we want to make it?"

I knew I wasn't going to get anywhere, but I gave it my best shot. *"Ça fait plusieurs fois qu'on vient,"* I began, assuring the waitress that we were regular customers. "I can taste the nutmeg, but there's a sweetness to the sauce that makes it exceptional." Maybe I could flatter her into a confession.

"Ah," she said, smiling coyly, "my husband caramelizes the onions. But he would cut off my fingers if I told you the rest."

Alexandre wandered back to the table for his dessert.

I raised my eyebrows at my mom. "See."

❦

WITH MY MOM and Paul here, Alexandre has acquired a jumble of new English words: *boat, red, turtle, moo, plum.*

Back from ten days at the beach, Jean found his plum tree groaning with fruit, several buckets of which he generously donated to my kitchen.

Not to sound ungrateful, but plums irk me. Something about the raw texture, the slightly acidic density, makes me feel like I'm biting into a juicy baseball. But the abundance of the Provençal summer doesn't leave a lot of room for discussion. Plums it is.

We have a new chest freezer in the cellar. I briefly considered tossing the whole lot in a Ziploc bag and shoving the issue downstream a few months. But another idea presented itself, inspired, of all things, by trips my mom and I used to make to a wholesale market in New Jersey. We would buy crates of overripe peaches and plums and come home and make compote. Where was that place? The details are a little fuzzy, for both of us. My mother was never a reliable narrator, and now that my grandmother's gone, I'm starting to realize just how much is at risk of being lost. As a writer, this terrifies me. I should have started recording long ago. Why didn't I know that my great-grandmother Rose was a milliner? Or that my great-grandfather Eddie entered the Jewish mafia by way of a Depression-era milk truck?

Gwendal's paternal grandmother passed away this week. There weren't many good memories; she and his grandfather were hard people, not particularly open to the wider aspirations of their children or grandchildren. But Gwendal still associates her with certain tastes. She would spend hours painstakingly shelling crabs to make him a *tartine* of bread and butter with crabmeat on top. A whole morning's work devoured in a matter of minutes. He remembers picking blackberries for her jam—two for him, one for the pot—and the smell of burnt coffee, sitting all day over a low flame on the stove. He remembers the meticulous rows of their vegetable garden (like Jean, Gwendal's grandparents demanded precision from their beans) and the tiny, rock-hard yellow apples from their tree.

Unlike me, my mother loves plums. This, coupled with some leftover red wine, leads to a fruitful development. I roasted the plums in a medium oven with the wine, added a split vanilla bean, a cinnamon stick, and the tiniest bit of sugar. The plums gave way, exchanging their springiness for a comforting sag. The wine bubbled into a spiced burgundy syrup, thick and glossy. I served it with *faisselle,* a mild spoonable cheese, though I sense that sour cream, Greek yogurt, or mascarpone wouldn't go amiss.

This summer feels like a golden time: we have a new project simmering, our son is small enough that I can protect him just by closing the front gate, my parents are well enough to sit at lunch on a sunny terrace and watch Alexandre eat chocolate profiteroles and get whipped cream all over his face and in his blond hair. I don't know what kind of food should mark this very simple gift. Something warm and sweet is a good start.

....

Recipes for Something Warm and Sweet

MULLED-WINE ROASTED PLUMS
Prunes Rôties au Vin Chaud

3 pounds of purple Sugar Plum plums
½ cup full-bodied red wine
1 tablespoon raw cane sugar or light brown sugar
1 cinnamon stick
1 small vanilla bean or ½ of a large vanilla bean, split down the middle

Preheat the oven to 350°F.

Halve the plums and remove the pits. In a 9-by-13-inch casserole, combine plums and all the other ingredients. Roast for 35 to 45 minutes, until tender. Discard the cinnamon stick and vanilla bean.

Serve warm or at room temperature with sour cream, yogurt, or lightly sweetened mascarpone.

Serves 6

HOMEMADE HOT FUDGE

I wanted a rich, thick American-style hot fudge sauce for the shop—the kind you could drown in. This recipe is adapted from fellow expat artisan ice cream makers Seán and Kieran Murphy of Murphy's Ice Cream in Dingle, Ireland. You'll find further inspiration in their book *Murphy's Ice Cream Book of Sweet Things* (Mercier Press, 2008). Guinness ice cream? Yes, please.

5½ ounces 70 percent cacao dark chocolate
7 tablespoons butter
1 cup unsweetened cocoa powder

⅓ cup milk
½ cup plus 2 tablespoons heavy cream
1⅓ cups sugar

In the top of a double boiler, gently melt together the chocolate and butter. Add the cocoa powder, and whisk to combine.

In a medium saucepan, heat milk, cream, and sugar, stirring until the mixture boils.

Add the hot milk mixture to the chocolate in several small additions—this will look like a mess at first, clumpy and goopy, but just keep whisking with confidence, and it will all come right in the end. Keep stirring until the sauce is smooth and shiny.

The hot fudge keeps in the fridge for weeks; it also freezes beautifully. Reheat in the microwave or in a hot-water bath.

CHAPTER 18

La Rentrée

Autumn is here, suddenly, vibrantly. Clouds swept by the wind cast giant shadows across the hills. The wind has pushed aside the summer haze; the sloping angles of the roofs against the sky are sharp, clear. Falling chestnuts are deadly (in a Bugs Bunny–cartoon kind of way). Alexandre has made a collection of the smooth dark globes, the perfect size for his small fist. It's crisp, do-something-new weather. It's *la rentrée*.

Like Bastille Day, and maybe the beginning of the January sales, *la rentrée*—the official start of the French school year—is one of those days when the majority of French people are doing precisely the same thing. The atmosphere is expectant, electric; an entire nation plugging in after three or four weeks of holiday.

On the way down the hill, Alexandre picked up a leaf bigger than his face. Today is his last day at the crèche. Tomorrow he starts full-day preschool, just across the street at *la maternelle*. I opened the gate to the crèche and waved to the team, still applying sunscreen to small faces despite the morning chill. Alexandre doesn't even say good-bye anymore; he just runs in. No looking back.

For the kids' last day, Charles brought in a makeshift bubble maker—really just two long sticks and some string. I stood across the street and watched the sun glinting off the giant bubbles as they wobbled into the air. Alexandre ran with his arms lifted to the sky, the sun shining through his blond hair. He won't remember this part of his childhood, but I will. His pants are too short; he's grown so much over the summer.

The night before, I decorated his *classeur*, the required binder where the new teacher will place all his drawings, collages, and little poems to give us at the end of term. I went to town with the pirate stickers; there's even a little parrot sitting on the *A* in his name. There are days when I think my mother and I live on different planets, and there are days, like this one, when I think we are the same person. I remember her sitting at the kitchen table wrapping math textbooks in brown-paper book covers made out of grocery bags, sketching my name in big graffiti letters on the cover. This is what was known in our house as Arts and Craps. She used to draw stick figures on my lunch bag for a field trip so I could easily find my meal among the pile of lumpy brown sacks. She sent me off to boarding school with a cardboard box to slip under my bed that was full of fuzzy pipe cleaners, construction paper, rubber cement, and an ancient tub of magenta glitter that never seemed to run out, no matter how many sparkly Valentine's Day hearts I gave away.

Once the goody-goody, always the goody-goody: we arrived for Alexandre's first day of school at 8:36 for a 9:00 start. I wanted to get a few pictures along the way. I imagine it's the same tumult in every preschool in the world, the choosing of hooks and hanging of bags. Although Alexandre had visited twice with the staff of the crèche, I'd barely seen the inside of the classroom; I'd never shaken hands with the teacher. She was a fixture, well liked. There were at least one or two young moms in the village who'd had her as their teacher twenty-odd years before.

Parents were being ushered out quickly, no introductions, no explanations. French education, like French pregnancy, is an all-enveloping system; teachers don't particularly need or want parental input. It was clear I was meant to drop him off and then good-naturedly get out of the way. (Gwendal and I have our own tricks to stay involved: I volunteered to give short English lessons to the kindergartners through the fifth-graders; Gwendal offered to teach a class in cinema history and technique—the teachers are planning a student film festival for the end of the year.)

Alexandre walked in and said *"Bonjour"* to the teacher (score one for the all-important *politesse*), then put a plastic stethoscope around his neck and went to stir something in the play kitchen. It's clear I was more nervous than he was. I backed away; he was already surrounded by pigtails and little hands. There's an expression that French parents use a lot to describe this kind of early independence: *Il vie sa vie*. He's living his life.

The French preschool day is long—9:00 to 4:30—and absolutely free for all children over the age of three, on the condition that they are properly toilet-trained. You can send them for half a day or take them home for lunch, but Gwendal and I both work full-time, and Gwendal thinks it's important that Alexandre eat at the *cantine* with the other kids. Besides, he's not likely to get the equivalent of a four-course lunch every day at home with me.

At the end of the day, when I came to pick him up, there was already a gaggle of parents waiting by the gate. There were plenty of familiar faces, but even so, I found myself fighting the instinct, left over from my own awkward first days of school, to hang back from the group, to hide behind a book. *La maîtresse* had them sitting calmly by the door. She handed the children out one by one, sending them down the ramp to the waiting parents. I couldn't help thinking of cattle going down the chute. When Alexandre grabbed my hand, his head was down; he looked so sad.

"Was it good?" I said. He hesitated, then shook his head and nodded at the same time, as if he were confused.

"Gâteau. Gâteau," he beseeched as we walked across the parking lot to the *boulangerie*. He looked like a tiny POW, dazed to see the sunlight.

"Let's get a cookie and you can tell me all about it." He still wouldn't look at me.

"Alexandre, are you sad? Why are you sad, sweet boy?" This is what makes me crazy. He's so private already. You can see he's deciding how much to tell me. How much to let me worry.

When we got home, he started wailing when I tried to open the bag of madeleines for him. He stuffed them into his mouth one after the other with a fierce concentration.

"Laisse-moi," he said. I was sitting too close. He just wanted to eat in silence. I adjusted my posture away from him, trying to give him some space. I have a vague memory of this feeling, how invasive and unnecessary it felt when my own mom would come home early from work and quiz me about my day. I just wanted to veg out in front of the TV. As Alexandre ate, his bone structure seemed to return, and so did his smile. He leaned forward and put his forehead against mine. What I took for a catastrophic first day at school was beginning to look more like a mild case of hypoglycemia.

GWENDAL IS ALSO starting school, ice cream school, this week. In order to produce your own ice cream in France, you need a diploma from the state, a CAP Pâtissier/Glacier. The course runs for one year, one week a month, and it's two hours away, in Toulon. Often these courses are a pre-professional track for students who decide not to finish *le bac,* the traditional French high-school diploma. There's a diploma for butchers, chocolatiers, even hairdressers. So ten years after finishing his PhD, Gwendal will be heading back to class with a group of sixteen-year-olds in plastic hairnets. I smiled as I watched him pack his neatly folded chef's whites and kit of knives and pastry bags. While he went to look for his plastic no-slip shoes, I tucked a little note into his Dopp kit. I used to do this when he went on his first business trips. Little postcards of odalisques and Degas prostitutes drying themselves with one leg perched provocatively on the bed. These postcards wished him luck, courage, told him that I loved him. I hadn't done it in a long time. All this commiserating, setting out on a new adventure together, is doing something good to our *vie de couple*. There is a sense of renewal, of building something together, which I always found the most exciting part of marriage. You and me against the world.

When he arrived in Toulon, he sent me a snapshot of himself in uniform in a gleaming industrial kitchen. He looked a little bit like the Swedish chef from the Muppets.

༄

CRAP. I MEAN, happy New Year. Like every year since I've been living in France, the Jewish holidays sort of snuck up on me. As we live out in the middle of nowhere now and as Gwendal no longer works in the cinema industry, where he had all his LA studio meetings canceled for the High Holidays, I forgot it was Rosh Hashanah. I got home from my driving lesson (I too have gone back to school) with a piece of Morbier cheese for dinner and five bars of hard-to-find dark chocolate with cocoa nibs. At least I bought apples yesterday at the market. Then again, I also bought my usual Monday-night pork roast. "Why apples and honey?" said Gwendal as I quartered a small yellow apple. When I couldn't give him a better explanation than "for a sweet New Year," I was forced to type *why apples and honey + rosh hashanah* into Google. The fourth site down was judaism.about.com, which ought to be followed by a site called lapsedjew.com/guilt.

These lapses tug at me in a different way since Alexandre was born. Over dinner (I shelved the pork roast for another day) I tried to explain to him what was going on. "This is a special day"—I hesitated—"because Mommy's family and Mommy and, therefore, you are Jewish. Rosh Hashanah. Can you say that?"

"Wosh Yahyahyah," he said, touching the picture of the giant Red Delicious apple on the computer screen. He has so many identities to absorb already, what's one more?

Since it's *la rentrée,* maybe I should start thinking about his religious education? At this rate, I don't know if Alexandre will feel the slightest identification with Judaism. He won't go to traditional Hebrew school or belong to a temple (neither did I). I went to a Yiddish Sunday school. My grandparents spoke Yiddish when they didn't want me to understand what they were saying—a perfect incentive to learn. Instead of having a bat mitzvah, I wrote a research paper on the tensions between the Reform, Conservative, and Orthodox Jewish communities in Teaneck, where I grew up.

If we stay in Céreste, Alexandre will probably know very few, if any, Jewish kids. Growing up in the New York tristate area, I didn't have deep feelings about being Jewish, the same way I didn't have deep feelings about being white. Those were the facts, matters of casual ease and generalized cultural identity, like bagels and lox. Being Jewish didn't require particular courage, inconvenience, or tough decisions. It's hard to explain why something should be important to my son, when I never quite asked, or answered, that question for myself.

Explaining to Alexandre how I'm Jewish is like explaining how I'm American—it has more to do with Grandma Elsie's mandel bread than God. I loved my Children's Bible, but I read it alongside Greek myths and classic fairy tales. I wonder if my mother still has those cassette tapes of David and Goliath and Daniel in the lion's den? Can you even buy a cassette player anymore?

As usual, the easiest thing for me to pass down is food. I called Aunt Joyce, keeper of the family recipes. She'd just finished making my Grandma Elsie's apple Bundt cake. Funny—when we moved to Provence, I vowed to wheedle the recipe for Madame N.'s homemade apple cake out of the local *boulangerie*. In fact, Grandma Elsie's cake looks very similar; Aunt Joyce showed me on Skype. Rosh Hashanah apple cake over the Internet. It's a modern-day miracle any biblical prophet would be proud to call his own.

Two years ago, Nicole gave me her grandmother's handwritten recipe notebooks for Christmas. I'm sure I saw a recipe in there for *gâteau aux pommes*. Why hadn't I ever made it? Life is like that. We are often chasing our tails, looking for stuff that was there all along. Alexandre and I would bake it together.

Of course, Alexandre can't eat cake over Skype, so I brought out the apples and some lavender honey from Reillanne market. Alexandre didn't take a nap at school today, so at first he wanted a whole apple and pouted when I gave him just a slice. He finally let me give him a piece after I peeled it and promised him he could lick the honey off the top. He seemed to enjoy it. I don't know if he understands being Jewish, but he understands dessert.

After dinner, I looked at my Facebook wall for the first time in months. I hadn't sent a single New Year's greeting. A solitary feeling overwhelmed me. Here I was in this tiny village, a million miles from home. I felt like an astronaut looking down at planet Earth, a glass marble, below. *EB phone home.*

I don't know if I feel far from my religion, but I feel far from my family, which may, in fact, be the same thing.

As the temperature drops, I've slipped into a mild culinary panic. We barely had time to begin our experiments with peach sorbet, and now it's too late. The last of September's abundant figs and plums are disappearing—the quince, herald of a long winter's simmer, are ripening on the hedges at the edge of the fields. These abrupt seasonal changes make me mourn (who knew you could mourn a tomato?). They also make me realize that I've gone yet another busy summer in Provence without learning how to can.

I may have mentioned this before, but fruits and vegetables in Provence don't leave a lot of room for free will. When the apricots are ripe, they're perfection. When they're gone, it's *hasta la vista, baby*. I used to wonder what the women here did all day, before cable television. Now I know; they were busy picking, cooking, and canning this summer plenty so they could sock it away for the long winter.

I thought a book might be helpful, but the books all make the same assumption—that your mother, your grandmother, and your grandmother's grandmother have been making jam and preserves since time immemorial. A book is simply an *aide-memoire* for something already in your blood. Sure, my grandmother's grandmother probably knew how to make jam, but somewhere on the journey from the shtetl to suburban New Jersey, we picked up Smucker's. The French recipes are patently unhelpful: "Put one kilo of fruit and one kilo of sugar in a pot. Boil. Jar." They never say much about timing, temperature—or botulism.

What I really need is a master class. When in doubt, I say, call a Brit. Mollie and David have been making their own jams and chutneys and sealing them in neatly labeled jars for years. I'd been politely bugging them about it since June. Like an afternoon with Maria Callas, one has to sign up early.

As I walked in the door, I was enveloped in the steam coming from the stove, the sharp edge of vinegar and fresh ginger softened by cinnamon and the sticky, slowly dissolving sweetness of the figs. David was standing over a large cast-iron pot measuring the level of syrup with a T-shaped wooden implement that had three distinct notches. "It's an old crepe spreader," he said. David has the longish, curly-white hair of a poet who works by candlelight, and great bushy eyebrows that could invent things all by themselves. I began to wonder if to master proper canning technique you had to be the kind of practical yet creative type who would think to fashion a measuring stick out of an old crepe spreader.

Mollie and David's kitchen is the stuff of dreams. There's a rustic front kitchen with heavy beams, well-scrubbed wooden counters, and a groaning red range with room for six bubbling pots. There are glass-fronted cabinets with crystal tumblers and a shelf of neatly labeled spices in squat glass jars. Discreetly hidden behind the stove is the doorway to a smaller room—a full pantry, lined floor to ceiling with white cabinets, an extra freezer, and a deep slop sink. It's like *Upstairs, Downstairs,* but without the servants.

By the time I arrived, they had the whole thing set up like a cooking show. There was an almost finished pot simmering on the stove. The glass jars were at the ready, fitted snugly into a large roasting pan, covered lightly with a paper towel to keep stray insects or dust from flying in. Just beside the jars were all the ingredients for the next batch: red wine vinegar, finely chopped onions, fresh ginger, ground allspice berries—ready to start all over again. Just like Nigella Lawson showing you how to make a chocolate cake and then, in the name of instant gratification and a half-hour time slot, whisking a finished one from the oven just as the other goes in to bake.

They clearly had this down to a science. About ten minutes before pouring the chutney, Mollie placed the roasting pan full of jars in a hot oven for ten minutes. Using a silicone oven mitt, she transferred the hot jars onto a foil-lined tray and got ready to pour.

"Normally, there's a lot of swearing during this bit. But maybe the fact you're here will keep us in line."

The chutney was thick, like the blob in a B horror movie. Big chunks of fig slid through the flowered ceramic funnel in satisfying gloops. Every now and then a drip would escape. "Oh, bul—" Mollie began, and then stopped herself. I saw one of David's Dickensian eyebrows shoot up and settle itself back in place.

"It makes the seal as it cools down, you see," said Mollie. "I just tried to open one of last year's jars in the pantry. Couldn't loosen it."

While Mollie was photocopying the recipe, I stared out the window of the office. The smell of a nearby pine drifted through the open window. I left the house, a warm pot of chutney in my hands, already dreaming of thick slices of sourdough bread and the butcher's *jambon aux herbes*. "If you can bear the suspense," said David, "leave it in the back of the cupboard for a few months. It'll be that much better for Christmas."

Not sure I can wait that long.

Back-to-School Recipes

MAMIE'S APPLE CAKE
Gâteau aux Pommes

I suspect most French families have a recipe like this one—a simple cake that tastes like home. This one comes from Nicole's grandmother. I make it with the fruit on the bottom, so it turns into a buttery apple upside-down cake.

10½ tablespoons unsalted butter, melted
1 cup flour
1 teaspoon baking powder, or 1 small packet French levure alsacienne
1 pinch fine sea salt
2 eggs
¾ cup plus ½ tablespoon sugar
3 small apples or pears, firm but ripe (two regular-size apples will do)
Squeeze of fresh lemon juice

Preheat the oven to 350°F.

Melt the butter; set aside. In a small mixing bowl, combine flour, baking powder, and salt.

In a medium mixing bowl, whisk together eggs and ¾ cup sugar until light lemon yellow. Wash and core the apples or pears—I never bother to peel. Cut into 1-inch pieces. Toss the fruit with a squeeze of lemon juice and ½ tablespoon of sugar to keep it from oxidizing.

Add flour mixture to the eggs. Whisk briefly to combine. Add melted butter, whisk to combine.

Line a 10-inch tart pan with parchment paper. Scatter the apples on the bottom and pour the batter on top. Bake for 45 to 50 minutes, until middle is firm and well browned and a toothpick comes out clean.

Cool 10 minutes. Flip out onto a cooling rack. Peel parchment paper off. Cool completely. Store covered with aluminum foil; an airtight container will make it soggy. Serve with a cup of your favorite afternoon tea.

Serves 8

MOLLIE AND DAVID'S FIG CHUTNEY
Chutney aux Figues

Though figs are a passion of mine, I suspect this would be equally good made with pears, quince, or even plums. With thanks to Mollie and David for sharing their recipe.

13½ cups (108 fluid ounces) red wine vinegar
2½ pounds light brown sugar
5 onions, finely chopped
5 ounces fresh ginger root, finely chopped
4 teaspoons Colman's mustard powder
Zest from 1½ lemons
2½ cinnamon sticks
2 level tablespoons coarse sea salt
1¼ teaspoons ground allspice berries
½ teaspoon cloves, crushed
7 pounds firm fresh figs, quartered

In a large nonreactive stockpot or Dutch oven (stainless steel or enamel), combine the vinegar, sugar, onions, ginger, mustard powder, lemon zest, cinnamon sticks, salt, allspice, and cloves and bring to a boil. Reduce the heat to a simmer and cook until mixture is thickened and reduced by two-thirds, forming a thick syrup. This will take at least a good 2½ hours. (I don't normally advocate recipes that require specialized equipment, but it's worth getting one of those flat metal-mesh pot covers they sell for making jam; it minimizes spit and sizzle.) When your syrup has reached the right consistency, add the figs and cook gently until the figs are very soft and beginning to fall apart and most of the liquid they've given off has evaporated, about 1 hour to 90 minutes more.

Chutney can be kept in a nonreactive container in the fridge for up to three weeks. Alternatively, hot chutney may be ladled into sterilized canning jars and processed according to manufacturer's directions.

Makes around a dozen 12-ounce jars

Tip: Just a small note to time-starved cooks: Chutney requires patience, though not constant supervision. Make sure you have a good 4 to 5 hours ahead of you when you start. It's an excellent rainy-day activity.

CHAPTER 19

I Scream, You Scream

We can't stop talking about ice cream. It's like some kind of sugarcoated Tourette's syndrome; we're constantly blurting out comments about quince sorbet in inappropriate contexts.

It's already October; we are aiming to open for Easter. The ideas are coming faster than our work. Definitely faster than our budget.

"What about petits fours," said Rod one morning, sitting on the sofa with a cup of tea.

I started thinking about tiny chocolate cups, no bigger than golf tees, each filled with a mini-scoop of ice cream and topped with *nougatine,* red peppercorns, candied ginger, dried figs.

"We could sell them like old-fashioned chocolates," I said, getting ahead of myself, "in flat boxes with paper doilies and a tiny silver pincher for serving."

"Do you know how much work that would be!" Gwendal looked like a vein was about to pop in his forehead. Like I said, I'm in charge of fantasy. He's in charge of spreadsheets.

If *la rentrée* is the season of new beginnings, it's also the season of unexpected costs. Christmas in reverse. Every day we add to the scroll-like list of really boring but essential things we have to spend money on. Like a professional water softener. Apparently, if we don't do something about the level of calcium in the water, our sorbet is going to taste like the ring around someone's bathtub.

Meanwhile, our dining room is starting to look like a badly dusted antiques shop. Everything Mom and I bought this summer is piled on the table, on the buffet, in every corner. I want to make homemade ice cream sandwiches for the shop, but are we prepared to pay extra baggage fees for five-pound bags of Domino dark brown sugar to make proper American cookies? Is that in the business plan?

It was still nice enough to work outside, so I was on my way to the café with my computer and a croissant when I ran into Tim and Bridget, well-heeled members of the Anglo crowd. A croissant is my treat when I'm having trouble getting started with my writing. I find the butter helps smear the fear of the white page.

"It's so exciting," said Bridget, giving me a kiss on each cheek. They must have heard the final bank loan came through.

"What's your favorite flavor?" I asked, always in search of new ideas.

"Rhubarb custard," said Tim.

"Ohhh. I love rhubarb." More fuel for the fire.

That afternoon I called Marion. *"Non, non, non.* Rhubarb doesn't grow here. It takes too much water. And the leaves are toxic. I'm always afraid I won't cut off all the bad bits and I'll poison someone."

Okeydokey. Ix-nay on the rhubarb.

WE BOUGHT AN ice cream truck today. Not just any ice cream truck; a banana-yellow Italian *triporteur*. If you've never seen one, a *triporteur* is an itty-bitty three-wheeled pickup truck, essentially a covered Vespa with room in front for one man and one dog and room in back for several crates of oranges and not much else. I've wanted one ever since I first saw a dusty model, with lights like cartoon eyes, chugging up a hill in Capri. It just goes to show, if you wait long enough, life presents an excuse to buy almost anything.

We'd found it on the Internet. There is a website in France called Leboncoin; it's basically a nationwide online garage sale.

"I can go on Thursday," Gwendal had said when we first spotted the ad, enlarging the picture to get a better view.

"No. You have to go tomorrow."

"But—"

I didn't let him finish. "Tomorrow. Call her right now and tell her you can be there any time after nine a.m." I've looked for an apartment in Manhattan, so I know you don't leave the good stuff sitting out there any longer than absolutely necessary.

The buyer was reluctant to let it go. It had belonged to her grandfather, who'd bought it in Italy in the early 1960s. She had painted it bright yellow thinking she would convert it into a juice business, but that didn't quite work out.

I got to the parking lot just as Gwendal and Rod appeared on the rise of the hill. The Piaggio—that's the Italian brand name of the *triporteur*—was loaded onto a flatbed trailer attached to the car. I admit it; I started spontaneously clapping. I've never seen a happier-looking object in my entire life. I think that was the day I realized that we were going into a business that was going to make a lot of people smile.

"It was amazing," said Rod. "People were honking and waving at us the whole way."

I put myself behind the wheel. *Vroommmmmm, vroom.* I've finally found a raison d'être for this whole driving thing. This must be how men feel about Lamborghinis. I want to go cruise for girls in my ice cream truck.

I couldn't wait to show Alexandre. "Daddy bought the coolest thing in the whole world today," I said when I picked him up from school. "Wait till you see."

He looked at it, got in the cab, pushed three levers and a button, then leaned his head out the window. "It doesn't work."

Details.

"You can serve us some ice cream," said Angela.

"More?" said Alexandre after ten minutes of handing pretend cones out the window.

Angela held her tummy. "Another one?"

"I'm American," I said brightly. "I'll have another one."

"So," I said, taking a large lick of my invisible triple chocolate cone with extra whipped cream and colored sprinkles. "We should find a night for you and Rod to come over for dinner and a movie—where we talk about anything except ice cream."

"Do you talk about it in bed?" she asked.

"Actually. We do."

Angela took a last bite of her imaginary double coffee cone. "We do too."

⟋❀⟍

THAT NIGHT, I sent around a picture of the Piaggio to my friends and family in the States.

Auntie Lynn was the first to write back:

Re: The yellow thing.

The content of the message was three little words.

Give us strength.

My mother couldn't stop laughing when I got her on the phone. "Never a dull moment with you," she said. "Are you going to have a bell?" This is my mother's finest quality, an unwavering confidence in my—and, since my marriage, our—nutty ideas. In between chuckles, she defends me to the naysayers and duds. "Do people really send their kids to an Ivy League college to drive an ice cream truck?"

"They do now."

⤮

Rockin' Saturday night *chez nous*. The kitchen looks like a bomb exploded in it. Two pots of quince compote and my Le Creuset of split-pea soup will not fit on the range at the same time.

It's getting chilly, so I'm stocking the freezer with soup—big pots of soup, all kinds of soup. Last week I made *soupe d'épeautre*. *Épeautre* is spelt, and though in the States it might still be confined to the health-food store, in Provence, whole spelt grains are used like barley, to make soup, risotto, and cold salads. My *soupe d'épeautre* is a conjuring of the beef and barley soup at the Kiev, a now defunct all-night Russian diner on Second Avenue. My dad and I used to go for cheese blintzes after a late movie. We always sat in the narrow brick-lined back room, connected to the main restaurant by a heavy steel door. I think it used to be the meat locker. The soup was so thick you could stand a spoon upright in the bowl.

Tonight, our house smells like a candy factory with a bacon department (I hear that's a trend). While I am frying the pork belly for my split-pea soup, Gwendal is in the dining room peeling and chopping quince to test a sorbet. Quince is somewhere between a very tart apple and a fuzzy pear. Some scholars believe it's the forbidden fruit from the Garden of Eden. People in Provence grow up with *pâte de coing*—a condensed quince jelly; it's the kind of thing grandmas make for Christmas. Despite the slightly grainy texture, we think it would make a superb sorbet.

Even though I've written a cookbook, nothing could be further from a professional kitchen than mine. I only just learned how to screw and lock the thingie on my food processor. I would have helped Gwendal with the quince, but we have only one peeler, and I surely would have hurt myself coring the tough fruit with one of my many dull knives. I know good cooks are supposed to have sharp knives—everyone says you are more likely to cut yourself with a dull one. My apologies to Escoffier and the rest, but that just doesn't sound right. It's not that I won't cut my finger off with a sharp knife; I'll just cut it off cleaner.

Alexandre, wearing his favorite truck pajamas, was playing with his blocks under the dining-room table. Every once in a while he would surface, lick the half lemon that Gwendal was using to keep the quince from turning brown, and disappear back beneath the furniture. No judge would believe me: *Your Honor, my son has eczema on his chin because he'd rather suck on half a lemon than eat a perfectly good* pain au chocolat.

Prince was the sound track for the evening. "'Pu-pu wain, pu-pu rain,'" repeated Alexandre, watching us boogying around the sink. He must think his parents are crazy. Neither one of us is Fred Astaire. But who needs to be Fred Astaire when you're dancing in your kitchen?

It was almost ten by the time we finally sat down to dinner. Alexandre insisted on tearing apart a piece of bread and stirring it into his soup.

"*Un vrai paysan*—that's the way my grandfather used to do it." Gwendal beamed. Only in France is the word *paysan*—"peasant"—used with such pride.

I thought back to other Saturday nights. Nights in black tie, nights reading or crying or studying, nights drinking margaritas or eating chocolate chip cookie dough out of the bowl. We may not get out much at the moment, but if I could be this happy every Saturday night for the rest of my life, I'd be lucky.

⁊

GWENDAL IS LEAVING for his second week of ice cream school in the morning.

He'd been warming up the bed for ten minutes when I crawled in. "Well, I guess we can't change the sheets tonight," he said, turning the page of his book, "or you're stuck."

"Hey, don't laugh at me. I'm a Jewish American New Yorker. I could be a lot more neurotic than I am."

The neurosis in question is a simple one: I don't like to let Gwendal go away on a trip unless we have slept, preferably *slept* slept, in the sheets currently on our bed.

My reasoning is straightforward, and rather morbid. If Gwendal were to die in a car accident or otherwise be eaten by wolves or abducted by aliens, my first instinct would be to spend several years in a wedding dress, Miss Havisham–style, sniffing his old pillowcase while the walls of the house crumbled around my ears. It's not a particularly flattering self-portrait, but there you go. Somewhere in the ancestral, talisman-littered portion of my brain, our musty sheets keep him safe. What can I tell you; we all have our little quirks.

⁊

WHILE GWENDAL IS away, Alexandre and I find our routine. I play piano concertos on my computer. Music seems to calm everything down. Alexandre lines up his knights for battle on the kitchen floor while I make dinner.

Tonight, after I read him a story, he crawled into my lap. *"Tu me berces comme un bébé."* As I held him in my arms, rocking him back and forth, he stuck his thumb in his mouth, something he does only when he is "playing baby." He's only three, but he's growing up and sometimes needs to go back. I wonder if he knows how much I enjoy these little regressions. It's like a do-over for me. A chance to savor something I rushed through the first time around.

"Yesterday," he said, "I got a haircut with Mamie Nicole." Lately Alexandre has been condensing time. Everything that happened in the past he talks about as if it happened "yesterday." I wonder if he isn't onto something. I read a play in college, J. B. Priestley's *I Have Been Here Before.* In the play, time is not linear, it's coiled, episodes stacked one on top of another like poker chips. The past is so near. You can take an experience from the bottom of the pile and slip it back in at the top. Relive it again and again until you get it right.

It's a pretty swift philosophical insight for a three-year-old.

WINTER IS BACK, along with my hibernation instinct, a slowing-down of the biorhythm. In Paris, the traffic, the streetlights, and ten o'clock showings of the new James Bond movie at the Canal-side cinema would keep this sensation at bay. In the village, there are no such distractions. At 6:00 p.m., the streets are deserted; eight in the evening feels like three in the morning.

I'm cold all the time. Each summer I forget, and each November I'm shocked again to discover I don't want to get out of bed because it's too damn cold to put my toes on the tile floor. I've discovered slippers, something I never thought would be a part of my fashion repertoire. I have fur-lined ones with bows and brown-and-white knit booties that, if I'm in a certain state of undress, Gwendal says make me look like a Swedish porn star. I've never seen Swedish porn, but if I were having sex in Scandinavia in the middle of winter, I see the merit of keeping your booties on.

⁓

TODAY I ACCOMPLISHED something. I finally put in my French nationality application. I've been stamped and stapled, fingerprinted and translated. It was definitely easier to complete this process in Provence than it would have been in Paris. There was only one person in one office to call with my questions. If I was getting the wrong answers, at least I was getting the same wrong answers every time.

My appointment was for 10:00 a.m. on Wednesday. But last week, when I'd called the official translator to retrieve my documents, she said she'd be away on Monday and Tuesday. We would have to pick up my papers on the morning of.

I cursed myself as we got into the car. There are only forty days of rain a year in Provence, but when it rains, it *really* rains. It doesn't rain cats and dogs; it rains camels and wildebeests. It rains like Noah's ark is about to float down the stream behind our house. We'd be lucky if we could crawl along the highway thirty kilometers per hour under the speed limit.

I must be crazy. A decade in France is long enough to figure out that leaving things to the last minute is a recipe for disaster. They shouldn't give you a French passport if you're not pessimistic enough to leave a little extra time for things to go mortally, catastrophically, wrong. But here I was, me and my American expectations, about to blow up the most important French process I'd ever been through. For some reason, this situation made me want to shout expressions I'd learned in junior-high-school French class and hadn't heard since. We're going to be late for the immigration lady! *Sacré bleu!*

The reason for my hubris is simple: I've been the recipient of too much dumb luck. Take my study-abroad application. It was the end of my sophomore year in college. I was at Kinko's at 10:00 a.m. on the day before the application was due, filling out a form for FedEx. When I handed it to the man behind the counter, he shook his head. "This is a PO box. FedEx doesn't deliver overnight to a PO box." I was just about to crumple with panic and self-loathing when the guy behind me in line said, "My mom lives there. I bet she knows him. Let me call her. Maybe you can send it to her house and she'll take it over." I sat on the floor of the Kinko's while the nice man behind the counter let my would-be savior use the phone. "Sure," he said when he hung up. "She'll get it to him. But anyway, he's not leaving till Sunday; his son has a basketball game." I almost kissed him. There are twenty thousand students at Cornell, and that morning, in that line, was the kid whose mom lived next door to the overseas admissions director, who happened to be leaving a day late because of his son's basketball game. It's the very definition of dumb luck, and it's made me residually cocky.

After nearly drowning on the highway and running through a muddy field to retrieve my documents from the translator, we pulled into the parking lot of the prefecture at 9:52.

The immigration lady didn't look friendly. Fifty-something with a blond pixie haircut, chunky bracelets, and high black boots, she didn't return my smile. I opened my notebook. Her face brightened when she saw my score on the French test. *"Très bien,"* she said, disappearing to make a photocopy. I thought of the Algerian man who took the exam with me who had never seen a bubble form before and who clearly needed glasses. No doubt his French was better than mine. No doubt his score was not.

Her mood improved again when she saw I had all my papers in order. She even apologized that we had to drive all the way back there next week for the official interview.

⌒

WHAT SHOULD I wear? I know they're not going to deny me citizenship if my scarf isn't tied correctly, but even so.

I feel like I need a relative with me today. I can't decide which of my grandmothers should accompany me. In the end I went with my father's mother, putting on a pair of her earrings—golden scrolls (brass, really, set with tiny green stones). She was an immigrant herself, and I think she would understand how I am feeling today. Both my paternal grandparents came through Ellis Island; my grandmother's Russian birth certificate is on display at the Ellis Island museum. When Gwendal and I took his parents to New York for our wedding, it was among the first places I brought them.

When we arrived at the prefecture (in plenty of time), there was another American woman in the waiting room with her three kids. She scolded in a singsong voice as they slid under chairs and kicked the counter. "They'll *never* give Mommy her French papers if you keep running around like this."

Gwendal took Alexandre to the bathroom—and the vending machine.

"Oh my *God!* What is that?" I stared in horror as Alexandre tore the wrapper off a Twix bar.

"They didn't have anything else." Gwendal shrugged. "He was hungry."

I watched Alexandre shove the chocolate happily into his mouth. I looked up at the other American mom and smiled meekly. "They'll never give me *my* papers if they see my son eating a Twix bar at ten in the morning."

Industrial chocolate for breakfast aside, the immigration lady softened at the sight of Alexandre. I guess he is living proof of my assimilation. He played his part by walking through the bright fluorescent-lit corridor to her office and saying, *"Oooh, c'est beau ici."*

Are you involved in any *associations?* This is an important question in French life. It's not enough to have a job and pay your taxes. You have to have hobbies, be involved in the local community.

"I give English lessons at the village school."

"*Bénévole?*" she asked.

"*Oui, bénévole.*" It's also important that you do it for free.

"Are there any children from a previous union?"

Gwendal looked up from the dinosaur he was drawing for Alexandre and smiled. "Not that I know of."

I looked at him, aghast. *Not that I know of?* Are you out of your mind? My mental telepathy was beaming his way. *Does this seem like a good time to be funny? My life is hanging in the balance and you're cracking wise with a French immigration official.* If it wouldn't have caused an awkward yelp, I would have kicked him under the table.

Her face was a block of stone. "No," I said. "No children from a previous union."

We went to a café when it was over. I ordered coffee, though I could have used a double vodka on the rocks. I ate *chouquettes,* shoving the choux pastry into my mouth until my heart rate slowed. (I'm not French *yet,* I have another year to kick my emotional-eating habit...) Suddenly I realized: it was done. Unless I murdered someone in the next twelve months, by next Christmas, I would be French.

Recipes for Winter Soups

SPLIT-PEA SOUP WITH PORK BELLY AND COGNAC
Soupe aux Pois Cassés

If I were stuck on a snowy mountaintop all winter, this is the recipe I would take with me. It can be a meal in itself with crusty bread and cheese, or served in a small cup, with crème fraîche and crumbled bacon on top, at the beginning of a multicourse meal.

1 large carrot, chopped

1 large onion, chopped

½ bulb fennel (including stalks and fronds) or 2 stalks celery with leaves,
*   chopped*

1 small cinnamon stick

3 cloves (or a large pinch of ground cloves)

1 ham hock or a 12-ounce slice of pork belly, slab bacon, or pancetta

3 tablespoons olive oil

½ cup white wine

2 tablespoons cognac or brandy

2¼ pounds split green peas

1 bay leaf

2 chicken bouillon cubes (I use Knorr)

14 cups of very hot or boiling water

In a large stockpot, sauté veggies, cinnamon, cloves, and ham or bacon in olive oil until meat is browned and onions are translucent, about 10 to 12 minutes. (It helps to stick the whole cloves into the surface of the meat, to keep them from getting lost.)

Add white wine and let sizzle. Add cognac. Add split peas and stir. Add bay leaf. Dissolve bouillon cubes in 1 cup boiling water. Add to the pot. Add remaining water. Bring to a boil and simmer over low heat with the cover slightly ajar, stirring occasionally, until the peas are tender, about 1½ hours.

Remove meat, bay leaf, cinnamon stick, and cloves. (If the cloves have gone missing, fish them out with a slotted spoon.) Blend soup with a hand blender. Serve with the shredded meat of the ham hock or slices of pork belly on top, or with a dollop of plain yogurt and a grinding of black pepper.

There's no point in making a small batch of this soup—there will always be another blizzard, and it freezes beautifully. To re-heat, dilute with a dribble of white wine. I sometimes sauté some extra bacon to crumble into the soup when I serve it the second time.

Note: You won't want to add any salt to the soup, as the ham/bacon and bouillon cubes take care of that.

Serves 8

BEEF AND SPELT BERRY SOUP
Soupe d'Épeautre

Whole spelt grains (spelt berries), an ancient ancestor of wheat, are a staple of Provençal cooking. You may have seen them sold under the Italian name farro. I love the nutty flavor and how the grains hold their bite through a long winter's simmer. My *soupe d'épeautre* is much like a traditional beef and barley soup, with slow-cooked chunks of meat and a thick starchy broth. I encourage you to go out of your way to try some—it will become a staple for your snow days.

3 tablespoons olive oil

2 pounds stew beef (chuck, chuck shoulder, chuck roast—you need a cheap
    cut with some fat and gelatin in it), cut into 1-inch cubes
Black pepper
4 carrots, chopped
2 large stalks of celery with leaves, chopped
2 trimmed leeks (white and light green parts), cut into ½-inch rounds, or
    two medium onions, chopped
1 pound, 2 ounces whole spelt berries (also called farro or petit épeautre)
15 cups of low-sodium chicken broth (as there is no canned broth in France,
    I use water with 3 bouillon cubes)
1 bay leaf
A few sprigs of fresh thyme (or scant ½ teaspoon dried)

In a large stockpot, heat 1 tablespoon of olive oil. Brown the meat
in two batches—add a good grinding of black pepper.

    Remove the meat and set aside. Add the remaining 2 tablespoons
of olive oil and scrape the bottom of the pot to make sure you get all
the wonderful meat juices. Add the vegetables and sauté until softened and just starting to color, about 7 to 10 minutes.

    Add meat and spelt berries; mix to combine. Add broth, bay leaf,
and thyme. Bring to boil. Then turn down the heat, cover, and simmer over low heat for 1 hour and 45 minutes, mixing occasionally
until the spelt berries are softened and the meat is tender.

Serves 8. Freezes well; reheat with a trickle of white wine.

Tip: If you cannot find épeautre or farro, you can make this recipe with barley—but not the precooked kind. The soup needs the long simmer to make
the beef tender. If you want to do a quick—and vegetarian—version of this
soup, you can use precooked barley and sauté a pound of sliced mushrooms
instead of the beef.

LENTIL AND SAUSAGE STEW
Lentilles aux Saucisses Fumées

This is a favorite dish in our house year-round—warm and comforting as a big bear hug.

2 tablespoons olive oil
1½ pounds high-quality smoked sausage, such as Jésu de Morteau, sliced
    into 1-inch rounds (or use Toulouse or Italian sausages, left whole)
2 medium carrots, finely chopped
2 medium onions, diced
½ small bulb fennel, finely chopped
2 branches celery, with leaves
3 sun-dried tomatoes, chopped
1 large handful flat-leaf parsley, chopped (use some stems as well)
2 cloves garlic, whole
2 pounds Puy lentils
1 cup white wine
1 bay leaf
Fresh ground black pepper
12 cups boiling water

In a large Dutch oven or stockpot, heat the olive oil and brown the sausages. Add the vegetables and garlic, stir to coat, and sauté until softened, about 10 minutes. Add lentils; stir to coat. Add wine; it will sizzle a bit. Add bay leaf and a good grinding of black pepper. Add 12 cups very hot or boiling water. Bring to a boil, turn down heat, and simmer, partly covered, until lentils are tender and most of the liquid is absorbed—50 minutes to 1 hour.

Serve a hefty bowl of lentils with the sausage on top. Accompany with Dijon mustard and more chopped parsley.

Serves 6–8

Tip: I nearly always get two meals for four people out of this. It freezes well; reheat with a bit of white wine. If you still have leftover lentils after all the sausage is gone, puree them with some white wine and chicken broth to make a thick soup. Serve the soup with a squeeze of lime, a dollop of crème fraîche (or sour cream), and lots of chopped cilantro.

CHAPTER 20

Christmas Present

There's no way you're going by yourself."

"Great," said Gwendal with a sigh as I tripped down the front step in my platform boots.

"I'm coming with you."

"There's no need."

"I don't want you to break the cake."

"I don't want you to break your ankle."

These were the darkest days of December, and Gwendal was practicing his ice cream cakes. Somehow I had trouble imagining this as an art form. The ice cream cakes of my youth were not sophisticated creations; they were layers of vanilla and chocolate soft-serve separated by crunchy chocolate kibbles and topped with my name written in transparent pink gel. As the birthday girl, I was entitled to the largest chalky icing rose.

The French take their *bûche de Noël,* the traditional Christmas Yule log cake, much more seriously. Gwendal had been training at school, and he came back with snapshots of his gleaming white *glaçage,* slick as black ice, decorated with a forest of bitty spun-sugar pine trees and spotted meringue mushrooms. Who knew my husband had such talents? I was bordering on jealous when he came home with a foolproof recipe for proper Parisian macaroons. We decided to use one of our signature flavors, honey and fresh thyme, for the outside of our *bûche,* with a layer of tonkabean mousse and a center of apricot sorbet for acidity and pizzazz. Though nothing was quite official, we already had orders for Christmas and New Year's—some friends, some prospective restaurant clients—but Gwendal still had no oven in his test lab, so we were stuck shuttling sheet pans of rich buttery *pâte sablée* base from our house down to the construction site in the middle of the night.

We drove down and parked the car next to the garbage cans, near the turnoff for Alexandre's old babysitter. The new building where our production facility would be was no more than a shell, so our new landlord had kindly loaned us a room near the site as a temporary test lab. Now all we had to do was get across the Route Nationale with our tray of pastry. Trucks, big trucks, drive this road at night. The only advantage of the darkness was that we would see an eighteen-wheeler coming from quite far away.

"How is it that you picked the spot with no crosswalk, no light, and a fifteen-foot drop?" I asked.

"There's a wall."

Is that supposed to be comforting?

Between the two of us, we managed to shimmy down the embankment with the sheet pan held reasonably level. For anyone watching through a slit in the curtains, we must have looked like a pair of clumsy cat burglars. I kept waiting for the gendarmes to pull up and arrest us for trespassing.

Gwendal unlocked the door to the temporary test lab and turned on the fluorescent lights.

I went to take off my coat, then thought better of it. "You realize it's the same temperature in here as outside."

"*Mer-de,*" mumbled Gwendal, his head in the freezer. When my husband is particularly frustrated, the French word for "shit" has two syllables. Our cookie sheet was a centimeter too large to fit. As we attempted a transfer, the *sablée* began to crack, fault lines appearing in the delicate layers of pastry. Eventually, using a system of cantilevers and waxed paper, we managed to get it all in the deep freeze.

Back on the embankment, Gwendal gave me a leg up, and my boots sank farther into the mud. "This must be in the fine print," I said, peering into the night for oncoming traffic. In situations like these, I tend to evoke our French marriage contract, the twenty-page legal document I signed during our civil wedding ceremony, that, at the time, I could not read.

"You know what I found out today," said Gwendal after we'd gotten into the car. "The guy from the ice cream machine company, the founder, Hubert Cloix, was a Résistant. I looked him up."

I wiped my muddy hands on my jeans. "Do you think if we told him René Char wrote poetry in our guest room, he'd give us a discount?"

✑

AFTER WE RAN our badges through the electronic barrier, we were confronted with a twenty-foot-high plastic cone topped with rainbow swirls of gelato. At least we knew we were in the right place.

We were on our first ice cream business trip—a weekend in Rimini, Italy, at SIGEP, the world's largest gelato-and-coffee trade show. Because we are chronically disorganized, we had to fly to Milan, rent a car, drive three hours to Rimini, and then, after we toured the trade show, turn around and do the whole thing in the opposite direction the very next morning. Our 4:00 a.m. start was just the beginning of a very long day.

There was a cacophony up ahead, cheering and loud whoops. We had stumbled on the international barista competition. Projected on a giant video screen was a close-up of two hairy hands making what looked to me like a portrait of Leonardo da Vinci in cappuccino foam.

We walked until we had blisters. Fascinating, how a single industry has its tentacles in so many things: cones and plastic cups, paper wrappers for cones and plastic cups, big neon signs of cones and plastic cups, metal garbage cans for cigarette butts and cones and plastic cups, not to mention the powders, pastes, and purees to fill the cones and plastic cups with artificial strawberry gelato. And, this being Italy, the most magnificent, shiny-like-a-Ferrari chrome espresso machines to accompany your cones and plastic cups.

There were not as many scantily clad women as I'd hoped. I've always had a soft spot for the Italian soupçon of vulgarity, and the women's uncanny ability to navigate cobblestones in stilettos. (They must teach it in high school, right after Dante.) One stand for industrial gelato mix had eight-foot-high sculptures of brightly colored macaroons; next to each one was a girl in a pleated black micromini, green-and-white-striped kneesocks, and platform heels. We sent a photo to Rod: *Wish you were here.*

Our central errand in Rimini was to shop for our ice cream display case. I imagine this is what it must be like to buy a sports car, considering line and color, modern or retro. It would be our most visible (and most expensive) investment. Too dinky, and no one would take us seriously; too grand, and you could blow a year's operating budget on curves and custom-made plexiglass. We spotted one model we had seen before, shiny white and curved on top like a space capsule. A thirty-something man with a shaved head, a well-cut suit, and chic, heavy black-framed glasses walked up to greet us.

We quickly exhausted our Italian greetings and switched to English. When he heard my American accent, he warmed up in a hurry.

"Where are you from?"

"New York," I said.

"Me too; I went to the French Culinary Institute. In another life I used to be a chef—so I have a lot of sympathy for people going out on their own."

"This is a nice model," he said, patting the display like it was a pet schnauzer. "But what we mainly do is these." He pointed to what looked like a cash machine recessed in the wall. "It's self-serve."

"Oh, I'm American, but he's French, so he wouldn't know from TCBY."

"Yeah, I figured."

"It's the new fad in the States." His tone changed, going to a pre-formatted sales spiel. "That way, you only need one person in the shop, and your employee doesn't have to know anything about making ice cream. The customer pays by weight—"

"So they feel virtuous," said Gwendal, cutting him off, "by choosing a small cup, and then they fill it with exactly as much as a large one."

The man nodded in silent (slightly embarrassed?) agreement.

It was, in its way, the ultimate American business model—absolute freedom, endless choice, maximum efficiency achieved with minimum skill, and all from a lever in the wall and a salad bar full of M&M's and broken Reese's Peanut Butter Cups. No ritual. No excellence. No interaction. No poetry. It was the absolute antithesis of what we were trying to do.

"It works," he said, a little bashful. What was a former chef doing selling ice cream ATMs? "Everyone's eyes are bigger than their stomach."

Well, not everyone's.

We couldn't explain that we were worried about exactly the opposite problem. How were we going to get very traditional French eaters to accept free tastes of weird flavors like ras-el-hanout ice cream and beetroot sorbet? How were we going to get French women, who spend their entire lives watching their figures, to order three scoops of anything? How were we going to make ice cream from high-quality local products and still be able to set a price that wouldn't feel punitive to local families with three kids? The whole idea of a French person walking up to a wall, pulling a lever, and strolling away down the street eating an overflowing tub of candy-covered soft-serve seemed unimaginable to me.

By lunchtime we'd been up for twelve hours; we were exhausted. I was dying for something savory to offset all the samples of pale pistachio gelato. Proget, one of the largest manufacturers of ice cream displays, had had a very smart idea; the company had set up a huge stand with a chef making focaccia with freshly grilled vegetables, cutting jagged chunks off a giant wheel of Parmesan cheese. We sat down at a table and waited for a sales rep to approach.

A half an hour and an excellent sandwich later, we bought our ice cream display. It was sleek but not flashy, with a flat top to put my three-tiered cake stand on. The list price for this model in France was twenty-three thousand euros; we paid just under nine thousand. That's still a very expensive sandwich.

ℴ

GOOD NEWS, OR at least crazy news, travels fast. Lisa and Johann, a Franco-American couple who host truffle hunts and tastings on their property, heard about our ice cream adventure and contacted us to see if we could partner on a black truffle ice cream for their clients. There was something incongruous about buying truffles with the last of Gwendal's unemployment checks, but hey—sometimes you have to spend money to make money. I know I read that somewhere.

It was a bright day in February. When we left for Cadenet, there was a low-hanging fog in the valley. The sun crept out as we climbed the hills behind Saignon.

The road to Lourmarin is one of the scariest—and most beautiful—roads I've ever been on. You are basically driving in a crevice between two cliffs, hugging the side of the mountain and hoping there's not a speeding local coming round the bend in the other direction. It had been raining nonstop; this was the first sunny day in what feels like weeks. Rays penetrated down into the canyon, making the wet leaves sparkle. There was water everywhere. Streams that are normally stilled to a trickle by the time the tourists arrive in May were rushing torrents.

We were told to wear our muddiest boots. (Now that I've lived in Céreste for a while, I actually have a pair of muddy boots.) We could see the house from the bottom of the hill, perched above a terraced field of olive trees, a beautiful two-story farmhouse with red shutters. Johann and Lisa shared the house with his grandparents. I knew his grandfather had been in the Résistance during the war; I wondered if he had known Char.

Gwendal, Alexandre, and I, along with another family, gathered by the gate. The morning started out with a minor disappointment. "When the dogs come," said Johann to Alexandre as he piled acorns in a corner of the yard, "you must not play with them." My son looked a little confused. "They are going to work. So you stay with us, and we will follow the dogs and watch them do their work." Alexandre accepted the rules with relative good humor and continued his collection of acorns.

The dogs arrived with Jean-Marc, a childhood friend of Johann's who is a part-time truffle hunter. Mirabelle and Pupuce circled excitedly around Jean-Marc's feet, no doubt as happy to see the sun as we were. They are part shih tzu, with shaggy coats and very short legs—a muddier version of the dogs you see accompanying older women on the rue Saint-Honoré in Paris. "You can use any kind of dog," said Johann as we walked toward the fields, "as long as they don't have hunting in their DNA. *Sinon,* they'll get distracted and go after a pheasant. If you have a Labrador, that's very good, because they always want to please you."

We stopped in the shade of a white oak. "The dogs start when they are tiny puppies. Jean-Marc puts a truffle inside a tennis ball. The dogs learn to identify the smell." I watched the pair of them, twenty feet ahead of us, sniffing and snuffing in circles, sometimes retracing their path before focusing on a certain spot.

"You can also hunt truffles with pigs. The problem with pigs is that they love the taste. You can always tell a farmer who hunts truffles this way," said Johann with a grin. "A piece of his index finger is missing." I thought back to Didier and Martine's nefarious porker, the one we'd met the day of the saffron harvest. I bet you could lose a hand trying to get a truffle out of his mouth. It's a long way from *Charlotte's Web.*

Every time the dogs started to dig in earnest, Jean-Marc knelt down and gently turned the earth with his hands and the prod of a large screwdriver. If he spotted a truffle, he extracted it. The dogs stood at attention, waiting for their treat. When Jean-Marc handed the first truffle off to Johann, he studied it, rolling it around in his hands, putting it to his nose, inhaling deeply. He passed it to each of us, getting us accustomed to the sweet smell of damp earth.

"Size doesn't matter. For me it's the smell." Johann pressed the truffle gently between his thumb and index finger. "And it has to be firm." He cut it open in the palm of his hand. Inside, it looked like a tiny brain, a dense black mass threaded with hair-width white veins.

"If the veins are very thin, that's how you know you have a real black truffle — *Tuber melanosporum.*"

Suddenly, out of the corner of his eye, Johann noticed a green jeep snaking slowly up the road. He frowned. "Don't look at the car," he said, as if we were undercover agents on a secret mission. "This is all our land. We have only two neighbors, and I know their cars. Most of the time we pretend we are looking at trees. But when they see the dogs, they know."

There's reason enough to be paranoid. Renegade truffle hunters often search on private land. Theft is common, and profitable. Depending on the year, a kilo of truffles sells for six hundred or seven hundred euros; it can be a thousand or twelve hundred around Christmas, when demand is high. It's impossible to secure the land without having someone complain that his grandfather's grandfather used to hunt wild boar on the property. And by *complain*, I mean "ram his jeep through your newly constructed barbed-wire fence."

The dogs moved along, having a rather successful run. Twenty minutes in, they had already found a small handful of truffles. The truffles were irregular in shape, like nuggets of black gold.

"You see that patch there, with no grass. We don't know exactly why, maybe the truffle produces a certain chemical or just uses all the nutrients in the ground, but you often find truffles in areas where there *should* be grass, but there's not. It's what *les anciens* called a witch's circle. They associated truffles with sorcery—black magic."

On the way back to the house, Johann walked us through his small vineyard and another olive grove. He stopped to show us a bird's nest he'd found in one of the trees.

When we got inside, Lisa, her boots very clean indeed, took over. I was looking forward to the tasting portion of the tour, because my only previous experience cooking with truffles had been underwhelming.

Our first winter in Céreste, I went with an Irish friend to a local truffle festival. Then, with much pomp and circumstance, I organized a dinner party where every course had something to do with truffles.

My champagne cocktails with truffle sugar syrup were a nice twist, but my rabbit breast stuffed with truffle ricotta and spinach didn't taste of truffles at all, and my truffle mashed potatoes were nothing special—maybe I didn't add enough? The only real success of the evening was poached pears with truffle crème anglaise. I let the shaved truffle infuse in the cream for a day before I served it. The morning after the party, I found Gwendal, in a violation of French protocol, eating the leftovers straight out of the open fridge.

"Truffles are best with a little salt and a little fat," said Lisa, passing around a silver tray of small white toasts spread with salted butter and topped with generous slices of truffle. "We first tasted truffles this way at Jean-Marc's birthday party. A piece of advice: If you ever get invited to a truffle hunter's birthday party, *go*."

I took a nibble. The truffle had bite, density. I was surprised—maybe I'd never tasted a slice this thick. Perhaps I had made my truffle meal unnecessarily complicated.

"You can cook truffles," said Johann, "but it's best to hide them, protect them. I've had them in puff pastry—like an apple turnover, but with ham and cheese, and the truffle in the middle."

After the other couple left, we were invited to stay for truffle burgers and fries—an impossible invitation to pass up if there ever was one. Lisa's recipe is a home cook's take on Daniel Boulud's $140 restaurant creation: a center of truffle and foie gras surrounded by ground beef. She and I had an instant, easy rapport. That nice American *click* that feels so great after the careful effort of French friendships.

While Lisa prepared lunch, I took it upon myself to smell each and every truffle we'd found that morning. Some were sweet and firm, and some smelled more of vinegar—maybe they were underripe. Some were grassy, herblike. There were mineral elements—quartz and slate. As I went through the pile, the associations mounted. Did I smell pine needles? Blueberries? The more I sniffed, the weirder it became. What did that sweet starchy smell remind me of? *That's it*—the beginning of a good rice pudding.

Lisa was cleaning the truffles with what looked like a boot brush, and as she massaged gently, the chocolate-colored soil gave way to cratered geological black; the truffle looked like a tiny meteor. We would have to choose a few to take home for our ice cream tests. If we could get the truffle to really infuse into the raw milk, we might even be able to make a limited edition for the shop.

"You can keep them for a couple of days in the fridge if you put them in a container with a paper towel on the bottom to absorb the condensation. You can also put eggs in with your truffle—the smell goes right through the shell. Or rice—that absorbs the moisture, and it makes the most incredible risotto."

"I'm trying that as soon as I get home."

While Lisa scrubbed yet more truffles to top our burgers, she told me a bit about the family history. "Johann's grandfather joined the Résistance in Paris. He escaped and rode all the way to the Alps on a bicycle with a wooden seat." That seemed to me an act of patriotic endurance in and of itself.

"His mother stalled the police with soup. The policemen sat down at the table to wait, and after a while, they were losing patience: 'Where are your sons?'

"'They'll be along any minute,' she said, setting the appropriate number of places at the table. '*C'est la guerre.* Do you think I would put out soup for people who are not coming to eat it!' Meanwhile, her husband and two boys were hotfooting it out of town."

There are people all over France living with this history, with these tiny accidents that made the future possible. For Johann, it is simply a family story. For me, it still feels like magic.

Recipes for a Truffle Dinner

CHAMPAGNE COCKTAILS WITH SHAVED TRUFFLE

Cocktail de Champagne aux Truffes

Champagne is like a magnifying glass for truffles, bringing out all their finest qualities. I first made this with truffle syrup, which I found at a local truffle market on a freezing morning in February. You can re-create the effect using shaved truffle and a small sugar cube.

1 small black winter truffle (you won't use all of it for this recipe, but you'll need the rest for your truffled crème anglaise)
6 small sugar cubes
1 bottle champagne

A day or two before: Store your truffle in a plastic container or glass jar with a paper towel on the bottom to soak up the moisture. Place 6 small sugar cubes in the container with the truffle. Leave overnight (up to 3 days)—the sugar will take on the truffle smell. Just before serving, finely grate some of your truffle; you'll need a small pinch per cocktail. Place a sugar cube in the bottom of each glass and top with a pinch of truffle. Bring the glasses out to your guests, top up each cocktail with champagne. Stir and serve.

Serves 6

Tip: For the best results, use black winter truffles, in season from November to February. To make the three recipes in this chapter, I would invest in two truffles, a small one to grate into your champagne cocktails and crème anglaise and a larger one to slice on your salted butter-truffle toasts. Look for fresh truffles at specialty food shops or online.

TRUFFLE TOASTS WITH SALTED BUTTER

Toasts aux Truffes et au Beurre Salé

The biggest lesson of the tasting we did at Lisa and Johann's: If you want your guest to truly *taste* a truffle, keep it simple. A little salt, a little fat, and decadent slices of truffle just thick enough to snap under your teeth.

1 dense brioche, cut into ¼-inch slices and then into 2-inch squares
Best-quality salted butter (if you can find butter with sea-salt crystals, so much the better), softened
1 black winter truffle, thinly sliced (aim for a bit thinner than an American dime)

Spread the brioche squares with a thin layer of salted butter. Top each toast with 2 or 3 slices of truffle. Serve with champagne, or your champagne truffle cocktails.

Serves 6 as an hors d'oeuvre

POACHED PEARS WITH TRUFFLE CRÈME ANGLAISE

Poires Pochées et Crème Anglaise à la Truffe

I'm not a fan of recipes that use truffles just for show, but this is without doubt one of the best desserts I've ever made. The truffle gives the crème anglaise an earthy quality that is a perfect match for the mellow sweetness of the poached pears. The truffle needs time to infuse in the cream—at least twenty-four hours for the full effect—so you can make this dessert in advance and be completely stress-free on the day of your big dinner party.

For the pears

8 Bosc pears, ripe but firm
1½ cups port
½ of a nice plump vanilla bean

For the crème anglaise

5 egg yolks
⅓ cup sugar
3 cups whole milk
½ of a nice plump vanilla bean
¼ to ⅓ of a black winter truffle, finely grated

Preheat the oven 350°F.

Peel the pears, leaving the stems intact. Place the pears in a large baking dish; pour the port over the pears. Split the vanilla bean down the middle, scrape out the seeds, and mix the seeds into the port as best you can. Tuck the vanilla pod among the pears so it's soaking in the port as well.

Bake for 1½ hours, basting and turning every half hour. Remove the pears from the oven and continue to baste as they cool so they absorb the maximum amount of syrup. Store the pears in the fridge with the port syrup.

Meanwhile, prepare the crème anglaise:

In a medium mixing bowl, beat egg yolks with sugar until a light lemon yellow. Set aside.

Pour milk into a medium saucepan. Split the vanilla bean down the middle, scraping the seeds into the milk with the tip of a knife, and toss in the bean too. Heat over a low flame, until just boiling.

Remove the vanilla bean. Slowly add the hot milk to the egg yolks, whisking continuously. Pour the mixture back into the saucepan and cook over low heat, stirring continuously with a wooden spoon, until the crème anglaise coats the back of the spoon, about 10 minutes.

Transfer custard back to the mixing bowl and cool briefly in an ice bath (a big bowl of ice cubes will do it). As the crème is cooling in the ice bath, grate in the truffle—the cream should be nicely flecked with black. Store in an airtight container in the fridge. Leave for 24 hours so the truffle flavor has time to develop.

On the day: Bring the pears to room temperature (I like to warm them up) before serving. I serve this dessert in shallow bowls, but you could also use parfait glasses. Place one pear in each bowl. Surround the pear with a generous serving of crème anglaise. Agree to look the other way if your guests want to lick the plate.

Serves 8

CHAPTER 21

Operation Scaramouche

Snails for breakfast. Barcelona is my kind of town.

A few weeks before the opening, Gwendal and I decided to steal a weekend together. We needed time. Time to talk. Time to do what grown-ups do in hotel rooms when there's not a three-year-old in the next room. Neither of us are yellers; when I take even the slightest tone, Gwendal shuts up like an oyster. We are both easily wounded. But there was no denying that in the past few weeks, there had been the occasional sarcastic nip. Gwendal was thinking of printing some new business cards for me: Critic in Chief. I'd heard these whisperings over and over again: Going into business with your spouse is asking for trouble. Along with calls about deliveries and hazelnut paste, we'd gotten a number of worrying calls in the last few months. A close friend was having a tumor removed. Another was spending the weekend in Paris "taking a break" from his long-term companion and newborn daughter. Another came home from work to find his wife had rented an apartment in the next town over and moved out, saying nothing to him or their three children.

Alexandre, Gwendal, and I took the train to Paris all together;

Alexandre was spending the weekend with Nicole. After lunch and a last-minute check for passports, we were ready to leave for the airport.

"I love you, sweet Boo," I said, bending to give him a hug and a kiss.

"I *not* love you too." He frowned, turning his attention back to his coloring book. This kind of comment doesn't panic me anymore. At least he was being clear about his feelings. I knew it wasn't a life sentence without parole. I think he could sense that Mommy and Daddy needed some alone time—and he was having none of it.

Gwendal and I travel well together. I always thought it was curious that the honeymoon comes after the wedding, because the way a person travels gives you a lifetime of information. Are you married to someone who makes a written checklist of all the sights he needs to see and who ticks them off one by one with grim satisfaction? Ten years later, woe unto you if you come home from the supermarket with the wrong brand of toilet paper.

Our travel philosophy consists largely of walking and eating. We wander in and out of churches and gardens, stop at cafés, drink a lot of coffee, study the local pastries.

On our last evening in Barcelona, we ate down by the port: sea snails and baby squid, razor clams and barnacles, langoustine and paella. I sucked the garlic and olive oil off my fingers and saved one of the spiky sea-snail shells for Alexandre. We got up to leave; our waiter helped me into my coat and then took my hands between his own. This was clearly his life's work, an almost holy mission, to surprise and delight and then send his patrons, fuller and wiser, back out into the night.

The world was slightly fuzzy around the edges from the wine, a Luis Cañas Rioja 2003. My husband is a cheap date. I can think of exactly two occasions when we've managed to finish a bottle of wine between us, and this was one of them. I love this about him; he gets silly and amorous. We walked back through the empty streets. After a meal like that I feel like we can conquer the world. I feel ready for anything.

∞

WHEN WE STOPPED by Angela and Rod's on Monday morning, the normally tranquil courtyard of the B&B looked like an Ikea storage depot. Wooden pallets were stacked with shrink-wrapped boxes as high as the ice cream truck—which we still hadn't found an appropriate spot for. Another two weeks and Angela was going to plant some geraniums in the front seat. I looked down at the vacuum-packed slices of cured ham we had brought back from Spain; it suddenly seemed a very small gift for their saint-like handling of the mess. Maybe we should have brought back two of those plastic halos with the flashing lights, the kind they use in the religious processions.

Angela came down the spiral staircase in jeans, well-oiled leather boots, a starched white blouse, and a turquoise cashmere sweater.

"I saw the courtyard," I said, with an apologetic half smile.

"Really?" she answered with perfect equanimity. "I haven't seen it in weeks."

It's possible that Rod and Angela are losing patience with the kids. Particularly as we are someone else's kids, and technically not their problem. Yet somehow, here we are, making a racket in their basement, squatting on their sofa, abusing their coffee machine, calling at all hours to complain about stuff they can't possibly fix. We stopped short of raiding the liquor cabinet.

Come to think of it, we've done that too.

Their inherent Englishness, combined with their incredible patience, generosity, and goodwill, makes it difficult to tell when you are about to fall off the edge of the politeness cliff and into the abyss. I am still a big American bull in the china shop, bolting through the aisles, trying not to knock anything over.

So far, we had gotten by with humor. For Christmas, I'd ordered the four of us Scaramouche aprons emblazoned with the slogan *Adventures in Ice Cream*. I'd also ordered a small stuffed toy in the shape of an ice cream cone.

"But we said no gifts," protested Angela.

"It's not a gift," I countered, "it's an anger-management tool. If Gwendal and I get out of line—and sometimes we are running so fast, we don't know when we are getting out of line—you just bop one of us, or both of us, over the head with the stuffed ice cream cone."

Angela looked down at the toy.

"I know," I said. "I tried to find a bigger one."

ALEXANDRE FELL ASLEEP on the floor in his plastic playhouse tonight, his baby doll wrapped carefully in the blanket beside him. Gwendal lifted the plastic house, and I lifted Alexandre. He was deadweight, not waking. I still love to carry my son when he's sleeping, but I no longer feel like I'm stealing a desperately needed hug. I am simply doing what a million mothers have done before me, tucking the covers around his chin and kissing him on the forehead. He rolled over and buried his nose in a stuffed koala.

I DON'T REMEMBER hearing an announcement on the news this morning, but apparently France has decided to suspend the Napoleonic Code and install Murphy's Law in its place.

Fortunately, Gwendal and I worry in different ways. I like to worry about things that might happen twenty years in the future, like if Alexandre will inherit my hatred of algebra or what kind of hat I might wear to his wedding. Gwendal can only worry from two minutes to approximately six weeks in advance. He goes postal when he can't find his keys.

I prefer to worry about things I can do absolutely nothing about. Gwendal is a solution-oriented individual and worries only about problems that have imminent resolutions, preferably ones he can oversee all by himself. This means we often have opposing definitions of an emergency, and, thankfully, we almost never hit the panic button at exactly the same time.

The town was building a traffic circle to give access to the new parking lot of the laboratory, and as a result, the main electricity line would have to be moved. The laboratory was due to be finished between April 3 and April 8—three weeks behind schedule. Until then, there was no electricity, and, worse, because of the position of the building, all the wastewater had to be pumped, so no electricity also meant no sewers. We had a three-ton ice cream turbine and a cold-storage room, not to mention an air-conditioning system due to arrive next week, and we had no way to test them. Until the main electricity line was installed, we were off the grid, which meant we couldn't even arrange to put in our own electricity line—EDF, the French power company, couldn't possibly make an appointment to come to a building that didn't exist (add another ten days). All this was inching us toward the busy holiday weekends of the first and the eighth of May—an opening boost our business plan simply couldn't afford to miss. We had an employee starting on April 8 and no lab for her to work in. There was also the fact that it had been raining for four days straight, and the construction site was as muddy as a pig trough. We were both wide awake at 3:00 a.m., Gwendal rubbing his hands obsessively back and forth across his scalp. I saw our leaky pirate ship slowly sinking into the waves. *Fifteen men on a dead man's chest, yo-ho-ho and a bottle of pastis.*

And then something curious happened. Twenty-four hours later, it was all solved. Gwendal met with the landlord in the morning, found the plumber early in the afternoon; the mayor would call to see if the electric company could install a temporary line. The interconnectedness, the proximity, the fact that everyone's success is so closely linked—all this makes for comparatively speedy solutions. In Paris, if you lose the plumber, you lose the plumber. He can avoid you for months. Here, it's like a benevolent mafia: *We know where you live.* Better still: *We know where you drink your morning coffee.*

∽

I GOT THE call a little after eight in the morning. Gwendal was at our newly finished lab, hysterical. "There was a mouse in here last night."

We are opening in one week. Seven days. This is just what we need. Apparently, this clever rodent got into the chocolate, went straight for the good stuff. If he's dead, he must have died of pleasure. I rushed down to the lab, thinking of a thousand euros' worth of vanilla beans. Our shiny packets of 68 percent cacao grand cru chocolate from the Dominican Republic stacked like gold ingots. I pictured an extremely acrobatic mouse, pure Cirque du Soleil, doing a triple pike straight into our twenty-kilo bin of sugar.

We spent the morning disinfecting the place from top to bottom. My parents are back in town for the opening. I sent them to the French equivalent of the dollar store to buy huge transparent storage bins, and we spent the afternoon arranging them. For once, my mother's obsession with sealed plastic containers seemed perfectly reasonable.

⁓

DID YOU EVER see ice cream make a grown man cry? I have. Today. The vanilla is overchurned—bits of ice and fat molecules clumped up into tiny grains of sand. The last time this happened was in September—months of experience and experiments ago. Gwendal was so upset, he had to go to bed and sleep it off. Meanwhile Paul and I took a trip to the local cemetery—the closest place with the tools to cut three inches off our new marble counter. I stood among the sample headstones, resisting the urge to tap my foot.

"*Une semaine,*" said the woman behind the desk.

"A week!" I screeched. "It's just one cut." She stared at me blankly. I could read her thoughts: *Most of our clients, madame, have eternity.*

I took a deep breath. *Remember where you are, Elizabeth. This is France; nothing can be done last-minute.* Or perhaps there's a broader point to be made: We're opening in six days—this *is* the last minute.

⁓

SO THIS IS what one hundred kilos of strawberries looks like: more than a bathtub, less than a swimming pool. When we arrived to pick them up at the farm, they were still warm from the sun. Our new professional juicer arrived yesterday. So we should be able to cut off the stems, juice the berries, and vacuum-pack the result for a whole summer's use.

The road to the strawberry farm was magnificent, lined with cherry trees in full flower. Red earth, blue sky, and, in between, the shimmering movement of millions of white blossoms shaking softly in the breeze. The strawberry man was, as Angela would put it, "a thinking woman's crumpet"—late twenties with a dark crew cut, tanned shoulders, and firm but not gaudy muscles on display in a dusty green tank top. I had a brief image of some kind of calendar: Sexy Farmers of Provence. Hello, Mr. May. He had been on his hands and knees since 6:00 a.m., gathering our order straight from the fields. I tasted one. If this doesn't make the world's most outstanding strawberry sorbet, I'll eat my espadrilles. Berthillon, here we come.

⁌⁍

WE WERE IN the lab till two in the morning decapitating strawberries, listening to the sound track from *Rent*. *How we gonna pay, how we gonna pay, this year's rent, next year's rent?*

When we got back, the light in my parents' room was still on. I poked my head in. "What are you doing up?"

"We were waiting up to see that you got home okay."

"Mom, we weren't on a date—we're married now. Anyway, the last time you waited up for me after a date, I came home at nine a.m."

"I remember it well."

⁌⁍

"I THINK IT's perfect," I said, licking our latest strawberry ice cream test off my spoon.

"It's an upstanding citizen," said Gwendal. Where does he pick up these English expressions?

"I'm just saying," I said, quoting my maternal grandmother, "you wouldn't kick it out of bed for eating crackers." Let him add that one to his repertoire.

Turns out there are cultural differences even in ice cream. Gwendal thinks our freshly churned strawberry ice cream doesn't have enough fruit to bear that name; I think it's heavenly. Apparently the

French like their strawberry in the form of a hot-pink sorbet. I prefer this, dense and creamy. The taste of the raw milk—even after a whirl in the pasteurizer—really comes through. I'd like to congratulate the cows. The color is the faintest blush of pink studded with chunks of ripe red strawberry that resist under your teeth. Must contain my American urge for unilateral action. We'll make both.

❧

I WOKE UP with a strawberry hangover. I must not be as young as I used to be. I need to order more plastic hats, or was it plastic tubs? Should the shopping bags have purple polka dots or purple stripes? I think I'll go with the stripes, in honor of Henri Bendel. Bed. Miss my bed. They're predicting rain right up until the opening and beyond. I had a dream last night where my teeth were falling out. That's chaos theory, right?

I was locked away in Gwendal's office translating the menu when Paul came upstairs. "There's a man outside. He said something like 'inspector' and 'Scaramouche.' He's wearing a dark blue jumpsuit. It looks very official."

Holy pistachio, I thought. *The health and safety people are here—in advance—and they got the wrong address.* I raced down the stairs, past the ants on the kitchen floor and the suitcases blocking the door and the toys scattered everywhere.

I stopped short. Thank God.

It was only Guy, the plumber.

❧

"WHAT DOES THYME look like?" asked my mother as we got into the car. She'd spent the morning scrubbing rings off our vintage water carafes with denture cleaner. This afternoon, the whole family is going to the field behind Marion's yurt. The thyme is flowering; we need another batch for the honey-and-thyme ice cream.

"Look at it this way," I said, evoking my mother's first trip to the French countryside, "it should be easier than trying to pet a chicken. At least the thyme won't run away."

Gwendal clicked Alexandre into his car seat. "And if it starts running, Karen, you know it's not thyme. It's a fox."

"I sense that I'm being made fun of," said my mom as we turned off onto a dirt track.

"Admit it. You love it."

We walked over to see if Marion was at the yurt. "See, Paul," I said, placing my hand on the tin coffee can covered with a plastic bag, "this is how she gets her Internet access." He looked unconvinced.

Marion was working in a nearby field; she waved her floppy straw hat in greeting. Alexandre ran to join her, following her sunken footprints in the freshly turned earth—a giant game of mulchy hopscotch.

"Come see my babies," she said, gesturing toward her brand-new greenhouse. She had baby Swiss chard, a dozen varieties of tomato plant. Outside, growing wild, were chives with tufted blue flowers. I always learn something when I come to visit Marion. I never knew onions had flowers.

"I love the green-tomato smell. I could wear this as perfume," I said, rubbing a leaf between my wrists. "We should make an ice cream out of this."

"*Non, non,*" said Marion, frantically waving her hands in the air. "*Toxique!*" My botany still has a ways to go.

We left the greenhouse and walked through the brush into a sunny clearing surrounded by small oaks and juniper. The spikes of *genêt* were showing their first bright yellow blooms. There was a warm green smell, like a cat sitting on a pile of clean laundry.

We were up on a small rise; you couldn't really call it a hill. There were patches of thyme everywhere, just starting to burst into purple flower. My mom held the shopping bag while Gwendal and I cut the branches. Alexandre, such a big boy at three and a half, insisted on having his turn with the clippers.

LAVENDER HONEY AND THYME ICE CREAM
Glace Miel et Thym

This ice cream reminds me of spring sunshine and the flowering green hills behind Marion's yurt. We use lavender honey from just up the hill in Reillanne. It's especially good with the season's first strawberries.

4 egg yolks
⅓ cup sugar
2½ cups whole milk
½ cup heavy cream
⅜ ounce (1 small handful) fresh thyme, left on the stems
⅓ cup lavender honey

In a medium mixing bowl, beat egg yolks with sugar until a light lemon yellow. Set aside.

Prepare an ice bath—a large mixing bowl full of ice cubes will do it. Set aside.

Pour milk and cream into a medium saucepan. Add the thyme. Heat over a low flame, until just about to boil. Shut off the heat, quickly fish out the thyme, and put aside for later use. Slowly add the hot milk to the egg yolks, whisking quickly and continuously to combine.

Pour the mixture back into the saucepan. Add the honey and cook over low heat, stirring continuously, until the cream coats the back of a spoon, about 10 minutes.

Immediately transfer the custard to the mixing bowl, add the thyme back in, and cool briefly in the ice bath, stirring for a few minutes until the custard has cooled a bit. Leave the thyme in the custard and store in an airtight container in the fridge. If possible, leave for 24 hours, so the flavor has time to develop. Remove the branches of thyme and, using a fine mesh strainer, filter out any stray thyme leaves that are floating in the custard. Freeze in your home ice cream machine according to the manufacturer's instructions. Transfer to your freezer to harden for 1 hour before serving.

Serve with plain sliced strawberries. Keep in an airtight container in the freezer for up to one week.

Makes about 1 quart ice cream

CHAPTER 22

One Thousand and One Nights

I'm going to film my own infomercial—"Lose Ten Pounds in Two Weeks: Open an Ice Cream Shop." No time to eat, and the number of steps back and forth between the sink, the ice cream display, and the terrace is roughly equivalent to the New York marathon. I'm thinking of buying a pedometer, just for fun.

Yesterday was the first of May. The sun came out in the afternoon, and suddenly there was a line. People came out of nowhere, filling up the terrace and perching on the stone staircase of the seventeenth-century house next door. I went home with a blister on my foot and whipped cream in my hair.

All this will be leading you toward the conclusion that I'm just coming to myself: in thirty-eight years on this planet, I've never done a real day's work. Owning the place makes the day more rewarding but no less tiring. Nor does it improve my memory, my math skills, or my dexterity with a squeeze bottle of homemade hot fudge. Why did I go to rare-book camp instead of taking a waitressing job in college? There are mornings when I think the coffee machine is more intelligent than I am.

Today was calmer; we found time to commiserate over photos

from the opening. We got lucky; after three days of rain, the clouds parted just long enough for a hundred and fifty people to crowd the street and line up for free samples in miniature cones. It was less a line than a merry-go-round; the kids in particular kept circling back to try new flavors. The honey-and-thyme ice cream was a hit, and so was the pastis sorbet. We decided we needed to change the name of our ras-el-hanout ice cream with grilled almonds. Even the adults wrinkled their noses at the idea of couscous-spice ice cream, but everyone loved it when it was called One Thousand and One Nights. The kids were attracted to the bright colors, so in addition to the strawberry sorbet (Gwendal was right), we had a lot of takers for our fuchsia beetroot sorbet. The vanilla was exceptional. Finally. I'm not sure I've ever been prouder to be a part of something than I was that night.

I passed the photos to Rod; our friend George got some great shots of kids with chocolate mustaches and toothy grins. I filled a broken cone with strawberry ice cream (have to use up those broken cones somehow) and sat down at an empty table. Two fourth-graders arrived with the director of the village school to hang a poster for the student film festival. Red carpet and everything. The sun set and the chill returned. Time to take the terrace in and close up for the night.

Angela leaned her head out the upstairs window. "Good day?"

I nodded and smiled. Good day.

✑

SPRING ARRIVED WITHOUT US noticing. When I walked Alexandre to school on Monday morning, the lilacs were in full bloom. The irises are out again along the Roman road. I used to pass this way every day on the way to Alexandre's nanny. Now that he's in school, I pass this way only when we forget a tub of saffron ice cream or a batch of toasted almonds at the lab. Because of all the rain, the grass is growing at a prodigious rate. Fields that were muddy brown only a few weeks ago have sprung to life, covered in knee-high grass. The tractor lines are still faintly visible, like someone has run a finger through an especially plush carpet.

Alexandre's suddenly become very popular at school. At that age, the only thing cooler than a daddy who's an astronaut or a fireman is a daddy who's an ice cream maker. I walk with him to the shop every day after school. He goes behind the counter and asks Gwendal for a cone of lemon or strawberry sorbet, sometimes coffee ice cream. Even if his parents have been a little preoccupied these past few months, he seems to be pleased with the net result.

There's a new crop of kittens in the garden across the way. When I opened the gate this morning, I found one sitting, still as an Egyptian idol, in a square of sunshine under the apricot tree. They are learning to jump. When I go to print something in Gwendal's office, I watch them take flying leaps from the longest branch to the sun-warmed *tuiles* of Denis's roof.

I'm still tired, but it's a different kind of tired, a better kind. One thing's for sure: writing has taken on a whole new meaning for me. A few hours to myself in front of the computer seems like a vacation.

I FORGOT HOW hard this is. Not since long division have I spent this much time trying to write neatly on a chalkboard. The flavors change every week now that fruits are coming in. Gwendal needs to take the truck up to Saint-Martin-de-Castillon this afternoon to get the first bouquets of fresh lemon verbena for sorbet. The mint that we can't control in our garden has finally found its raison d'être—fresh mint and shaved chocolate ice cream. I'm looking forward to the cherry sorbet. I think we'll make a sundae with hazelnut and vanilla ice cream, cherry sorbet, and Jean's cherry marmalade sauce—with a fresh cherry on top, of course.

The shop looks exactly the way I'd hoped it would. I commandeered the wrought-iron chairs from our dining room and found some bright stripy cushions. The exposed stone vaults of the cellar are cool to the touch, even in the midday heat. On the marble bar, there's a candy jar full of pastel Smarties that are doled out with one of my mother's silver gravy ladles.

If I think about it, there's almost no one we know who hasn't contributed in some way. The logo—Scaramouche with his sword inside an ice cream swirl—was done by a local graphic designer, the husband of the director of the village crèche. The sewing lady across the street made the cushions for the bench inside the shop. We get the three-liter *bidons* of fruity olive oil for our rosemary–olive oil–pine nut ice cream at the butcher, and the saffron, *bien sûr,* from Didier and Martine in Reillanne. Mr. Simondi, whose farm is down the hill near Marion, has promised to hand-pick our melons for sorbet when the time comes. Angela has become our gardener in chief, making sure the terrace is full of bright spring flowers.

✍

"JUST TO LET you know," Gwendal said over lunch. "Laure is coming on Friday."

"Laure. Laure?" I repeated, searching my internal Rolodex. Oh. *Laure.* Laure is his ex-girlfriend. More specifically, the girl he dated for five years, lived with for three, and left just before he met me.

"I know you like to be aware of these things."

"Okay," I said, trying my best to sound nonplussed. "I'll remember to brush my hair."

There must be something sexy about this ice cream business, because both of Gwendal's serious ex-girlfriends have popped up in the last six weeks. I'm not the jealous type. But Laure is recently divorced, and, frankly, I'm suspicious of her motives. The fluid nature of French relationships means that no one ever completely hangs it up, throws in the towel. There's always the possibility, the frisson of sex. It's what makes the air crackle. It probably makes the cheese taste better. One reason why French women always look so good is that nobody ever stops looking.

I admit it, I dressed with more care than I usually would on a random Friday afternoon: my most flattering jeans, a white eyelet fitted blouse, and my favorite crocheted mohair cardigan. Jewelry: simple, tiny diamond studs and, of course, my engagement ring. I slipped on my new Matt Bernson ballerina flats. The idea, the lesson, if you will: Start every day as if your husband's ex-girlfriend is coming to dinner—and knock her out of the water. There is no such thing as a French MILF; all mothers are meant to be inherently fuckable. I made sure my bra and underwear matched—for inner confidence.

The anticlimax was inevitable. Laure arrived with her new boyfriend in tow. She was taller than I expected and not quite as pretty as I'd made her in my head. She does have a beautiful, infectious smile. She also has a PhD in history, spent a year or two at Cambridge, did a graduate fellowship at Princeton. We clearly share a passion for the past, for text, for the ivory-tower life.

She was so much more open and enthusiastic than your average French girl, leaning in to ask me questions, tasting the ice cream flavors with abandon, waving her sample spoons in front of herself like Madame de Pompadour with a fan. If it weren't for the slightly suspicious reappearing-French-ex thing, we could be friends.

She'd arrived with a bottle of champagne to celebrate the opening and two books for Alexandre. She had clearly told the new boyfriend quite a lot (too much, perhaps) about Gwendal. Women are idiotic that way.

Just after six o'clock, Nicole arrived at the shop with Alexandre.

With only a few tiny gaps, either my parents or Nicole will be here through the end of August. We are working nights, weekends; we could never do this without them.

Even after a whole day spent taking care of a small child, Nicole still has her red lipstick in place. My mother-in-law would no sooner go out of the house without her lipstick than she would without her pants.

Of course, Laure had known my mother-in-law for years, and they fell into easy conversation. I sat to one side as Laure leaned in — she had a nice way of leaning — and asked my mother-in-law questions I'd never dared. "Nicole, *si c'est pas indiscret,* would you like to meet someone?" Her tone was warm, conspiratorial.

"*Mais oui,*" answered Nicole. "But men of my age, *c'est des ordures.*" It was like she was talking to a close girlfriend.

I walked inside in a huff. Turns out I *was* jealous, not about Gwendal, but about Nicole.

Three years had passed, and she and I never quite talked about the book. Never really talked about how it felt to lose her husband, what she hoped for from her new life in Paris. We talked a lot about the past, family history, recipes, but not about the future.

"*Ça va?*" I said to Nicole when she walked inside with the champagne glasses to rinse.

"*Et toi?*" said Nicole. "If it had been me, I would have been—" I forget the exact French word she used, but it meant something between "icy" and "apoplectic."

For whatever reason, this encounter made me feel sad, and a little brave — so I jumped off the cliff. "I saw the way you were talking with Laure, the questions she was asking." I hesitated, searching for language and feeling. "I sometimes wonder if it would be easier for you to have a French daughter-in-law." *Someone who knows all the lyrics to Brassens and could read Lacan in the original. Someone who always knows what's appropriate and what's not. Someone who isn't constantly in danger of tripping over these cultural lines in the sand.* "And sometimes, I want to…"—already my French was getting jumbled—"say things, ask things." I took a minute to collect my words. "I don't know if it's a question of culture or temperament, but sometimes I just don't dare."

She looked at me in surprise. Whatever qualities she attributed to the American girl who had wandered into her life, I'm pretty sure a lack of daring wasn't one of them. *"Tu as tort,"* she said kindly. You're wrong.

"Oh," I said, taken aback that it might be that simple. It was an invitation, one I desperately wanted to accept.

Tu as tort.

Maybe I was; maybe I had been all along.

When I got home that night, I was full of questions, openings. It must have shown on my face.

"Was that okay?" said Gwendal.

"It was fine for me. Not sure what Laure's boyfriend thought."

"Yeah."

"Actually, I feel lucky. People that are really happy don't normally drive an hour and a half out of their way to see an ex."

"Wow." He looked up from his computer. "I never thought I could get points off a meeting like this one."

"I'm just saying," I said, walking up behind him to put my arms around his neck. "I'd rather be married to the coolest guy I know than talking about the coolest guy I know with another man."

∽

We had minimal time to set up before the paparazzi arrived. We have an ice cream stand at the student film festival tonight. The nineteenth-century schoolhouse is decked out with banners, and a red carpet stretches from the wrought-iron gate to the stage.

There's a barbecue, a crepe stand, someone making homemade waffles. The teachers and the kids have done an amazing job.

The parents, all in dark shades, made a convincing crush of celebrity photographers. Dozens of flashes clicked away as each class paraded up the red carpet. Some of the boys were wearing white dress shirts and bow ties with their jeans and sneakers. The girls had all been allowed into their *mamans'* makeup drawers.

It's May 25, and two hours south of here, the real Cannes film festival is ending. I remember how excited Gwendal was the first time he went. One year I called him; he had cut himself shaving just before the premiere of the new Indiana Jones movie. Holding the phone to one ear, he tried not to drip blood on the collar of his tuxedo shirt.

"Do you miss it?" I asked.

"No," he said without hesitation. And I knew he didn't. We had stumbled into an unlikely life. All the five-year plans in the world wouldn't have gotten us here. Yet it's exactly the right place to be.

Perhaps René Char said it best:

Impose ta chance, serre ton bonheur et va vers ton risque. À te regarder, ils s'habitueront.

Impose your chance, hold tight to your happiness, and go toward your risk. Looking your way, they'll follow.

The translation is mine, and rather liberal.

Gwendal handed me the ice cream scoop and walked toward the stage. He'd been asked to present the award for Best Director. Alexandre sat on the ground beside me with a cone of lemon sorbet. The wind started to pick up. I squinted into the evening sun and turned toward my next client, a little girl wearing too much of her mother's sparkly green eye shadow.

Recipes for an Ice Cream Evening

ONE THOUSAND AND ONE NIGHTS
(RAS-EL-HANOUT ICE CREAM WITH GRILLED
ALMONDS)

Glace Mille et Une Nuits

Gwendal's mom was born in Casablanca, and this recipe is an homage to his *pied-noir* roots. Ras-el-hanout is a North African spice blend often used to flavor couscous. There's ginger, cinnamon, cardamom, and clove, but also cumin, coriander, and pepper. The flavor is a tiny bit like chai tea, but with a kick. It's especially good with apple pie, a pear tart, or mince pies for Christmas.

⅓ cup sliced almonds
4 egg yolks
¾ cup sugar
2½ cups whole milk
½ cup heavy cream
1½ teaspoons ras-el-hanout

Toast the almonds in a small frying pan, until golden. Let cool fully and set aside.

In a medium mixing bowl, beat egg yolks with sugar until a light lemon yellow. Set aside.

Prepare an ice bath—a large mixing bowl full of ice cubes will do it. Set aside. Find your fine-mesh strainer and leave it near the ice bath.

Pour the milk and cream into a medium saucepan and add the ras-el-hanout. Heat over a low flame, until it's just about to boil. Turn off the flame, then slowly add the hot milk to the egg-yolk mixture, whisking quickly and continuously to combine.

Pour the mixture back into the saucepan and cook over low heat, stirring continuously, until the cream coats the back of a wooden spoon, about 5 minutes.

Immediately pour the custard through a fine-mesh strainer back into the mixing bowl. Cool briefly in the ice bath, whisking for a few minutes until the cream has cooled a bit. Store in an airtight container in the fridge. If possible, leave for 24 hours, so the flavor has time to develop. Freeze in your home ice cream maker according to the manufacturer's instructions.

After churning, mix in the toasted almonds. Freeze in an airtight container for an hour or two before serving. Keeps for about a week, but in terms of texture, it's best eaten on the day it's churned.

Makes about 1 quart of ice cream

Note: Ras-el-hanout can contain any number of different spices: galangal, rosebuds, black pepper, ginger, cardamom, nigella, cayenne, allspice, lavender, cinnamon, coriander, mace, nutmeg, and cloves to name a few. But I have also seen ras-el-hanout with curry powder mixed in—definitely to be avoided. The curry will overwhelm the other spices.

JEAN'S CHERRY MARMALADE
Marmelade de Cerises

A decadent, old-school cherry sauce. Serve over hazelnut or vanilla ice cream, with whipped cream and a fresh cherry on top!

2¼ pounds fresh cherries
1 pound, 10 ounces sugar (I use half white, half raw cane or light brown sugar)
½ cup of kirsch (cherry liqueur)

Pit the cherries and cover with the sugar and the alcohol. Stir to combine; let the mixture sit for 12 hours or overnight. In a heavy-bottomed saucepan, bring the mixture to a boil, lower the heat, and simmer for 20 minutes. Fish out the cherries, set aside. Continue to simmer the syrup for 1 hour—a bit longer won't hurt—until reduced by half.

Distribute the cherries between 3 or 4 sterilized jars. Pour the boiling-hot cherry syrup over them, leaving ¼ inch of space at the top. Tightly close the jars and sterilize in a hot-water bath according to the manufacturer's directions. If, like me, you haven't mastered the intricacies of proper canning, the syrup keeps in the fridge for a week or two, or you can freeze it for up to 6 months.

Makes 3 to 4 12-ounce jars

Thanksgiving

W hat's a 'pick and pie'?" I said, scanning the menu that Marion and I were scribbling on the back of an envelope.

"Lili wants to make pick and pie."

"Pecan? Pecan pie?"

Marion looked at me, confused. *"Noix de pécan."*

"Yes."

I had decided that if I wanted holiday traditions in France, I would have to create them myself. Marion's sister and her Irish husband had just returned with their baby girl from three years of living in California. It seemed like the perfect opportunity to suggest a communal Thanksgiving dinner.

Lili walked in with the baby, who was eleven months old, just the age Alexandre was when we arrived in Céreste. She looked at home already, plucking bayberries off the trees and giggling as she stuffed them into her aunt's décolletage.

We went down the list:

Brussels sprouts with lardons
Stuffing

Salt cod with leeks
Pumpkin puree
Roast potatoes
Mashed potatoes
Corn soufflé
Dutch apple pie
Pick and pie (pecan pie)
Pumpkin cheesecake
Chocolate-dipped physalis

"*Mais c'est trop!*" said Dominique, Marion's mother, wiping her boots on the mat.

"*Trop* is good," I said. Too much is the whole point.

"*Et la dinde?*" said Marion.

"I vote for no turkey. Nobody eats it anyway. All the good stuff is on the side."

"My brother wants a turkey," protested Marion. "He's seen too many American TV shows."

I was wondering how we might get a *Desperate Housewives*–size turkey into a French oven while Marion wrapped up a thick slice of her favorite Durban pumpkin and put it in my bag. There's no such thing as canned pumpkin in France, so if I want to make my favorite cheesecake, I will be roasting, mashing, and draining my own.

⁓

BACK IN THE States, we don't eat lunch before Thanksgiving. I'm too busy picking the crunchy bits of stuffing out of the bird every time I baste it. If any concession is made at all, it's a Hebrew National salami with school-bus-yellow deli mustard that sits on the counter where everyone can walk by and grab a piece. Having seen the menu, Marion's family had gotten the idea, and no one wanted a big midday meal. But this is France, so there was no question of skipping lunch entirely.

We made a salad. I sliced half a green cabbage while Marion went into the garden to get some carrots and beetroot. Among the carrots were two that had grown stuck together. Rounded at the top and tapered at the bottom, they resembled the hips and legs of a zaftig chorus girl. I smiled at the memory of the naughty carrot photos that began our friendship. The wet beetroot was dark as ink, with a hairy little tail. As Marion peeled the beets, I popped the ribbons of skin into my mouth. The purple juice stained my fingers. *Pourquoi pas?* I rushed over to the mirror, pressed the peel to my lips. The color was a little Elvira, but it worked.

We walked up the path to Marion's mother's house, about a hundred yards as the crow flies. Dominique was stirring her salt cod with slow-cooked baby leeks, which she normally makes for Christmas. The codfish, dried and preserved in sea salt, had been soaking for two days.

"How many times did you change the water?" I asked.

"Three times," said Dominique. "Or there's a trick: You can put the fish in the toilet tank, that way the water runs over it continuously."

I pursed my lips. Try explaining that on the Cooking Channel.

∽

"Is THERE CORN in this?" Dominique asked.

I held my breath. Dominique had just served herself a big spoonful of my corn soufflé. In France, corn is food for the animals; I'm never quite sure what will happen when I serve it to humans.

"*C'est délicieux!*" she said, closing her eyes with relish. I exhaled. Another Thanksgiving convert.

My fingertips were still stained from the beet juice. "Marion and I made lipstick out of beetroot peelings this afternoon."

"Didn't they do that during the war," said Lili, "when there was no makeup—rub beetroot on their cheeks?"

I took a bite of the flaky white cod together with the mellow green of the leeks. Wonderful fireside food. It's supposed to snow tonight, which makes me think of Jean. Our neighbor, our friend, passed away suddenly in July. He went down to Marseille to have a pacemaker put in, and three weeks later he died in his sleep. I'll always think of him checking the temperature in his bathrobe and slippers when I step outside on a frozen winter's morning. Would his thermometer say $-8°C$, $-9°C$? The same way I think of Marcelle when I see the bright bloom of the roses in the garden or the lilies of the valley on the first of May. From the beginning, this place has been a collage of the past and the present—and now, for us, the future.

Alexandre is nodding off in front of his mashed potatoes. I still love to watch him sleep. I go into his room every night, replace the covers he has kicked to one side. Sometimes I find him upside down or sideways, his legs climbing the wall, like he fell asleep in the middle of a circus routine. I understand better now what my mother means when she says to me, "You're the best thing I've ever done." If I can launch a happy human being out into the world, as my mother launched me, it *will* be the best thing I've ever done, certainly the most important. I'm not afraid of it anymore—this lay-down-in-the-middle-of-the-road kind of love. If I was late in getting there, if I wasted time, stood back when I should have leaned in, then I hope it makes me vigilant, careful to cherish everyday moments with my son. When I think of the childhood Alexandre has had here, at the foot of Jean's cherry tree, I am so thankful—for some of the peace that I've recovered, some of the fear that I've put away, some of the lacks I've understood. I'm not a perfect parent, but I'm a better one.

Scaramouche has quickly taken on a life of its own. Word of mouth this summer was superb, and Gwendal has just started on orders for Christmas Yule log cakes. When the numbers are in, we will survive the winter—which, speaking with French *prudence,* is all you can ask from a new business. That said, the American half of my brain is already wondering how we can get our banana-yellow ice cream truck up to the Canal Saint-Martin in Paris.

Iain took a piece of the braised leg of lamb and passed it to me. "Wow," he said. "I'm glad you couldn't find a turkey."

He raised a glass:

"Cheers."

"*Santé.*"

"Happy Thanksgiving."

It was exactly what the holiday was supposed to be: cooking, sharing, talking—and eating way too much. After dinner, Marion and I sat together at the end of the table, cutting slivers off the pumpkin cheesecake. It was even better than I remembered. I was glad I'd reduced the sugar by a third to suit the French palate.

Gwendal wanted to get home before the snow started, so we left the dishes—and all the extra food—at their house. When I got up the next morning, there was nothing in our fridge. In that way, it was a uniquely French holiday—a Thanksgiving dinner with no leftovers.

∽

Today, I am French. Or, rather, today it's official. The Frenchness has been seeping in for a while now, like olive oil into a leg of lamb. I've lost some of my hard edges. I'm full to the brim with a feeling that would have made my younger, cosmo-drinking self snort with derision. I'm content.

When you become a French citizen, the first thing the government does is issue you a French birth certificate, as if you were a French baby who'd just *happened* to be born abroad. My name and birthday are the same, but the address on my new birth certificate is in Céreste. I've been reborn here. The metaphor's a bit heavy-handed, if not entirely untrue.

The letter itself was a letdown. It's not like getting into college. There was no *Welcome, Elizabeth, to the class of 2013!* I don't know what I was expecting. A musical card that sprays confetti and plays "La Marseillaise"? A pop-up figure of Charles de Gaulle?

Like most French administrative mail, this was a letter with instructions to write another letter. It asked me to verify the enclosed birth certificate and send the papers listed below, but if I *didn't* send them within three months, it would make no difference at all, and my details would be recorded as stated therein.

"Let me get this straight. They're asking me to send papers they already have and that they don't really need but that I'm going to send anyway because I'm too paranoid not to." Involuntarily, I lifted my shoulders and let them drop with a sigh. The whole thing was maddeningly, undeniably French.

I called Marion. I'd promised to alert her at the first official sign of Frenchness. She's been rebuilding a tiny stone cabin on her land. It's shaded by an enormous oak tree and has a view of the surrounding hills.

"It's just an administrative letter," I said, trying to keep the disappointment out of my voice. "I don't know what I was expecting. It lacks...gravitas. I'd like to do something to mark the occasion. Maybe I could plant a tree."

"What kind of tree?"

"I'm not sure."

"I'm ordering some *figuiers* for March."

A fig tree. I had a flash of Alexandre and me twenty years on, making a fig and almond tart with fruit from our very own tree. The French woman inside me nodded.

"Perfect," said the American.

Recipes for a Franco-American Thanksgiving

RAW BEET, CARROT, AND CABBAGE SALAD
Salade de Betteraves Crues, Carottes, et Chou Vert

Along with a slice of Hebrew National salami, this is the only thing I can think of that I'd want to eat *before* Thanksgiving dinner. That said, it would also make a lovely salad served with dinner itself—the raw vegetables are a bright, crunchy contrast to some of the more stodgy holiday sides.

1 pound green cabbage or Chinese cabbage (half of 1 small cabbage)
10 ounces (about 4) organic carrots
10 ounces (about 2) medium organic red beets (raw!)
2 tablespoons olive oil
2 good pinches of coarse sea salt, to taste

In a food processor or by hand, grate all the vegetables. Store in an airtight container. If making in advance, keep the beetroot separate from the carrots and cabbage until the last minute. Just before serving, toss the vegetables together with olive oil and salt.

Serves 8 as a side dish, 12 as part of an appetizer

Tip: Try this salad with grilled meats or as part of a meze plate with hummus, falafel, and yogurt dressing. I sometimes substitute a teaspoon of sesame oil for part of the olive oil and sprinkle toasted sesame seeds on top. I served a tiny portion of the sesame version with a slice of foie gras as an appetizer on New Year's Eve.

DOMINIQUE'S SEVENTY-TWO-HOUR SALT COD WITH WILTED LEEKS

Morue aux Poireaux Fondues

This recipe is an in-depth holiday project; if you count the soaking of the dried fish, it's about three days from start to finish. That said, the combo of creamy leeks and cod is an inspired one, nursery food in the best sense. Below is the lengthy Provençal recipe followed by the streamlined American one (appropriate for a chapter about my new Franco-American self).

1 pound, 12 ounces morue *(salted codfish fillet)*
6½ pounds untrimmed leeks
3 tablespoons olive oil
1 bay leaf
A few peppercorns
A few sprigs of fresh or dried thyme
Black pepper
½ cup white or rosé wine
½ cup bread crumbs
1 pat of butter
⅓ cup cured black olives, pitted and chopped (optional)
½ cup Gruyère cheese, grated (optional)

Put your salt cod in a large plastic container covered with two or three inches of water. Leave it in the fridge for two full days, changing the water each morning and evening. By the time you are done, the water shouldn't taste salty at all.

Preheat the oven to 350°F. Cut off the hairy bottoms of the leeks as well as the tough dark green leaves at the top. You want to use only the white and light green parts. Cut the trimmed leeks into ½-inch rounds; rinse thoroughly to remove any dirt. In a stockpot, blanch the leeks in boiling water for 3 minutes. Drain.

In a Dutch oven, heat the olive oil, add the blanched leeks, stir to coat. Please don't add any salt—the cod will take care of that. When the leeks are heated through and sizzling (about 3 minutes), cover and put in the oven for 1 hour.

Meanwhile, poach the fish. Discard the soaking water and place the salt cod in a stockpot of fresh cold water. Add the spices and bring the water slowly to a simmer over medium heat. When you see small bubbles form on the surface, turn the heat off and cover; leave to rest for 10 minutes. The fish will be cooked again with the leeks, so better to undercook it slightly than overwork things. Remove the fish to a plate, let cool.

When the fish is cool enough to handle, break the cod into small pieces (each about the size of a dime). When the leeks come out of the oven, add the fish to the pot along with a good grind of black pepper and the wine. Stir to combine. Heat on the stovetop until the wine starts to bubble, then cover and return to the oven for ½ hour.

Meanwhile, toast the bread crumbs in a pat of melted butter until nicely browned.

Transfer cod and leeks to a 9-by-13-inch casserole dish. Mix in olives and cheese, if using. Top with the bread crumbs. Return to the oven for 10 minutes. Serve piping hot.

Serves 6–8

TWENTY-MINUTE COD AND CREAMY LEEKS
Dos de Cabillaud et Fondue de Poireaux

This is weekday comfort food.

For the leeks

3 pounds untrimmed leeks
2 tablespoons olive oil

2 good pinches coarse sea salt
½ teaspoon Dijon mustard
2 generous tablespoons crème fraîche or sour cream

For the cod fillets

½ tablespoon olive oil
¼ cup white or rosé wine
4 pieces of thick cod fillet, about 5 ounces each
Coarse sea salt
Black pepper

Cut off the hairy bottoms of the leeks as well as the tough dark green leaves at the top. You want to use only the white and light green parts. Cut the trimmed leeks into ½-inch rounds; rinse thoroughly to remove any dirt. In a stockpot, blanch the leeks in boiling water for 3 minutes. Drain.

In the same stockpot, heat the olive oil, add the blanched leeks and salt, stir to coat. Cook over medium heat with the cover ajar for 10 minutes, moving the leeks around every 3 minutes or so. I like to leave them until they brown a little and I see some charred bits when I scrape the bottom, but they will be tender before that. In a small bowl, stir together mustard and crème fraîche. Just before serving, add the cream mixture to the leeks and cook just long enough to heat through.

While the leeks are cooking, in a medium frying pan, heat ½ tablespoon olive oil and ¼ cup wine. Add the fish fillets and sprinkle with a bit of coarse salt and a grinding of black pepper. Cover and simmer until the fish flakes, about 7 to 10 minutes. I always err on the side of caution, turning off the heat before the fish is fully cooked and leaving it covered so it continues to steam for a while in its own juices.

~~Serve~~ the fish on a bed of leeks.

Serves 4

CORN SOUFFLÉ
Soufflé au Maïs

The French may think corn is for the chickens, but once they taste this, they usually change their tune. This soufflé is adapted from *Fonda San Miguel: Thirty Years of Food and Art*, by Tom Gilliland, Miguel Ravago, and Virginia B. Wood (Shearer, 2005). I like to serve it with braised meat dishes and sautéed Brussels sprouts.

¾ cup flour
1 teaspoon baking powder
1 teaspoon coarse sea salt
2 pounds of frozen or canned corn kernels, thawed or drained
¾ cup whole milk
6 eggs, separated
⅓ cup sugar
6 tablespoons butter, melted
4 ounces Comté cheese (white cheddar will do), grated

Preheat the oven to 350°F.

Butter a 9-by-13-inch casserole dish. In a small mixing bowl, combine flour, baking powder, and salt.

In a food processor or using a hand blender, puree corn and milk until smooth. Add the egg yolks one by one, mixing for 30 seconds after each addition. Add sugar and mix until dissolved, about 3 minutes. Add melted butter and mix until smooth.

If using a food processor, transfer corn mixture into a large bowl. Fold in flour mixture, until just combined. Fold in cheese.

Beat egg whites until they hold stiff peaks. In two additions, fold egg whites into the corn mixture. Pour into the casserole dish and bake for 50 minutes to 1 hour, until golden brown on top. The soufflé is great warm, or even at room temperature, so if you need your Thanksgiving oven for other things, bake this first.

Serves 8–10 as part of a larger holiday dinner

PUMPKIN CHEESECAKE
Cheesecake au Potimarron

Mary McCollough of Burlington, Massachusetts, sent a version of this recipe to the November 1996 Cooks' Exchange column in *Bon Appétit* magazine. I've adapted it, cutting the sugar by a third—even before they gave me a French passport, I'd lost my yen for sickly-sweet desserts. Using fresh-roasted pumpkin is extra effort, but it does make a tremendous difference.

Crust

1½ cups speculoos cookie (or gingersnap) crumbs
¾ cup ground pecans
¼ cup unsalted butter, melted

Filling

1 4- to 5-pound slice of raw pumpkin
3 8-ounce packages cream cheese, at room temperature
1 cup (packed) light brown sugar
1 tablespoon quatre épices or pumpkin-pie spice (or 1 teaspoon each
*   ground ginger, cinnamon, and nutmeg)*
1 large pinch of ground cloves
1 tablespoon vanilla extract, or one vanilla bean, seeds scraped
3 large eggs

Preheat the oven to 350°F.

The day before: Roast your large slice of pumpkin (no need to peel or cut it) in a 350°F oven for 1½ hours or longer, until sweet and absolutely tender. Cool, remove and discard the skin, and mash. Press through a fine-mesh strainer to remove the maximum amount of water. You'll need 1½ cups of mashed pumpkin.

For the crust: In a medium mixing bowl, combine cookie crumbs, ground pecans, and melted butter.

Press crust mix into the bottom and 1 inch up the sides of a 9-inch springform pan. Refrigerate until filling is ready.

In an electric mixer, beat the cream cheese with the sugar until smooth; add pumpkin, spices, and vanilla. Beat until well blended. Add eggs one by one, beating after each addition.

Pour batter over crust, bake until top is golden and center is softly set, about 1 hour and 15 minutes. Transfer to a baking rack, cool completely. Chill overnight.

Serves 10–12

Reading René Char

If you'd like to further explore René Char's poetry, there is a side-by-side English / French translation of *Feuillets d'Hypnos* in *Furor and Mystery and Other Writings* (Boston: Black Widow Press, 2011). If you read French, Mireille Sidoine-Audouy recounts her childhood memories of Char in her book *Darwin fera la mis en scène: Une enfance auprès de René Char (1940–1950)* (Paris: Editions du Sextant, 2009).

Acknowledgments

I'm once again blessed in the sound advice and magic touch of my agent Wendy Sherman, my editor Judith Clain, and the dream team at Little, Brown. So many friends contributed their valuable time and comments: Afra, Betsy, Jenny, Sarah, Zizi. Courtney Rubin, there's simply not enough monogrammed stationery in the universe. Both Gwendal and I have been buoyed by the strength of our ties in the village: Cindy and Pierre provided a warm welcome and an office away from home. A special thank-you to Mireille Sidoine-Audouy, who was kind enough to share her personal history with us, and Marion Peyric, with whom I discuss tomatoes and Homer. We miss Jeannot and Pierrette Cappelletti each day, particularly when there's a frost. Though they shun the spotlight, *mille mercis* to Rod and Angela Heath; from our first visit to our most recent cone of quince sorbet, none of this would have been possible without you. To my parents, who have seen us through yet another round of crazy ideas, and particularly to my mom, who proved throughout this process that she is not only a terrific mother but also a very good sport. Finally, to my husband and my best boy, who have given me happiness beyond anything I could have imagined. You make my heart full every day.

Index to Recipes

About the Author

Elizabeth Bard is an American journalist and author based in Provence, France. Her first book, *Lunch in Paris: A Love Story, with Recipes,* was a *New York Times* and international bestseller, a Barnes & Noble "Discover Great New Writers" pick, and the recipient of the 2010 Gourmand World Cookbook Award for Best First Cookbook (USA).

Also by Elizabeth Bard

Lunch in Paris

A Love Story, with Recipes

"A charming memoir.... If you enjoyed the Julia Child romance that made the *Julie & Julia* film so entrancing, you'll love this voyage into the gastronomic soul of the French—complete with luscious recipes."
— Carol Memmott, *USA Today*

"*Lunch in Paris* has got it all: romance in full on the front burner, with delicious French recipes for sustenance. Elizabeth Bard's voice is filled with lust and longing—it's *Eat, **Stay,** Love* with a side of spiced apricots."
— Adriana Trigiani, bestselling author of *All the Stars in the Heavens*

"A love story is always delightful, and one with recipes is also useful in the long run, part and parcel of a real French relationship."
— Diane Johnson, author of *Le Divorce* and *L'Affaire*

Back Bay Books
Available wherever books are sold